The
Stars and Stripes

World War II
and the Early Years

The
Stars and Stripes

*World War II
and the Early Years*

KEN ZUMWALT

EAKIN PRESS ★ Austin, Texas

FIRST EDITION

Copyright © 1989
By Ken Zumwalt

Published in the United States of America
By Eakin Press, P.O. Box 23069, Austin, Texas 78735

ISBN 0-89015-658-1

LIBRARY OF CONGRESS
Library of Congress Cataloging-in-Publication Data

Zumwalt, Ken, 1914–
    Stars and stripes: World War II and the early years / by Ken Zumwalt.
        p.   cm.
    Bibliography: p.
    Includes index.
    ISBN 0-89015-658-1 : $16.95
    1. Stars and stripes (European ed.) — History. 2. World War, 1939–1945 — Journalism, Military — United States. 3. Journalism, Military.   I. Title.
D731.S726643Z86 1988
071'.3--dc19   88-16314
                                                                                CIP

For Paulette,
who was nearby
when much of this
took place.

★ ★

Table of Contents

★ ★

Acknowledgments		vii
Introduction		ix
1	Paris	1
2	Liege	27
3	Nice	49
4	Pfungstadt	72
5	Altdorf	105
6	Business	125
7	Cheesecake	138
8	Griesheim	144
9	Trouble	158
10	Berlin	169
11	Staff	182
12	Critics	201
13	People	213
14	War	224
15	Taps	233
16	Brass	238
Epilogue		253
Roster		260
Bibliography		273
Index		275

Acknowledgments

Ken Zumwalt, managing editor of The Stars and Stripes *in Europe, is writing a book on the U.S. occupation in Germany that is expected to stir up a diplomatic storm . . .*

Danton Walker
Daily News NYC

Well, Danton, here's the book. It took me more than thirty years to prove your syndicated gossip column item correct. I don't know where you got the tip, but at the time it wasn't so. I don't know about the State Department, but Col. Edward Ott, chief of the Armed Forces Information and Education Division, called me to his office in Heidelberg to ask about it and seemed greatly relieved when I denied the report.

Since I left *The Stars and Stripes* in 1955, I have thought often about writing of my eleven years with the GI newspaper, but it wasn't until after my retirement in 1979 from the staff of *The San Diego Union* that I gave it serious consideration. John Livingood and Jim Quigley, golfing buddies who played the courses in Pennsylvania, were the ones who initially persuaded me to tell my story. Jim, who was a National Broadcasting Company news executive in New York after he left *Stripes,* put me in touch with an agent. That was the first step.

Col. William G. Proctor, editor in chief from December 1945 to November 1947 and now living in retirement in Vancouver, Washington, put me straight about the magazine business that still is the lifeblood of the present-day *Stripes* in Europe. Francis "Red" Grandy and Roland Thrush, at the time with the newspaper in Germany, helped jog a fickle memory, as did Ernie Reed of Vienna; Barney Kirchhoff of Paris; Henry Toluzzi of Newport, Australia; Betty Luros Knorr and Stan Emery of London. I thank them.

Harold "Hal" McConnell, who was with me in Altdorf, Pfungstadt, Griesheim, and later at *The San Diego Union*, did the editing despite a full workload in the Sunday department of *The Union*, a mild heart attack, and then those last hectic days prior to retirement. My daughter, Sheri Frances, corrected my spelling and prose. My daughter-in-law, Suzanne, typed some of the chapters, while my wife, Paulette, who is in much of the book and to whom it is dedicated, helped recall some of the events.

The book couldn't have been written without the back issues of the wartime *Stripes*, which I acquired in the early 1950s when Tony Biancone, then in distribution at Griesheim, diverted them from the dump to my basement. Tony telephoned to say that he had been ordered to get rid of the bulky files because they were taking up too much space in the warehouse. I asked if he would send them to my billets instead, and within an hour a six-by-six pulled up in my driveway and unloaded its contents.

When I returned to the States, the bundles of newspapers and bound volumes followed to San Diego along with my household goods. I have since donated one set to the Smithsonian Institution in Washington, D.C., another to the Hoover War Memorial at Stanford University, and my bound volumes to the James S. Copley Library in La Jolla, California. All this I owe to Tony, since deceased. Without those files that he had been ordered to destroy, this book could never have been written.

But you, Danton — you called it. Although it took me all these years to write *Stripes*, here it is.

Introduction

The *Stars and Stripes* forever?

It could happen.

What started out April 18, 1942, as a weekly newspaper for American troops in Northern Ireland, the European edition of *The Stars and Stripes* is now in its fifth decade and inching its way to a half century of service to the U.S. armed forces abroad. The Pacific edition in Tokyo dates from October 3, 1945, and it too is still going strong.

Both editions serve Americans who are in the military or who are employed by the military. Tourists and U.S. civilians living abroad who do not have access to military installations cannot purchase the English-language tabloids.

Neither carries advertising, so the newspapers pose little financial threat to English-language publications overseas. How can the two military papers exist without the advertising dollar? The answer: both are subsidized.

The European edition, which is published at Griesheim, near Darmstadt and a few kilometers south of Rhine-Main airport, has what amounts to a franchise to sell American magazines and books in *Stripes*-built and operated newsstands inside PXs on military property. The markup is the usual forty percent, which grosses *The Stars and Stripes* several million dollars a year. Out of this money, *Stripes* pays salaries, buys newsprint and ink, purchases fleets of automobiles and trucks, and contributes to its employees' retirement. In turn the Central Welfare Fund, consisting of army, air force, and navy representatives sitting as a board of directors, monitors the operation. When the balance reaches a certain point, the directors siphon off excess profits for the welfare of the services, such as the purchase of sports equipment and the payment of teacher salaries in the dependent school system.

Tokyo *Stripes* is not as fortunate, since it doesn't have a like arrangement with U.S. magazine publishers, and as a result depends on subsidies from the American taxpayer. Both editions lose money on the sale of the newspaper; it costs approximately twenty-five cents to produce one copy of the twenty-eight-page, seven-day-a-week newspaper in Germany, for which the GIs pay fifteen cents.

The future? Probably indefinite — and certainly as long as American troops are based overseas.

Not so with *The Stars and Stripes* of World War I. That *Stars and Stripes* lasted just seventy-one issues — from February 8, 1918, to June 13, 1919. The standard-size weekly carried advertising, cost its reader fifty centimes, and had three major dailies in Paris as competition — *Chicago Tribune*, *The New York Herald-Tribune*, and the *Daily Mail* of London's Continental edition. The dailies did not circulate up-front. *Stripes* did, and its press run was over a half million. Having no wire service, the paper depended on staff-written material. And what a staff it had: Harold Ross, Grantland Rice, Alexander Woollcott, Steve Early, and Franklin P. Adams, to name a few.

The present *Stripes* boasts big names too: Bill Mauldin, cartoonist; Andy Rooney, author and television personality; John Sharnik and Ernie Leiser, CBS executives; Jack Raymond and Shirley Katzander, who own New York public relations agencies; Sterling Lord, New York literary agent; Creed Black, publisher, the *Herald* and *Leader*, Lexington, Kentucky; Robert Donovan and Jack Foisie, *Los Angeles Times;* Herbert Mitgang, *New York Times;* Warren Phillips, board chairman, *Wall Street Journal;* and Otto Friedrich, *Time* magazine.

Pulitzer Prizes? Mauldin has two, the first in 1945 for "Willie and Joe" and the second in 1959 for his "Boris Pasternak" cartoon. Russell Jones, one of the founders of the London edition, won a Pulitzer for his reporting in Hungary in 1956. Mark Watson, a captain for the World War I edition, was awarded a Pulitzer for his work on the *Baltimore Sun*.

There were at least four different editions of *The Stars and Stripes* in the Civil War. A private newspaper of that name was printed at Tobacco Factory, Virginia, in August 1861. The first military *Stripes* was published at Bloomfield, Missouri, on November 9, 1861, for members of the 18th and 29th Illinois Volunteer Regiments.

A copy of the Bloomfield paper, which is owned by the University of Michigan, carries this slogan: "The Union, it must and shall be preserved." On another page is this reminder: "Persons wishing *The Stars and Stripes* can obtain it by leaving their names with the carrier."

Another edition, called *Stars and Stripes in Rebeldom,* was published by prisoners of the Confederacy. The issue dated November 28, 1861, published by the Union Lyceum at Parish Prison, New Orleans, listed George T. Childs as editor.

The fourth *Stars and Stripes* was published at Jacksonport, Arkansas, and its volume 1, number 1, dated December 1, 1863, said: "The officers requested us to edit a loyal paper here, which we agreed to do, till somebody else could be got to run the machine. If anybody thinks they can get up a better paper under the same circumstances, they can occupy our editorial chair." The Arkansas publication reported "there was no paper on hand, or obtainable, but wallpaper."

The existence of the Civil War papers may or may not have influenced Guy T. Viskniskki, an army second lieutenant in Paris. He came up with the concept for a newspaper for the U.S. troops and sold it to Gen. John J. Pershing. This is what Viskniskki, by then a captain, wrote in the newspaper's first anniversary issue:

> It fell to my lot to propose *The Stars and Stripes,* to give the paper its name, to set forth its aims and its policies, to organize it and then to manage it as officer in charge until some weeks after the armistice.
>
> But (barring an officer or two, who had to be around to satisfy Army tradition) *The Stars and Stripes* has actually been produced by enlisted men, many of the lowly, or buck, variety. A handful of enlisted men has written and illustrated the greater part of the paper — I believe, for its size, the most brilliant and er-erratic *[sic]* editorial staff ever possessed by an American newspaper.

William K. Michael sheds more light on the name selection process. A lieutenant with the 101st Machine Gun Battalion, 26th Infantry Division, he and Hudson Hawley, a buck private who had worked for the *Springfield* [Massachusetts] *Republican,* were sent from Neufchateau to Paris to work with Viskniskki.

Michael recalled: "Visk, Charles P. Cushing, a Marine lieutenant who had been a free-lance writer and photographer, and I got together to select a suitable name like Liberty, Independence,

U.S.A. and then chose *The Stars and Stripes* because it was long enough to go over the full seven columns of the front page."

Although mostly civilian now, the staff of both the European and the Pacific editions still retains the military flavor: Both have officers in charge and some enlisted personnel on the staff. Both are geared for the long haul. Both are set up to live forever.

When I joined the newspaper in Paris in October 1944, the only longevity I was thinking about was my own.

I was to remain with *Stripes* for the next ten years — the rest of the war in Paris; Liege, Belgium; and Nice, France. After the fighting ended, I was sent to Germany to be the managing editor of the Pfungstadt edition. While there I took my discharge from the army at Frankfurt and continued working as a civilian on that edition, another at Altdorf in Bavaria, and the last few years in Griesheim near Darmstadt.

The history that would form during my years with *Stripes* was phenomenal, and we tried to cover it all . . .

1

Paris

Leaves were falling from the chestnut trees as I walked up the Champs Élysées and turned onto Rue de Berri that late October day in 1944. I entered the *Herald-Tribune* building, where *The Stars and Stripes* was located and where I hoped to get a transfer to keep me out of the infantry.

My one concern was that I was AWOL. Well, perhaps not technically absent without leave, but certainly in Paris without a pass.

I had a pass from my SHAEF (Supreme Headquarters of the Allied Expeditionary Forces) outfit at Camp Satory near Versailles to go to the dispensary on the outskirts of Paris. For some reason the bus driver never stopped, and the next thing I knew I was staring up at the huge arch, which I soon found out to be the Arc de Triomphe de l'Étoile.

There was an elevator in the lobby at the *Herald-Tribune* but since *Stripes* was on the second floor, I walked up. I had been in the army two years and I was used to walking.

A hand-painted sign that read "Abandon Your Stripes All Who Enter Here" greeted me as I opened the door to the newsroom. Since I had only the two stripes of a corporal, I wasn't too concerned. I asked a GI seated behind a desk for the officer in charge.

"Oh, I guess you mean Max. He's in charge today," and he pointed to an office across the hall. I entered and saluted a blond captain at a desk in a very small room.

"At ease, Corporal. I'm Max Gilstrap. Sit down."

When I told him I had heard that *The Stars and Stripes* was looking for copy desk help and that I had experience on a daily newspaper in California, he excused himself and left the room. A few minutes later he returned with a tall, balding man I assumed to be a major or a lieutenant colonel. He wore no insignia on his shirt.

"This is Bud Hutton, one of our managing editors," the captain said.

"What rag did you work on?" Hutton asked.

"*The Sacramento Union,* sir. It's a daily, and I was there five years before I was inducted."

"Don't call me sir. It's a Scripps-Howard sheet, isn't it?" he said.

"No, sir . . . I mean no," I stammered. "It's an independently owned paper, but Charley Lilley, the editor, is an old Scripps-Howard hand. He used to be editor of the *Cleveland Press.*"

"Well, if you're trained by Scripps-Howard people, we can use you. Max, can you get him a seven-day TDY buck slip? Listen, Zumwalt, take the buck slip back to your top kick and get your ass here as fast as you can."

I later found out that Hutton was a master sergeant but never wore his stripes. At least I never saw him with them. He did wear a Canadian army jacket, also without stripes or insignia, a souvenir of service in that branch as a photographer prior to transferring to the American army while in England. I also found out that his full name was Oram Clark Hutton, but I never heard anyone call him that.

After my interview with Gilstrap and Hutton, I walked back to the Étoile to see about transportation to camp. I was certain there would be a bus. If there wasn't, I was in big trouble.

Missing the bus to the dispensary that twenty-eighth day of October changed my life. I had been in the European Theater of Operations (ETO) five months, having left Boston June 6, the day of the Allied landing in Normandy. Our ship, the USS *Wakefield,* docked in Liverpool following a six-day solo crossing.

After a brief stay in Devon, I was assigned to Headquarters Company, Headquarters Command, SHAEF, in Bushey Park east of London. My assignment was with the training and security section. Our job was to track incoming buzz or robot bombs as they crossed the English Channel and to alert the headquarters of Generals Dwight D. Eisenhower and Carl Spaatz, Air Marshal Sir Arthur W. Tedder, and two nearby airplane factories.

As the invasion progressed, General Ike moved his headquarters to Portsmouth and then to Versailles, but by the time I got to France he had shifted farther east to Rheims. When the Germans were pushed back to their own borders, there were fewer V-1s and V-2s aimed at London. So our outfit was transferred to Camp Satory near Versailles, where most of us were slated for the infantry.

I was headed for the dispensary that day to take a physical exam in order to transfer to the paratroops. A buddy, Cpl. Richard Harding, who was in his early twenties, was going to join. One night, over a few pints of ale, he convinced me that I should too despite my advanced age of thirty. Missing the bus saved me; I never heard how Harding made out.

When I arrived earlier that morning, I could not believe that I was in Paris. Not having a pass was damn inconvenient, but I decided to brazen it through. I stepped up to the nearest of several military police and asked how to get to the Scribe Hotel, the headquarters of the Public Information Division, where another buddy, Cpl. Ken Conybear, had recently been assigned.

The MP told me to follow Avenue Friedland until it joined Boulevard Haussmann and then to keep going. I did and finally reached the Opera and the nearby Scribe. It was a long walk, but the alternative was a ride on the Metro. Since I knew no French, let alone how to buy a ticket or how to get off once I was on, it was better that I walked.

Conybear was on duty and he showed me about. He also suggested that I give up the idea of jumping with the paratroops and try to get into his outfit.

"In the first place, you're too old for that sort of thing. Those guys are all kids. It would be better for you to try and get on here; all the accredited newspaper and radio correspondents work out of here. Ernest Hemingway, Ernie Pyle, Charles Collingwood, and all the rest. This is the place for you," he said. He didn't have to twist my arm: I was ready when he led me to his commanding officer, a lieutenant colonel whose name I have forgotten. The colonel said his table of organization was filled, but he did say that *The Stars and*

Stripes was looking for copyreaders. The newspaper had been in Paris about two months and was planning to expand from four to eight pages.

He told me how to get to the *Herald-Tribune* building. I thanked him, said goodbye to Conybear, and off I went back to the Étoile. I could see the buses lined up, but I skirted the area, walked up the Champs Élysées, and made a left on Rue de Berri.

With the buck slip that Captain Gilstrap had given me, I hurried to the bus and sat down in one of the last remaining seats for the ride back to Versailles. I had walked about twenty miles or so across Paris and back, and I was exhausted.

I intended to return to newspaper work when the war ended, so *Stripes* was the answer. If I made it, I would be doing in uniform what I did in civilian life; not every GI could make that statement. I had been reading the London edition for the past three months while I was stationed outside of London. It was a good paper and, I thought, very professional.

I was aware that *Stripes* had started in Paris during World War I and had many on its staff who later became famous — men like Harold Ross, Steve Early, Alexander Woollcott, and Grantland Rice. The World War II version began as a weekly, first published on April 18, 1942, to serve American troops stationed in Northern Ireland. It became a daily on November 2 that same year and was printed in the London *Times* building.

I found out that I hadn't even been missed when I reached Camp Satory. The next morning I told the first sergeant what had happened and he took the buck slip into the major, who gave his approval for seven days' temporary duty. I got the impression that they didn't care where I went, as long as my name was deleted from their duty roster.

★   ★   ★

I sat down at the same copy desk that had been used by the *Herald-Tribune* before the Germans captured Paris. The news editor was Bob Moora, a first lieutenant who, like Hutton, didn't wear his insignia while on duty. Hutton was nowhere in sight. I found out later he had returned to the States for duty in the New York news bureau and for a thirty-day furlough. Moora had formerly been on the desk at the *New York Herald-Tribune,* and he was as quiet as Hutton was brash.

The office was abuzz that day with news of a meeting in General Eisenhower's headquarters between the supreme commander and Gilstrap and Hutton. Maj. Arthur Goodfriend, head of the information and education orientation section and *Stripes* editor, was out of town, so Gilstrap, his assistant, filled in. That meeting, it turned out, was held the day before I had my talk with the captain and the master sergeant.

Hutton told staff members gathered around his desk that the general was displeased over an editorial printed in late September entitled "So You Wanna Go Home, Eh?". Goodfriend, a former women's wear fashion writer from New York, should have been at the meeting because it was he who had written the editorial, Hutton said.

Thousands of letters from GIs and officers alike protesting the editorial were received by the B-Bag editor. (B-Bag, with its subtitle "Blow It Out Here," was a daily feature.) A full page of some of the letters was printed October 2. One, for example, objected to a key sentence, "It looks like our great big American supermen are ready to leave this legalized murder to the nurses, Wacs, and clubmobile girls."

Gilstrap wrote about the October 27 meeting with the supreme commander a year later in the *Christian Science Monitor*, the newspaper he had worked for prior to joining the army. Here is what he said:

> General Ike was cordial. He merely wanted to get a few ideas off his mind.
>
> Recalling that he had made a practice to leave *The Stars and Stripes* alone, the general emphasized, as he did later for publication, that our soldiers' paper must remain free as long as it lived. However, he said he expected us to play ball in using discretion on anything that might be detrimental to the best interests of the Army. On editorial policy he thought it important occasionally to remind the soldier of what he is fighting for, but to be careful in expressing opinions which might not be those of the soldiers in the field. He cautioned us on printing anything which might undermine confidence in command.
>
> General Ike said he read our letters column first of all since it gave him an idea of what the soldier was thinking about. At the end of our 45-minute conference he emphasized again that he didn't want us to feel we were being told how to run our paper; that he considered it the greatest influencing factor for the soldier in the Army.

These assurances from the lips of the Supreme Commander were extremely heartening to newsmen in uniform striving to publish an Army newspaper in the tradition of the press. His words were to be our Magna Charta, a protection against influences which might curb our freedom in the days ahead.

From the very start of the London edition of *Stripes*, editorials caused problems. The presentation of straight news and news features was the easy part of getting out a newspaper for the men on the ground and the men in the air — men the writers called Joe, as in GI Joe or Combat Joe, but mostly just Joe.

The editors, all with a number of years' experience working on civilian newspapers, thought that presenting the news was what was required when they took the assignment. It would be easy: they didn't accept ads, so there would be no advertisers breathing down their necks, and no business office concerns.

When the first edition came out April 18, 1942, as a weekly, Gen. George C. Marshall, the army chief of staff, set the policy in a Page 1 article by pointing out that during World War I, on Gen. John J. Pershing's authority, he had assurance that "no official control was exercised over the matter which went into *The Stars and Stripes*" and that it "always was entirely for and by the soldiers."

"That policy," Marshall declared, "is to govern the conduct of the new publication. . . . A soldier's newspaper, in these grave times, is more than a moral venture. It is a symbol of the things we are fighting to preserve and spread in this threatened world. It represents the free thought and free expression of a free people."

Heady and important words, but certain rear echelon generals and colonels felt otherwise. They, on their own, decided that *Stripes* would make a fine propaganda organ. The editorials appeared on a regular basis and continued even after the meeting between Eisenhower, Gilstrap, and Hutton.

★   ★   ★

It was good to get back on a copy desk, a bit like old times in Sacramento, where I had been first a reporter and then my last two years state editor.

The Stars and Stripes was a five-column tabloid, while I had been used to a standard eight-column format. It didn't make much difference because Moora passed me up on the important stories and gave me only shorts. It would be like that until I learned the paper's style.

The headline the second morning I was there read: CRACK ANTWERP BLOCKADE. That head was probably written by Lester David, who later in the week took over the desk when Moora returned to the States for a brief stay. Les had worked on the *Brooklyn Eagle* in civilian life. When he had a day off or was on a writing assignment, the slotman was Sid Gans, also a New York newspaperman.

Reporters working out of Paris included Charles W. White, Joseph B. Fleming, Richard Lewis, Arthur White, Fred Mertinke, and Walter B. Smith. The field staff included Jules B. Grad, Earl Mazo, G. K. Hodenfield, Russell F. Jones, Allan M. Morrison, Jimmy Cannon, Andy Rooney, Ralph Martin, Morrow Davis, and Dan Regan. Morrison was the only black soldier on the staff.

The news headlines were terse and to the point. The feature heads were something else. A couple of days after I arrived, one of the deskmen turned in this gem on a four-picture layout of Adolf Hitler: WITH A HEIL NAZI NAZI AND A HOT BLAH BLAH.

News copy came into the office by teletype, some of it written in cablese to save transmission space. Other typewritten articles arrived in a courier pouch from the 1st, 3rd, 7th, and 9th armies' press camps where *The Stars and Stripes* staff writers, wearing the dark green and gold war correspondent patches on their caps and shirts, were attached as accredited reporters. Air Force copy was sometimes flown to Paris by fighter planes.

My first brush with cablese was a disaster. The story came in on the teletype from Mazo, who was just outside Metz in eastern France with the 95th and 5th infantry divisions of Gen. George S. Patton's 3rd Army. I was given his cable by the slotman and was told to unscramble it and write a headline. The story started out with "ninetyfifthetfifth," and I being new at this form of news writing assumed that the "etfifth," which meant "and fifth," was garbled, so I just left it off.

The next day hell was to pay all the way from Metz to Paris and a couple of way points. Needless to say, Mazo caught the brunt with the 5th Division brass and GIs alike. *Stripes* published this box on Page 1 the next day, November 21:

Fifth, 95th and Metz
An error in transcription of a cabled story by staff writer Earl Mazo telling of the taking of Metz listed the 95th Division but failed to mention the Fifth Division in *The Stars and Stripes* Mon-

day. As Mazo said in his story it was the "blood and guts of the Fifth and 95th Divisions" that won at Metz.

"You had better stay the hell away from the 5th Division because they'll kill you. I almost got it myself and I didn't do a thing," Mazo told me a week later when I met him in the office.

I was always extra careful from then on and turned in the original with the finished copy so the desk could check it out. The best example of cablese was the famous reply of foreign correspondent Reynolds Packard to his desk in New York: "Upstick job asswards."

Despite my goof, the 5th did all right, and Mazo didn't have to hide out after his story about the "foxhole surgeon" was published on Page 1 November 30. The space above the name of the newspaper, sometimes called the masthead, was reserved for extra special stories, and that was what Mazo's story was.

Medic Private Saves Dying GI
With Knife and Pen Surgery
By Earl Mazo
Stars and Stripes Staff Writer

WITH THE FIFTH DIV., Nov. 29 — Using a GI knife and fountain pen, Pvt. Duane N. Kinman, 19 year-old medic from College Place, Washington, D.C., accomplished what might be the most remarkable piece of battlefield surgery of this war when he performed a windpipe operation to save a dying man during a concentrated mortar barrage.

It was during the drive on Metz. An aid man in B. Co., Second Regt., Kinman was finishing the job of bandaging chest wounds and the shattered ankle of one soldier when he saw another drop close by and thresh the earth with his arms and legs as though choking to death.

Quickly he went over and examined the wounded man who was turning blue in the face because a shrapnel wound in his throat prevented him from breathing. Remembering a lecture in basic training months before, Kinman calmly opened his GI knife and began probing for shrapnel in the wounded man's throat.

The injured man, almost in his last breath, continued threshing his arms and legs. Platoon Leader Lt. Edwin Eberling, of Lincoln, Neb., crawled over to hold him while Kinman worked.

Carefully missing the jugular vein, Kinman cut into the wounded man's throat. Feeling for the windpipe as blood squirted out and dripped onto the mud which was the operating table, the young medic found what he thought was the right spot and made a one-and-a half inch incision just below the point where the shrapnel went in.

Then to keep the "breather hole" open, Kinman slipped his fountain-pen into the hole. The wounded man, now breathing more freely, was moved to a clearing station.

Doctors all the way up to the evacuation hospital marvelled at his skill and said medical schools in the States might offer him a surgical scholarship.

And that is just what happened. A few days later the United Press reported that Kinman, at that time a T/4 (technician fourth-grade), had been offered a free medical education at Case Western Reserve University in Cleveland, Ohio, provided he could pass pre-medical exams. I never heard of him again.

★   ★   ★

The Paris edition of *The Stars and Stripes* was the third on the Continent. The first was at Saint-Mere Eglise, the second at Rennes.

When the invasion of France seemed certain, Lt. Col. Ensley Maxwell Llewellyn, a Tacoma, Washington, advertising man who started the London *Stripes* as a major, announced to some of the staff that he had a plan for a Continental edition. "We'll go in the first day with the second or third wave of troops," he said.

They landed at Omaha Beach on D plus 12 and made their way to Carentan, which had just been taken by the 101st Airborne Division.

The colonel hired a sign painter who came up with a huge wooden panel that said "Stars and Stripes Continental Edition." He hung it on the front of a print shop, but a German shell brought it and the building down a few days later. The staff moved to Saint-Mere Eglise, where they had located a small printing plant, and brought out a single sheet printed on both sides on July 4.

"The first print order was 100,000, and we were able to up that to 150,000, but that was it," Warren F. McDonald, circulation manager, recalled later. McDonald, who had been with *Stripes* since its days as a weekly serving GIs stationed in Northern Ireland, said they also depended on receiving some papers from the London edition but that they didn't always get through.

In addition to Llewellyn and McDonald, the first landing

party included Maj. W. C. McNamara, Charles Kiley, Jacob Miller, Earl Mazo, Robert Collins, Jack Melcher, Ralph Noel, Claude Briscoe, and Wally Newfield.

The headline on that first Continental issue was YANKS LAUNCH NEW ATTACK ON PENINSULA, all in capital letters just under the legend PRINTED SOMEWHERE IN FRANCE.

Since a larger printing plant was required, Llewellyn, Collins, McDonald, and Lt. Stan Thompson of *Yank* magazine drove south to Rennes and found the facilities they wanted. The next day the staff arrived: Bob Moora, Melcher, Andy Rooney, Bryce Burke, and Herb Schneider, among others.

The last Continental edition appeared August 19; the first Rennes papers came off the press August 21. Its last issue was September 2, two weeks after the Paris edition started.

★   ★   ★

Lou Rakin, a lawyer and police judge in Linden, New Jersey, before the war who became a T/5 (technician fifth-grade), edited the letters that appeared in B-Bag, but he had other duties as well. He rode herd on a help-wanted column and a feature listing births.

One memorable letter was from 2nd/Lt. Frances Slanger, a nurse in a U.S. Army Field Hospital. It was so meaningful that it was printed in the editorial space alongside the regular B-Bag column. In it she thanked the wounded for the privilege of easing their pain and sharing some of their hardships. She said she was proud to be there as they were brought in "bloody, dirty with the earth and grime and most of them so tired."

"For a change," she wrote, "we want the men to know what we think of them." She signed the letter along with three other nurses and mailed it October 21.

That same evening Frances Slanger was killed by a German shell. Her obituary and photograph were published November 22 on the same page as her letter under this headline: 1ST ETO NURSE KILLED IN ACTION.

Two months later, another story reported that the first Red Cross girl had been killed. She was Ann Kathleen Cullen of Larchmont, New York, and she died when a German bomb fell on a U.S. Army hospital in Belgium. "Katie" Cullen, twenty-six, joined the ARC in June 1943 and came to the Continent after a year's service in Britain. Both stories were under Arthur White's byline.

★   ★   ★

The first few nights I was in Paris I slept in a room in the Hotel Haussmann, assigned to another staffer but not being used at the time. I came home a couple of nights later and found my gear in the hall, so I took over the room of a reporter I knew was in the field. The next day I was given my own quarters in a loft in Montmartre and walked back and forth to work.

The *Stripes* brass wanted the troops nearby, so on a cold and damp Christmas Eve, about twelve of us were moved into a vacant building on the Champs Élysées not too far from the Étoile. It had been a hotel, an apartment building or, perhaps, a department store, but now it was completely devoid of carpets, drapes, and furniture. There were wooden bunks and the inevitable straw ticks on the second floor. There was no heat but there were fireplaces in each room, and the unoccupied wooden bunks made great firewood. We called the place Pneumonia Manor.

★   ★   ★

The most popular page with the troops was sports. It was edited by Gene Graff, who also wrote a column entitled "Once Over Lightly." Graff prided himself in packing as much news and scores in that single page as he could, despite one or two pieces of art and a comic strip across the bottom.

The lead story the next morning after I went to work said: "Ensign Sid Luckman of the Maritime Service got off his boat long enough to pass the Chicago Bears to a 29–21 triumph over the Cleveland Rams in Chicago."

Two and sometimes three comic strips were used in the four-page paper: "Li'l Abner," "Terry and the Pirates," and "Blondie." Later, when the paper expanded, "Popeye," "Abbie and Slats," and "Dick Tracy" were added. Late in December, "Jane," a London *Daily Mirror* feature, joined the comic family and became an instant hit because Norman Pett, the artist, took delight in lifting Jane's skirts and frequently her entire dress.

A two-column cartoon appeared daily on the page with B-Bag and the editorial. It was either "Up Front" by Bill Mauldin or "Hubert" by Dick Wingert. Mauldin, working on the Rome edition of *Stripes*, sent his original art to New York, where it was dispatched to Paris. Later, a panel by 1st/Lt. Dave Breger was used in the Paris edition.

One of the best-read features was "Hashmarks," a column of brief stabs at humor and recycled old jokes. It carried the initials

J.C.W., which stood for John Cornish Wilkinson, a South Carolina captain who had been told by his commanding officer earlier in London to write a daily humor column. "It will be funny, Lieutenant — that's an order," the CO said.

It usually was funny, helped along with drawings by Dick Wingert, Curtis Swan, and Ralph Newman in London and Bert Marsh in Paris.

★   ★   ★

Shortly after I arrived, a general came bustling into the newsroom. He had been there before, I was later told. A hush came over the large room, the typewriters fell silent, everyone looked up as he strode to the news desk.

"I have a great idea for the top of page one. It's something like the 'Buy American' and 'Buy Bonds' that the Hearst papers use back home. It could run every day," he said as he shoved a piece of paper across the desk.

The note said: Have You Killed Your German Today? The general stood waiting, smiling at his contribution. The room remained quiet. Finally, the general left.

"Who the hell is that?" I asked.

"That's O. N. Solbert, chief, special service officer, ETOUSA. He's the big boss; he's over Goodfriend. Last month he was chicken colonel. That's the first time we've seen the new star," my friend said.

I never saw the general in the newsroom again; the slogan he suggested never saw print in *The Stars and Stripes*.

★   ★   ★

The big story in *The Stars and Stripes* was always the war. The second biggest that November was President Roosevelt's victory over Thomas Dewey. It was the first wartime presidential election campaign since the days of Abraham Lincoln.

As far as the election campaign was concerned — the speeches, the handshaking, the promises — our readers were spared. There was an Associated Press story published on an inside page October 21 which said the soldier vote was expected to hit 2.3 million.

The next week Elmer Roessner, a civilian in officer's attire, sat down at the desk. A longtime newspaperman, and now with the Office of War Information, he asked for and was given all campaign copy off the teletype. He sifted through the wire service articles and then put them in a file. Nothing about electioneering was printed between that October 21 AP story and the day before the November 6 election. That day readers were told: CANDIDATES WIND UP VOTE DRIVE.

The lead story reported the Allies nearing Rotterdam. The election story was the off-play or secondary and jumped to an inside page that featured photos of the two presidential candidates and a sidebar that said bettors were laying $17 to $5 for an FDR victory.

On election day, *Stripes* was in the hands of its readers before America turned out to vote. The headline: 50 MILLION VOTERS HEAD FOR POLLS; FDR CEDED EDGE.

The complete story was reported in Wednesday's issue under a five-column banner: FDR WINS FOURTH TERM.

Moora's byline was on the Washington-datelined story that read out of this two-column head: DEWEY BACKERS CONCEDE DEFEAT ON GROWING TIDE.

Thursday's edition reported that President Roosevelt had a 2,401,000-vote edge and that he led in twenty-eight states. A picture of Harry S. Truman, the new vice-president, appeared with that of the president.

On election day, the B-Bag editor received a letter from lst/Lt. Melville E. Watson and he turned it over to the news desk. The letter asked, "Will you as soon as possible publish the complete returns by state with particular reference to Hancock County, Indiana?"

The lieutenant's request was cabled to Ben Price in the New York news bureau, who must have thought the guy on the desk in Paris was crazy but, nevertheless, acted on it the following day. Price, one of the early staffers on the London edition, later returned to the Paris edition as picture editor.

Price's reply was published on Page 1, November 11:

Hancock County Briefs
Ira Fisk Elected Sheriff

Hancock County, Indiana — Sheriff, Ira Fisk, Republican; Coroner, Charles Pasco, Republican; Surveyor, Chris Ostermier, Democrat. Bertha Kirkpatrick, Democrat, won something — we think county clerk. Now that we've shown we can do it, we rest on our laurels. No more please.

Roessner stayed around for a few days and then returned to his OWI job. I met him in New York some years later and he told me the reason he was sent to Paris was that the Roosevelt administration wanted to be certain that Dewey's campaign was given no more or no less news space than the president's. As far as I know, there were no complaints from the GOP about campaign coverage.

★   ★   ★

Another major story that November was about cigarettes. Like most GIs, I smoked, but I soon learned that cigarettes were worth money on the black market. The only problem was that we were permitted to purchase only five packs a week at the post exchange, and if you had a heavy habit you didn't have anything to sell.

A shortage was revealed in a front-page story November 14 that Communication Zone troops in Paris would get no cigarettes that week, so that combat men could continue to get their seven-pack-a-week ration.

A sign in the Paris PX said: "No cigarettes, cigars or tobacco of any kind until further notice."

Ten days later sales resumed, with combat men cut from seven to five packs a week and Com Z personnel limited to two packs. Two packs a week could hardly satisfy a normal smoking habit, but it sure slowed down the black-market process. The only alternative was to ask the folks back home to mail an occasional carton, but that took time and conditions were not all that great in the States.

Secretary of War Harry L. Stimpson said November 16 in Washington that the cigarette shortage overseas would be corrected. Then two months later, it all became clear. Staff writer Ernest Leiser reported that the men of the 716th Railway Operating Battalion in Paris had been stealing cigarettes by the case, selling them on the black market, and sending the money home in the form of money orders which an officer must sign. In his story, Leiser said two officers and 182 enlisted men were charged with theft and black-market sales.

Four prison terms of forty years at hard labor and a fifth of forty-five years were ordered for the five enlisted men tried January 11. All were dishonorably discharged; all were from Company C of the 716th.

Black-marketing was not the only crime taking place that fall in wartime France. There were a number of cases of rape, for which punishment was much more severe. This appeared on Page 3, November 20:

2 Soldiers Hanged
After Rape Convictions

Two soldiers were hanged last Saturday at Fort du Roule, Cherbourg. Both were sentenced to death by a U.S. court martial. One was convicted of rape and assault with a dangerous weapon. The sentences were reviewed and confirmed by Gen. Eisenhower.

Two days later another story, this one only one paragraph, reported the hanging of a U.S. soldier at St. Lo for the crime of rape. His sentence was also reviewed and confirmed by the supreme commander.

★   ★   ★

As Christmas neared, *Stripes* launched a shopping service for combat troops. Sgt. Ralph Noel of the business office and Wac Pfc Mariam Jean Brody set up and operated the service which provided lists of stores, gifts, and prices.

If Joe happened to be in Paris on leave, all he had to do was to drop by the newspaper, make his selection, and leave some of his combat pay. The volunteers would do the shopping, wrap the gifts and take care of the duty, if any, and pay the shipping costs.

If he was unable to get to Paris, as was usually the case, he could send a note and money and the gift would soon be on its way. The American Red Cross performed a similar service for troops stationed in and near Paris. Both were popular with GIs and officers.

★   ★   ★

Capt. Rader Winget, an Associated Press reporter before the war, had reason to be proud of his communication setup located on the top floor of the *Herald-Tribune* building. It was probably the best on the Continent, the envy of the U.S. Army Signal Corps and other news agencies in Paris — but it wasn't always so.

The captain had followed an American cavalry recon outfit into Paris the day the city was liberated. He took over the office even while German soldiers were running down Rue de Berri. His big problem — other than the Germans — was that he didn't have any equipment.

As fate would have it, a bewildered French underground fighter wandered into an office downstairs where Bob Moora was arranging desks for his editorial staff to use when the switch was made from Rennes. The Frenchman told Moora he knew where he could get some German communications equipment and wondered if the Americans wanted it. The Americans most certainly did. Moora sent for Winget, and the result was that the captain borrowed a six-by-six from circulation and he and the Frenchman took off.

They drove to St. Cloud where, in the hills, they found a German radio station complete with transmitting and receiving equipment including hellschreibers, the German version of teletype machines. It took several trips to get the priceless haul downtown to the *Herald-Tribune.*

The Signal Corps couldn't provide a line from London to Paris — said it would be at least a month — and refused to give him a GI operator, so Winget hired a Frenchman. Soon he had the entire Reuters news report rolling in, the AP and UP on Morse code, and for good measure the German DNB news file.

Later, the Signal Corps put in the necessary lines and one teletype machine but still refused to provide military operators. Winget got around that by bringing in AWOL soldiers from the street and putting them to work while he bucked transfer papers around the command like crazy.

"We got our only fully qualified operator on a fluke; he was busted for throwing a piece of paper on the floor, and the Signal Corps couldn't refuse him a transfer to *Stripes* after the bust," Winget wrote in a story for the tenth anniversary edition of *Stripes* in 1952.

On the night of November 21, just minutes before the paper went to press, Winget charged into the newsroom with a bulletin that he dropped on the desk. It quoted Swiss Radio as saying French forces had bypassed Mulhouse and Colmar and were in Strasbourg. The bulletin, set in boldface type, led the front page the next morning. Three days later the headline read: 7TH ARMY IN STRASBOURG.

It wasn't until January 11 that we knew for certain what Vic Dallaire and Ed Clark were doing in Strasbourg. We knew that the two Rome-based staffers were putting out a paper there, but we didn't know how they were doing until a story by Helen Kirkpatrick of the *Chicago Daily News* came in on the teletype. Here is her story:

2 S&S Men Publish Paper
In Strasbourg As Soldiers
Staff Leave Town By Order
By Helen Kirkpatrick
Chicago Daily News Correspondent

STRASBOURG (Delayed) — Two sergeants who refused to quit prevented "the great fear" of Strasbourg from turning into panic.

Now that the threat to Strasbourg is officially declared over, the story can be told as it came out on "the day of the great return" — Saturday, Jan. 6. The German New Year's Eve attack necessitated some changes in disposition of Seventh Army forces. For some 30 hours the capital of Alsace, across the Rhine from Germany, was held by two *Stars and Stripes* sergeants and a company of MPs.

On Tuesday, Jan. 2, the people of Strasbourg saw the Americans pulling out. To them, this was a disaster. And nobody bothered to explain to them that it wasn't.

Wednesday morning is now known as "the day of the great fear." Strasbourg thought the Germans were coming back in and they knew it would mean mass slaughter. They began piling up such possessions as they could in carts and baby carriages. They took to the roads.

Staff Ordered Out

In Strasbourg, the two sergeants heard the order to move and decided to stay put. These men had been editing and publishing *The Stars and Stripes* in Sicily, Italy, southern France and Alsace. They thought the troops needed it at that moment. All their staff were ordered out and had to go — reluctantly and with anger in their hearts.

For three days *The Stars and Stripes* was published by these two sergeants and a French linotype operator. It came out as one sheet printed in English, French and German, and it was the only news Strasbourg had.

The Frenchman monitored BBC news in French and German and set it up. The electricity faded often during the night and it was five o'clock in the morning before the paper was off the press. The boys slept a few hours and then distributed the army newspaper throughout the city.

Walked About Town

Because of that — according to testimony of dozens of Strasbourg citizens — panic was prevented. *The Stars and Stripes* team

and the MPs made a point of walking around town showing
themselves.

Former UP man, now Staff Sgt. Victor Dallaire, of Medford,
Ore., gives all credit to his assistant, Sgt. Edgar Clark, of San
Francisco, and three boys of the Third Div.: James Lee, of Pine
Bluff, Wyo., Red Bell, of Pecos, Texas, and Arthur Simpson, of
New York. But they all think Vic Dallaire is the man to be
praised. And they are all in favor of the 163rd Signal Photo Det.
which supplied pictures.

Dallaire says there were a lot of reasons why they couldn't
walk out. There's Lucien Detiere, the 14-year-old FFI lad with
three Germans to his credit. He became *The Stars and Stripes* office
boy when the French Army decided he was too young to be a regular soldier. He and his family would have been murdered by the
Germans.

Couldn't Leave Mascot

And there's 16-year-old "formidable" Anna Marie from
Saint Die, whose house was burned when the Germans fired the
entire town. She's *The Stars and Stripes* mascot and they couldn't
leave her and her mother who is dying of cancer.

Slowly Strasbourg is coming back to life. Saturday was "the
day of the great return."

"The worst moment for us," said Dallaire, "was the day we
went around with the people of Strasbourg and helped them take
down the French and American flags. We were so ashamed we
couldn't look each other or the people in the face. And they were
ashamed and unhappy too. After all you can't blame them. Look
at the way the Germans treated them when they were here. They
knew what would happen if the Germans returned."

Dallaire later said that the three 3rd Division GIs were putting
out their weekly newspaper in the same plant at the time of the
evacuation order and decided to stay and help *Stripes*.

There were also two civilians attached to the Psychological
Warfare Division in Strasbourg, and both thought it a good idea to
keep publishing since the civilian papers were closed. The PWD
men provided French and German texts of SHAEF news broad-
casts. Radio was the only other source of news.

As each issue came off the press, Dallaire and Clark loaded
their jeeps and made the rounds of the closed newsstands. In front
of each they deposited a stack of papers, and the townspeople
snatched them up, leaving behind five francs, which the two ser-

geants used to buy food, since they hadn't been paid in months. Their pay books were in Rome.

Conditions returned to normal, and the Strasbourg staff was transferred to Nancy when that edition started up January 22. But Strasbourg never forgot the two sergeants — a street in that city across the Rhine River from Germany was renamed "Avenue des *The Stars and Stripes*" in their honor, and the grateful French awarded Dallaire and Clark the Croix de Guerre.

That decoration came along just in time to nip plans of some American officers to court-martial the pair for disregarding orders. Some months later Dallaire and Clark did receive the Bronze Star from the U.S. Army.

★   ★   ★

One of the features of the 1918 newspaper was revived with the establishment of the *Stars and Stripes* Orphan Fund. Started in World War I, it was launched again on November 30, 1944, on Page 1.

The first French orphan to be sponsored by GIs was Guy M., a ten-year-old youngster whose right foot was permanently injured in a bombing raid. To help care for Guy for five years, soldiers contributed $400.

The response was good. Approximately 630 orphans had been cared for in England. The lighter side was some of the letters that accompanied the contributions, such as: "For our $400 we would like to select a redheaded, good-looking, feminine little French war orphan about twenty years of age."

It wasn't long before a clause was inserted in the conditions of sponsorship specifying that no orphan would be more than twelve years old. The fund had been approved by the French Ministry of Health and was administered by the American and French Red Cross. During World War I, 3,444 orphans were sponsored.

★   ★   ★

One of the stories I recall working on wound up with this head: DATES WITH GIS TO GET HOLLAND GIRLS IN DUTCH.

John M. Mecklin of the *Chicago Sun* reported that church officials in Maastricht, Holland, were warning Dutch girls not to associate with American troops. Unsigned posters were also tacked up about the city warning that girls seen in the company of GIs would have their heads shaved, as would women who collaborated with the Nazis.

The church campaign started soon after the Americans liberated Maastricht on September 14. The newspaper *Veritas* published editorials supporting the church's position. The newspaper warned that there would be an increase in illegitimacy and venereal disease if the Dutch girls yielded to "temptations of Americans" with chocolate and cigarettes.

So much for romance.

★   ★   ★

A four-page feature section called *Warweek* made its appearance each Saturday starting a week before I joined the staff. The first issue contained a double-page spread written by Ed Wilcox and entitled "I Saw Aachen Die." Other writers on *Warweek* were Hamilton Whitman, John Christie, Frances Herron, Joseph Wechsberg, Joe Weston, Jack Caldwell, Simon Bourgin, and Igor Cassini.

A second section, *Tomorrow*, was included in the paper in mid-December. It appeared each Wednesday with stateside features designed to make the transition easy for the GI when he returned to civilian life. The drawings of the pretty girls were usually worth a second look.

All this — *Stripes*, *Warweek*, and *Tomorrow* — had to be trucked to the forward areas in the cold and wet of December. The paper's six-by-six trucks, and some of the trains that were operating, were hauling about 800,000 newspapers six days a week. The problem was that Paris was just too far in the rear to insure morning delivery.

On December 16 six staffers set out in two jeeps to reconnoiter Liege, one of the largest cities in Belgium. More importantly, it was just behind the 1st and 9th army fronts and was being used by Peter Hansen and his circulation crews as a distribution point. Bud Hutton headed the group, which included Charles Kiley, Al Ritz, Joe McBride, Charles White, and Bill Spear. Capt. Max Gilstrap and Fred Mertinke drove up the next day.

As they entered Liege, they found the railroad yards smoking from buzz-bomb hits and a convoy of army trucks blazing in the streets. Bombers of the Luftwaffe streaked across the sky before the anti-aircraft artillery guns could open fire or the sirens sound the alarm.

For nine days the eight men scoured the burned city for printing facilities. Then right on the main street they located *La Meuse*, a

Belgian newspaper which had one of the most modern plants in Europe. It was undamaged.

They made arrangements with management and located a garage to maintain and house their jeeps. Living quarters were found across the street, down two buildings from a public bathhouse. The restaurant owner next door promised to feed the staff provided the army issued the rations. The 1st Army agreed and also threw in PX supplies.

Gilstrap was busy filling out the requisition forms for typewriters and office supplies when the word came from Paris to abandon Liege. He knew why, and it wasn't too difficult to convince the others. They packed up their personal gear, locked the office, and drove back to Paris. There was hardly any traffic on the usually busy thoroughfare.

The following day two *Stripes* couriers — Morris "Blackie" Blackman and Tom Dolan — were bringing back copy from G. K. Hodenfield and Russ Jones at the 1st Army press camp. The pair, both veterans of the 1st Infantry Division who had fought in North Africa, Sicily, and Normandy, and who were now with *Stripes* in a supposedly noncombatant job, wound up in a fight with a German armored car. Blackman described the encounter:

> We were coming down the road, and it was deserted as a skunk's picnic, when Tom saw an armored car pull into a crossroads up ahead. We'd both seen that kind of armored car before. For a second we didn't know whether to turn and get the hell out before that 37-millimeter cannon on the car opened up, but they hadn't seen us yet.
>
> We drove the car off the road, grabbed the tommy guns we've been hauling ever since we left the line, and started stalking the sonofabitch. And was he dumb!
>
> The guy in the turret apparently figured he was all right, or maybe he had seen us and was trying to locate us, but anyway he unlatched the turret and stuck his head and shoulders out just as we got within gun range. Tommy cut loose on the guy and just about chopped him in two while I made a dash to get in close, under the gun. It worked, and even better, the other Kraut in the car got so panicky he opened the escape hatch in the bottom of the car and started to crawl out. I was waiting for him and that was that.

Blackie and Tom arrived in Paris wearing fancy German winter-issue white fleece jackets, watches on their wrists, and Lugers stuck in their belts when they delivered their copy.

★   ★   ★

The reason for the withdrawal from Liege by the *Stripes* group and the two couriers' fight with the German armored car was the early stages of the Battle of the Bulge, although, at the time, no one was calling it that.

The headline Thursday, December 21, told the story of the German counteroffensive: BIGGEST BATTLE SINCE D-DAY; GERMANS' ASSAULT ON 60-MILE FRONT IS HALTED IN NORTH.

Dan Regan reported from the 1st Army headquarters that the Germans were using their best western front troops, and the German officers were promising their men that they would spend New Year's Eve in Paris.

Jules Grad reported from Belgium that "American troops are fighting in the eerie atmosphere of an Alfred Hitchcock movie thriller . . . After hacking through Normandy hedgerows and slugging it out in Germany's snow and mud, they are now up against their strongest natural enemy — fog."

A story in the same issue said the Paris *Herald-Tribune* resumed publication after an absence of four years. The staff, under managing editor Eric Hawkins, took over a desk in the rear of the newsroom. When their duties on the *Stripes* copy desk were finished, several staffers shifted over to help Eric get out his standard-size, four-page paper.

★   ★   ★

The headline December 23, a Saturday: FOE 38 MILES FROM FRANCE; NORTH LINE HOLDS; LIEGE-BASTOGNE HIGHWAY SEVERED.

Carl Larsen, working in the New York news bureau, wrote that American editors had trotted out their largest headline type.

The *Buffalo Evening News:* NAZIS GAINING IN LUXEMBOURG; U.S. LOSS WORST SINCE BATAAN. The *St. Louis Globe Democrat:* TANKS SWARMING THROUGH BREACH IN U.S. LINES.

On Sunday the Germans were reported to have taken Stavelot and St. Vith in Belgium but had lost 178 airplanes in a series of fierce aerial dogfights with U.S. and British pilots.

On Christmas Day the word "bulge" appeared in a *Stripes* headline for the first time. Grad reported from Belgium that German parachutists, carrying small phials of sulphuric acid, dropped behind the U.S. lines to sabotage communications and to kill high-ranking officers. The phials were in match boxes and the plan was to toss them in the face of anyone who tried to intercept the parachutists. They were clad in American uniforms taken weeks before from captured U.S. officers who were forced to strip to their underwear and then shot.

The headline Christmas Day read: YANKS STOP NAZI ATTACK, UNLEASH BIGGEST AIR BLOW; BULGE STABILIZED; COLUMNS HALTED 29 MI. FROM SEDAN.

A story on the same page revealed another side of the war.

Maj. Glenn Miller Lost
On Flight From England

Maj. Glenn Miller, director of the USAAF band which has been playing in France, is reported missing while on a flight from England to Paris. The plane, in which he was a passenger, left England Dec. 15.

Maj. Miller lived in Tenafly, N.J., where his wife resides. No members of the band were with him.

Also in the Christmas issue were stories by Bud Hutton and Jimmy Cannon, both reporting from Belgium. Hutton said the troops he talked to didn't even know it was Christmas. "Must have lost a day," one told him. Cannon wrote about Pvt. Robert C. Mastin of Detroit, who had set up a tiny Christmas tree in a former German barracks and trimmed it with stars cut from milk cans. That was Christmas at the front.

Conditions were better the next day with U.S. and British air fleets out for the third time in a row. Grad reported that the Luftwaffe lost 196 planes to 78 for the United States. Pat Mitchell flew with 1st/Lt. John W. Anderson of Nashville in a Black Widow which stung a German JU88 in a sky duel over the counterattack zone. From the observer's seat in the P-61, Mitchell reported this conversation:

"Pete night, Johnny-bogie at three o'clock. Go get the bastard," said Radio Observer 2nd/Lt. James W. Mogan, of Boston, on the ground.

"I see him. I see him. It's a JU88," replied Anderson.

For twenty minutes high-speed teamwork between Anderson and Mogan kept the Widow on the trail of the evasive Nazi fighter. Finally, a burst from the Widow's guns hit the JU's right engine. The Nazi plane trailed groundward in a screen of smoke.

That same day, Paris had its first air raid since August. Two

German planes dropped bombs, reportedly causing damage and casualties at a hospital and other targets. We didn't hear the sirens when they sounded shortly after the planes flew over around 11:00 P.M. because we were inside. The next day we saw a few damaged buildings near a railroad station. We didn't see the hospital.

Thursday's headline: YANKS REACH BASTOGNE. Friday's said: U.S. GAINS ON 35-MILE LINE; 3RD ARMY CRACKS BASTOGNE SIEGE; NAZI FLANK REELS.

The Friday, December 29, issue will be one I will always remember because a photograph of the ever-so-secret Norden bombsight was published for the first time and nearly drove our resident censor crazy.

Yes, *The Stars and Stripes* was censored. News from the front was delayed forty-eight hours so as not to disclose troop movements, but staff-originated articles had to be cleared by a censor — an officer — who had a desk in the *Herald-Tribune* building. In addition, full-page proofs of news pages were pulled so that the censor could take them to his headquarters for closer reading by others including his superior. A telephone call thirty minutes or so later would clear the pages and the press could start.

Engravings of photographs were not run through the proof press because of the possible damage to the zinc plates. However, the cutlines were proofed. In this case a wire service photograph of the U.S. Air Force's most carefully guarded secret had been cleared in the States and had been sent to Paris by *Stripes*'s New York bureau. The editor positioned it at the bottom of Page 4 under the caption "Third Eye of the Bombardiers."

"Everything looks fine. Let the presses roll," the voice at the censor's office said.

"Gee thanks. We got off easy tonight. I sure as hell thought you'd nix the pix of the Norden bombsight though," the editor said and hung up the phone.

A few minutes later the censor called back, but the editor had gone down to the press room, and it was some minutes before he could come to the phone.

"What the hell do you mean — Norden bombsight?" the censor demanded.

"Sorry, captain. You're too late. The press has started. See you around," the editor said and hung up.

★　　★　　★

The headline on Saturday, December 20, reported that Gen. George S. Patton's 3rd Army had retaken thirteen towns and his 4th Armored Division, which broke the siege of Bastogne, was pouring into that city and widening the corridor.

On the back page (in retrospect it should have been on the front) was a box which said:

"Give Up," Said Nazis;
"Nuts!" Said General

When the Germans demanded the surrender of the American forces holding besieged Bastogne, the 101st Airborne's acting commander, Brig. Gen. Anthony C. McAuliffe, according to the Associated Press, gave the enemy one of the briefest replies in military history.

"Nuts," he said.

Three days later there was another box pertaining to McAuliffe's comment, and this one rightly made the front page.

No Compris "Nuts,"
Say Paris Papers

The French press was full of praise for the American stand at Bastogne but it was a little baffled by the word "Nuts" with which Brig. Gen. Anthony C. McAuliffe rejected the Germans demand for surrender.

"Vous n'etes que de vieilles noix," was the way Paris papers rendered it: "You are nothing but old nuts."

"This phrase," wrote *L'Aurore*'s New York correspondent, "is entered in the American vocabulary forever."

C'est vrai!

McAuliffe made it clear in a press conference that the 101st Airborne Division was not "rescued" at Bastogne.

"Anyone who says we were rescued or who thinks we needed rescue is all wrong. On Christmas night, I called my regimental commanders together and told them we now were ready for pursuit."

The text of his reply to the Germans was terse:

22 Dec. 44 To The German Commander:
N-U-T-S. (Signed) American Commander.

★　　★　　★

That pretty much was the story of the Battle of the Bulge, which was later known as the Battle of the Ardennes.

That New Year's Eve we sat around on the floor of a room in the Hotel Haussmann (also called Le Flea Bag) and drank champagne someone had liberated. Jimmy Cannon was there, and so was Russell Jones. Russell brought his brother, Dick, along. Dick had just joined *Stripes*, was feeling a bit blue, and proposed a toast to his wife back in the States. That went over so well, we drank toasts to all the wives in the States. Except me. I had to decline because that day I had received word that my divorce was final.

"A new member of the Brushoff Club," Cannon said, and we all drank to that. My permanent assignment to *Stripes* had finally come through, so I proposed a toast to army red tape. I guess we drank to just about everything that night as 1944 slid into 1945.

2

Liege

The Liege edition published its first issue January 21, and I received orders to go to Belgium six days later. At 5:00 A.M. on a cold and bleak January 27, I checked into the garage, in the Shell building on Rue de Berri just down from the *Herald-Tribune,* and climbed into the back of a jeep. The driver and his assistant, both French, had the benefit of the engine's heat to keep their feet warm.

Although the top was up and some ill-fitting side curtains were in place, the rear seat of the jeep, where I sat with my duffle bags, was drafty. Even before we got out of the garage, I was damn near frozen. The sun did come out from time to time, but it did nothing to warm us up. Frost was everywhere; patches of snow dotted the fields as we rolled east. At some point before we reached Charleroi in Belgium, we stopped for French coffee and *calvados,* which helped some.

I was now in my third month on the army's daily newspaper and enjoying work on the copy desk. Of course, I wanted to be a reporter, to get out into the field and cover the war. I have never met a copy reader who didn't think he was a better reporter or writer than most of those whose copy he edited.

I sat there in the jeep, wearing an officer's lined raincoat that one of the *Stripes* brass had bought for me in the quartermaster store. Civilian war correspondents were permitted to wear officers' clothing; but, of course, I was not a civilian. I had the dark green and gold war correspondent patches on my cap and shirt, and I thought I looked like the real thing — like a short Ernest Hemingway.

But I was still a corporal in the army, one whose stripes were on another uniform in the duffle bag. I avoided whenever possible a confrontation with officers on the Champs Élysées and discovered that most of them had their minds on something else, usually a pretty *mademoiselle*.

★   ★   ★

At the time Liege started, there were five other *Stripes* editions in the European Theater: London, Paris, Marseille, Dijon, and Strasbourg. The last three had been started by personnel operating out of Rome, but as of November 1, 1944, the command of the three French editions had shifted to SHAEF's Information and Education Division in Paris.

The Mediterranean *Stripes* began with the November 1942 invasion at Algiers, Oran, and Casablanca, and had its genesis in England. When U.S. troops landed in North Africa, a number of business and editorial men from the London *Stripes* went ashore to start a newspaper. Among them were Capt. Harry Harcher, Robert Neville, Russell Jones, G. K. Hodenfield, Dean Hocking, Earl Ericson, Robbie Robinson, and Ralph G. Martin.

Neville and Milton Lehman located a printing plant in Algiers and were the first to start publishing. Other editions followed in Casablanca, Oran, and Tunis under the command of Lt. Col. Egbert White, a New York advertising executive.

Following the invasion of Sicily in July 1943, an edition was started up at Palermo. When the troops landed in Italy, other editions followed in Naples, Rome, Leghorn, and Milan.

Some of those prominent in the Mediterranean *Stripes* were Victor Dallaire, Edgar Clark, William De Mazo, Harry Shershow, Herb Mitgang, Ben Dean, Wade Jones, Jack Foisie, George Dorsey, Hugh Conway, James Burchard, Paul Green (a photographer), Bill Mauldin, Greg Duncan, and Al Kohn. Duncan, an artist, lost his life while making sketches at Anzio; Kohn, a reporter, was killed during the invasion of southern France.

Jones and Hodenfield didn't remain long in North Africa; they returned to London and participated in the invasion of Normandy and the establishment of *Stripes* editions at Saint-Mere Eglise, Rennes, and Paris.

★　　★　　★

Anthony "Tony" Iannacio was the GI driver for Col. Robert L. Bacon, a five-foot-three-inch World War I veteran who commanded special troops in the North Africa invasion.

"We had a tiny French-made Simca in Algiers and even as small as the colonel was," Tony recalled, "he was always banging his head getting in and out. One day he called me in and said, 'Goddamn it, Tony, I'm the laughing stock of this command. When I go to Allied Forces headquarters everyone makes fun of this car. I don't care how you do it, but I want something that I can be proud to ride in.' "

Iannacio and Sgt. George Laque went car hunting. They came upon a locked stall in a garage off Rue Michelin in downtown Algiers; the garage owner said it was empty. Tony figured the man was lying, so he told the sergeant to shoot off the lock. Since each had a tommy gun, the owner saw that they meant business. He took out a key and opened the stall. Iannacio described what happened:

> In the stall was the most beautiful 1939 Lincoln sedan I had ever seen. It looked like it had just come from Detroit. I told him this was it, and I sent Laque back to headquarters to get a battery. The garage owner pleaded that the sedan belonged to French Admiral Jean Darlan, vice-premier in the Vichy government, and if we took the vehicle something terrible would happen. I told him to hell with Darlan, and when George came back with the battery, we installed it, ... drove [the car] to headquarters, and proceeded to paint it GI green with white stars.
>
> Bacon was in his glory and very proud of the car, but that wasn't the end of the story. A few days later Darlan showed up in Algiers and, when he discovered his car gone, he blew his stack. Finally an order came down from Ike's headquarters that the Lincoln would be returned to Darlan on 25 December. On 24 December some student put a few bullets into Darlan. On Christmas morning, Bacon called me into his office and said, "Damn it Tony, we could have given him the car, you didn't have to go to such extremes."

The war advanced, the troops moved up, and so did the 1939 Lincoln. Soon after he transferred to *The Stars and Stripes* and was assigned to the circulation department, Iannacio saw Darlan's sedan on the streets of Rome, still GI green with white stars but with another colonel in the back seat.

Rome fell to the U.S. 5th Army on June 5, 1944, and the next day marked the debut of the Rome edition of *The Stars and Stripes*. The headline on Paul Green's lead story in the four-page paper which rolled off *Il Messaggero*'s presses screamed: WE'RE IN ROME.

It would have been the top story in newspapers around the world on any other day, but June 6 was also the date of the Normandy invasion. The story from Rome rated a paragraph at best in most U.S. newspapers. Tony recalls the event vividly:

> We had our sheet but we didn't have any wheels. We only had two jeeps, so Bill Mauldin and I went to see a buddy of mine — a Captain Johnson whom I knew as a second john in England. He was with Military Government and had just taken over the Questura garage and had plenty of civilian cars parked there because of the wartime shortage of gasoline.
>
> He played hardnose, said his colonel had just taken inventory and he would get his butt in a sling if he gave us any transportation. I said bullshit and reminded him that he owed me a few. He finally agreed to give us one vehicle. That was all right with me because I had my eye on the one I wanted. It was a Lancia Imperial with a glass-partitioned back with all kinds of buttons. He yelled bloody murder, but we put gas in the car and drove off. I couldn't figure out why the natives were gawking as we drove to *Il Messaggero*, but I sure found out the next day. The car belonged to Count Galeazzo Ciano, Mussolini's son-in-law, whom the dictator had shot earlier in the year.
>
> That car didn't stay long enough in our possession to get the GI paint job because Johnson's one-star boss called *Stripes'* Maj. Robert Neville and ordered him to have it turned over to his headquarters. But a funny thing happened to the Lancia on the day I was supposed to give it back to the MG. I ran into three GIs from the 34th Inf. Div., who were AWOL and wanted to get back to their outfit. I told them to take the car and when they got close to their outfit to ditch it over the side of the mountain or burn it. They took off, two up front and the third sitting in the back as big as Ciano himself. I reported to the MPs that someone had cut the chain and stole the car from in front of the *Stripes* office.
>
> Two cars that had to belong to two of the biggies in history. That's some batting average.

★   ★   ★

The driver pulled up in front of the building that housed the newspaper *La Meuse,* and I got out dragging my duffle bags behind me. I was still about half frozen when I put them just inside the door and took the elevator to the newsroom on the fifth floor, where I spotted Capt. Max Gilstrap.

Max introduced me to Bill Spear, the news editor and a former Associated Press reporter in civilian life. I also met Art Force, Paul Horowitz, Frank Waters, and Al Ritz. Then he took me across the street to my billet on the top floor of a building that also housed the officers' club.

We had dinner in the restaurant next door to the newspaper. The food was exceptionally good, I thought. Although GI issue, it was prepared by Belgian chefs. It tasted even better than the French fare we had at Chez Mercier, just off the Champs Élysées, where the Paris edition staffers ate. Even the Spam, served with a piquant mustard sauce, was excellent.

Working hours were different from those in Paris. We went to work earlier, and then as soon as the first edition was out of the way, the deskmen had two hours off for dinner and a quick visit to the one good nightclub and the dozen or so sleazy bars in the neighborhood. That is, if we had the money to spend.

The bars came complete with B girls who started out their shift sitting alone at tables. They were not permitted at the bar, but with the steady stream of GIs in Liege for an overnight pass they didn't sit alone for long. At the end of the two-hour period we were back at work on copy for inside pages for the following day. If there was a late-breaking story or an update, it was taken care of and then it was letter writing time or, because of the 10:00 P.M. curfew, we would return to our billets to play poker with Capt. Victor "Molly" Meluski, the resident censor, or any other "pigeon" who happened by.

★   ★   ★

There was a slowdown at this time in ground action, as both the American and German forces regrouped after the fierce fighting of the breakthrough. The Germans continued to fire buzz bombs at Liege, and the first three nights I was there I spent part of the time under the desk.

Buzz bombs were not unknown to me. I had my fill of them in England, where approximately 8,000 landed in the southern part of the country in 80 days — an average of 100 per day. The roar was frightening, but as long as you heard it you knew you were all right. It was when the engine cut out and the bomb started its descent that you were in trouble.

I had been assigned to the Training and Security Section of Headquarters Command, SHAEF, and saw much of the cigar-shaped, stub-winged missile of death and destruction. The British press also called it the Doodlebug, flybomb, robot bomb, or ro-bomb.

One of them landed near a hospital site where I was on a sand-bag detail, and I dived into the nearest slit trench just in the knick of time. Although I was unhurt, the captain gave me extra time off, which I gladly accepted.

★   ★   ★

My first day in Liege was similar to my early days in Paris; I didn't get to write the top heads, only the briefs and some copy for the next day's paper. The main headline for that Sunday, January 28, was: 300,000 NAZIS KILLED IN 2-WEEK DRIVE.

A story by Richard Lewis at SHAEF said the 3rd Army was at the Luxembourg-Germany border and that the bulge was completely gone after six weeks of fighting.

Jimmy Cannon reported two days later that 3rd Army infantry crossings were made on the Our River, while Dan Regan wrote that the 1st Army had captured Bulligen in eastern Belgium, a mile from the German border.

A map by 1st/Lt. Bob Brown showing the Russian advance on Berlin was spread across the top of the page. Brown, originally from Los Angeles, had recently joined the Liege edition and turned out a map a day. His counterpart in Paris was Jean Baird, a pretty, blonde Britisher.

★   ★   ★

Photographs of General Eisenhower wearing his recently awarded fifth star appeared for the first time that month of January. He also had a new title, general of the armies, which Congress had approved and President Roosevelt had signed. The five stars, worn in a cluster, were also given to Generals George C. Marshall, Henry "Hap" Arnold, and Douglas MacArthur. The new rating went to Admirals of the Fleet Ernest J. King, William D. Leahy, and Chester W. Nimitz as well.

★   ★   ★

The Paris edition began to receive recognition in the States, and none other than FDR mentioned one of its editorials in his annual message to Congress.

"I quote from an editorial in *The Stars and Stripes,* our soldiers' newspaper in Europe. 'For the Holy love of God let's listen to the dead. Let's learn from the living. Let's join ranks against the foe, the bugles of battle are heard again above the bickering. That is the demand of fighting men. We cannot fail to heed it. The new year of 1945 can be the greatest year of achievement in human history.' "

Another Roosevelt appeared in *Stripes* that same month: Col. Elliott Roosevelt, his wife, and their dog, Blaze. A navy gunner called home by his father's death and a marine hurrying to the bedside of his sick wife said they were put off an army transport at Memphis, Tennessee, because a huge crate containing a mastiff consigned to Mrs. Roosevelt, the former actress Faye Emerson, had a higher priority.

The War Department said the men actually were put off to make room for higher priority freight; that putting off the dog would not have corrected the weight. The men said the crate took up the space for four persons. The flap didn't bother the president's son; he was promoted to brigadier general a few weeks later.

★　　★　　★

Adolf Hitler rated a Page 1 story that last day of January when he told his people "We will not surrender." In a nationwide radio broadcast, on the occasion of the start of his thirteenth year in power, he said: "Any suffering our enemies may inflict on the German towns and countrysides, and especially on our people, are nothing beside the irretrievable suffering and misery which would follow victory by a plutocratic-Bolshevist conspiracy."

He added that "now more than ever it is necessary to strengthen our solemn determination to fight on, no matter where and no matter under what circumstances, until final victory crowns our efforts."

Adolf was up to his funny mustache in trouble. As soon as he finished speaking, Berlin Radio reported that the Red Army of Marshal Gregory Zhukov was within eighty miles of the German capital. If that wasn't enough, he had forty-seven American divisions facing him where his forces, under Field Marshal Gerd von Rundstadt, had just taken a beating in the Ardennes. Joining with the Americans were fourteen British, eight French, one Polish, and three Canadian divisions.

★   ★   ★

Seymour Sharnik joined the staff early in February, and we became roommates. He came up from an anti-aircraft artillery group in Belgium and insisted that we call him "Sharkey," though he used Seymour when he signed his stories. After the war ended, and he went to work for CBS in New York as an executive producer, he called himself John Sharnik. Others there then were Walter B. "Wally" Smith, Johnny Brown, "Tex" Thomas, Nick Cinquemani, Cray Platt, Dick Jones, Bert Marsh, 1st/Lt. Bob Brown, and William R. Frye.

One day Ernie Leiser stopped by en route to the front, where he had been assigned to cover the war. His first story, about the 78th Infantry Division, was printed February 5. It told of fighting in the little town of Kesternich, where there were only 112 houses and each of them was knocked down. Leiser, too, joined CBS in New York after the war.

The lead story that same day, about the fighting along the Roer River, was written by Russell Jones, who later won a Pulitzer Prize for his United Press report of the Soviet takeover of Hungary.

★   ★   ★

I never thought the headlines in the Liege edition were as sprightly as they were on the Paris paper. The best we could do was "Sour Kraut," a stock head used several times a week over a collection of briefs mostly about the captured German soldiers.

Our page size was different from that in Paris too. That was understandable, since there was no certain source for newsprint and we used what we could get — some of it from captured stock. Our five-column tabloid page was an inch wider and an inch shorter than the Paris page. While I was in Paris we printed on two different sizes; in Liege we had three different measurements.

"It'll look better when we get our new blankets for the press," Gilstrap said. "They'll be here any day now."

★   ★   ★

On one of my days off, I went along with Gilstrap and Larry Riordan, the OWI photographer, for a jeep ride to the front. We dropped by the 9th Army Press Camp in the Hotel du Levrier at Maastricht, which was run by Maj. Barney Oldfield, to visit with Russell Jones. Jones was out with the troops, so we drove to the XIX Corps Headquarters at Heerlen, forty kilometers from Maastricht. While Max had lunch with the public relations brass in the officers' mess, Larry and I ate in the enlisted men's area. After taking a look at the 180-foot Schwammenauel dam, which posed a real threat to American forces if the Germans ever decided to release the water, we returned to Liege.

It was my first trip to the combat area, and I told Max that I would like to get out from time to time to write features about frontline troops. He was sympathetic, but said the paper needed copyreaders more than it did reporters. In fact, a few days later a box was printed on an inside page asking for soldiers with copy desk experience and suggested they stop by the Liege paper for an interview. Well, anyway, I tried.

I later visited the 1st Army's forward press camp in the Hotel Portugal at Spa, a pretty little tourist resort tucked in the hills of the Ardennes. It had been Kaiser Wilhelm's imperial headquarters in World War I and just missed being overrun by the Germans in World War II's Battle of the Bulge. Its press facilities were under the command of Maj. Casey Dempsey, and day-to-day operations were directed by 1st/Lt. Charles Rhodes.

Danny Regan, who covered the daily briefings for *Stripes*, showed me about and talked the billeting officer into giving me a bed for the night in a loft in the upper reaches of the hotel. While I was asleep, another soldier came in, and the next morning we had breakfast downstairs together. He was Sgt. Broderick Crawford, correspondent and announcer for the Armed Forces Radio. We talked about his playing the character Lennie on stage in John Steinbeck's classic "Of Mice and Men." Years later, I saw much of him in motion pictures and on television.

★ ★ ★

In late February, all hell broke loose. The tip-off was the February 23 issue which revealed that 6,000 Allied planes had hammered railroad installations throughout Germany.

Next day the headline read: 1ST AND 9TH ARMIES ATTACK; CROSS ROER, DRIVE ON EAST PLANES, ARTILLERY AID TROOPS; NAZIS SAY BIG PUSH ON.

Sharnik reported from 1st Army that its units had crossed the Roer and were fighting their way into the streets of Duren. Leiser, with the 9th Army, said its troops had crossed the Roer in assault boats, and Riordan's photograph showed GIs practicing boarding the craft. Other bylines that day, all from the Roer sector, were Bud

Hutton and Andy Rooney, again writing as a team, Ralph G. Martin, and Ray Lee.

Two days later, Duren fell and Bob Moora, at 12th Army Group headquarters, said the 1st and 9th Army units were fifteen miles from Cologne and moving. Rooney visited Duren and found the town leveled. Because of the bombing, the statue of Otto von Bismarck (the creator and first chancellor of the German empire), which once looked toward France, was now completely turned around. "Like all Germans, the statue was now facing the Rhine," Rooney said.

The drive continued with Munchen-Gladbach, the home of Joseph Goebbels, Hitler's propagandist, falling to the 29th Infantry Division. That was the lead story March 2. The following day Leiser wrote that the 83rd Infantry Division had reached the Rhine River south of Neuss and that the 2nd Armored Division had smashed through to the river south of Gartenstadt.

Hutton's story on the fall of Munchen-Gladbach was pure Hutton. His lead sentence said it all: "In the streets where Paul Joseph Goebbels spent a loud-mouthed boyhood and grew up hating even the kids he went to school with, there isn't a sound." The head on the story: NO SIEG HEILS FOR GOEBBELS, JUST WEIRD SILENCE TONIGHT.

★   ★   ★

March 6 was my day off and it turned out to be a big day in my life. It was the day the 1st Army was fighting in Cologne, and Ed Clark was there. So were three American divisions: the 104th Infantry, driving in from the west, 3rd Armored from the north, and the 8th Infantry from the south.

It was Bert Marsh's day off too. He had his sketchbook under his arm when the two of us hopped into the back of the courier jeep to get as near Cologne as we could. The driver took us as far as he dared. So we got out and walked in with a platoon of the 8th. When it stopped we kept on toward the cathedral, which loomed high over the smoking city.

Heavy stuff was flying overhead and there was plenty of rifle and machine-gun fire as we skirted the plaza. Rounding the corner of the cathedral on rubble-filled Comodien Strasse, we saw that a 3rd Armored's tank had just been hit by a shell from a German Mark IV hidden behind some bricks. The Mark IV's shell punched a hole through the gun turret of the Sherman tank, one of the five that were pushing through to the Rhine about 200 yards away.

Bert and I arrived just in time to see Lt. Col. C. L. Miller (who commanded the five Shermans) run with 1st/Lt. Ferdinand Le Doux to the damaged tank. With the help of the assistant driver, they dragged the tank commander from the vehicle. His right leg was off above the knee, and he died as they pulled him into a crater for protection from sniper fire. The driver and another tanker died in the Sherman.

Bert stayed there to finish his sketch, which later was published under the caption "Greater love hath no man . . ." He signed it Sam Marsh, Sam being the name he called the little character he used in the illustrations in "Hashmarks," the humor column, and other articles on the unit news pages. Rooney's story and Riordan's picture of the cathedral appeared the next day under an all-capital-letter headline: YANKS TAKE COLOGNE.

Andy's story told how the German crew in the Mark IV fared: "Meanwhile, on the side, coming along parallel to the Rhine, a third force commanded by Lt. Col. Matthew W. Kane of Des Moines, Iowa, was approaching the same intersection. The lead tank fired three shots point blank into the German Mark IV and destroyed it before the Germans could move again."

We didn't see them, but there was a team of U.S. Signal Corps photographers taking movies of the tank battle. S/Sgt. Norman Garrell of Beverly Hills, California, didn't know it at the time but his movie camera caught the German tank as it fired the actual shot that knocked out the Sherman.

While Bert was busy, I decided I wanted to see the inside of the cathedral and found a door fastened with only a piece of heavy wire. A *Time* magazine writer, whose name I never got, had the same idea and we entered together. The pews and all the fixtures and the pieces of furniture in the altar area had been removed; chunks of plaster, brick, cement, and glass littered the floor. It was eerie as the dust and smoke from the shelling and fires outside hung over us like a dark cloud. The building, at least from the inside, looked in good shape.

The *Time* man and I spent about twenty minutes inside. Then, as we were leaving, we saw some American medics with Red Cross armbands moving toward another entrance to the cathedral on a lower level. Since the firing had stopped, we followed them and found ourselves in a converted hospital.

My story about what I saw in Cologne, on my day off from the copy desk, was published along with two of Larry Riordan's photos of the aftermath of the tank battle.

Bert and I hitchhiked a ride back to Liege in a jeep driven by Max Lerner of *PM*, the New York newspaper. He drove with his lights off, as did everyone at the front, and the thought crossed my mind that we were really safer in Cologne than we were on the road that night to Liege.

I returned to the desk with the feeling that I could better handle copy about the Joes who were doing the fighting. I had seen firsthand what some of them were doing, and I was impressed. I also returned to work for a new editor; Bill Spear had left for the States and he was replaced by Carl Larsen, who had worked for Chicago newspapers before joining the army.

Larsen seemed to understand my feelings about getting off the desk from time to time to do some writing, more so than did Spear.

"You have just been to Cologne. You'll have to wait awhile and let some of the others go out if that is what they want to do," he said. He did let other desk types go. Sharnik had written several pieces, Bill Frye went out with an armored infantry outfit, and Art Force traveled with the 314th Regiment of the 79th Infantry Division.

We were also getting full production from the reporters in the field — sometimes two stories each per day — and I know that some of them resented seeing deskman's copy in the paper when theirs didn't make it.

"You guys got it made. You sit there on that damn desk and when there's a hole in the page you get your copy in and ours goes in the bin," one of them told me. "We do better in the Paris edition; at least they use our stuff," another said.

★   ★   ★

The capture of the Ludendorf bridge over the Rhine at Remagen was the big news, really a turning point of the war, in early 1945. It happened at 3:50 P.M., March 7, when forward units of Brig. Gen. William Hoge's 9th Armored Combat Command B crossed a bridge that the Germans forgot to destroy. Hoge pushed his tanks across, and once across, they never looked back. The story came to light two days later under big, bold capital letters: IST

ARMY ACROSS RHINE; FORGES BRIDGEHEAD SOUTH OF COLOGNE IN SURPRISE MOVE.

General Eisenhower's message, "Please tell all ranks how proud I am of them," to General Hoge of the 1st Army was printed at the bottom of Page 1.

★ ★ ★

It didn't happen often because there was always the war news, but from time to time we printed a bit of "in house" material. In this case it was about our sister paper in Italy. The subject didn't have anything to do with *Stripes* editions in England, France, and Belgium, but it was our news editor's thought that the story might just give a few of the brass some second thoughts.

GI Editors Protest B-Bag Restriction

ROME, Mar. 13 (AP) — The entire staff of enlisted men on the Rome edition of *The Stars and Stripes* has protested against newly-imposed restrictions on the newspaper's Mail Call column.

Restrictions, they contend, would make the column a device for "official instruction and orientation."

A written protest was handed to Maj. Robert Neville, publications officer, after a directive which the staff contended, circumscribed the field of discussion in published letters, was issued from Army headquarters in the Mediterranean theater.

The directive, it is understood, insisted that letters on controversial subjects should be published only when official replies could be made on the subject.

The controversy over the degree of free expression troops should have in the paper came to light when a war correspondent visiting *The Stars and Stripes* office saw the protest posted for signatures of soldier editors.

(The *New York Times* said Maj. Neville "is known to disagree with the ruling.")

★ ★ ★

American and British planes pounded the Ruhr in the north while the Russians kept up the drive on Berlin in the east. The ground forces of the British and Canadians struck in the north, the American 1st and 9th in the middle, and the 3rd and 7th in the south.

There was more big news March 25: AIRBORNE, 9TH CROSS RHINE.

In the northern elements of the 1st Allied Airborne, the British 2nd Armored, the Canadians, and the U.S. 9th crossed the Rhine in the greatest combined operation since D-Day. Paratroops dropped five miles east of the Rhine just north of Wesel after U.S. and Royal navies softened up the Germans with artillery bombardment.

That night, Russell Jones came into the office with a hitchhiker — Richard C. Hottelet, a CBS war correspondent — who had to bail out of a Flying Fortress at 600 feet when it lost its port inboard engine. It was Hottelet's first jump. Both he and Jones had participated in the U.S. 17th and British Airborne drop north of the Ruhr; Russell flew in a C-47 of the 436th Carrier Group towing gliders.

After calling Paris on the phone to report that he was all right, Hottelet sat down and wrote his story. Jones had his ready, and both versions were published side by side in *Stripes*. It was the first time Liege *Stripes* had ever used anything from a radio network reporter.

In the days following, the armored spearheads of the three American armies — the 1st, 9th, and 3rd — burst through the outer crust of the German defense east of the Rhine. The 4th Armored Division blasted out of Remagan and drove twenty-seven miles east of Darmstadt, crossing the Main River at a point forty miles from where it started. A day later, Lt. Gen. Alexander M. Patch's 7th Army crossed the Rhine near Karlsruhe while units of the 1st Army moved into Frankfurt.

I could hardly sit still at the desk; I was afraid the war was going to be over before I could get away. Finally, Larsen said I could go for a couple of days — "no more than three" — and off I went to pack. I caught the *Stripes* courier and that night I, too, crossed the Rhine on a pontoon bridge near Konigswinter, where the VII Corps had set up headquarters.

1st/Lt. Bill Maxey, the Corps public relations officer, said he would get me forward the next morning. So I crawled into my GI-issue sleeping bag and listened to the Rhine gurgling just outside my window.

"The Spearhead Division is hot, so you should go along with it," Maxey told me at early chow. Twenty minutes later, I was racing east in a jeep — the tanker Joes called them peeps — with Dog Company, 83rd Reconnaissance Battalion of the 3rd Armored Division, through the hills and valleys on the south rim of the Ruhr Valley. Spearhead was the nickname for the 3rd Armored, which I had seen in action at Cologne. There was no opposition from the Germans, and we made record time. That night, I slept in a big bed in a house I had all to myself in the little town of Altenkirchen.

I awakened to gunfire and was told that some German armored vehicles had been spotted in the trees on the hill above town. After a couple of hours we were on the move again, rolling east to Herborn where the main force of the division had seized bridges over the Dill River. Dog Company stopped off in Holzhausen, for it was getting late in the day and the company had run out of maps.

Here is the story that I wrote and which Larsen put at the bottom of Page 1:

Races Right Off the Map
By Ken Zumwalt, *Stars and Stripes* staff writer

HOLZHAUSEN, Germany, Mar. 28 (Delayed) — Dog Company of this armored reconnaissance battalion is well out in front after racing 90 miles in a little more than 60 hours, but that's about all the CO, Capt. Herbert Zimmerman, of Williamsville, N.Y., knows about his position.

Holzhausen is somewhere in the Hesse-Nassau district, but just where Zimmerman can't tell because he has outrun his maps.

Dog Company took out after the Germans early today and passed through five villages before reaching Holzhausen, largest place the company has entered since it left Altenkirchen.

The district is mountainous and many of the towns have steel smelters and railroad terminals. There was a large mill at Oberscheld, while at Herrnberg there was a large railyard and several intact freight cars.

White flags fly from the windows. At Trigenstein the streets were filled with civilians. Wallenfels was just a wide place in the road and Bottenhorn was a little larger.

At Holzhausen Zimmerman's troopers were cheered as they passed through — the first time they've been acclaimed since their race across France. There were many Poles and Russians — forced laborers — in the streets here. Out to greet the company was the burgomeister, who is not a party member according to his school teacher niece. Holzhausen's population is about 1,360.

The town yielded 32 prisoners after Dog Company doughs fired a volley into the woods above the town.

It was Easter week and the mayor's niece had her students filling baskets of spring flowers as our armored column halted in front of the schoolhouse. The baskets were lined up on a table in the schoolyard and looked very pretty; they added a gay touch to an otherwise somber moment.

I had forgotten about Easter, and I remember thinking it strange that the enemy would be honoring the same God.

New maps were available the next morning when Task Force Richardson moved out at 0600. Lt. Col. Walter B. Richardson, CO of the 3rd Battalion, 32nd Armored Regiment, said it was okay for me to string along with his outfit, so I climbed in the back of a half-track along with some armored infantrymen. Instead of going east, as we had for the past two days, Richardson's and three other task forces like it — four huge columns — turned north and rolled along on separate routes, each three to five miles apart from the other.

We had good roads all the way, mostly paved, but the other columns were forced to go cross-country in some cases. There were burning German vehicles along the roads and long lines of German prisoners of war marching back to collecting points. We saw many freight cars on the sidings of the railroad that paralleled part of our route. A couple of times we came upon a locomotive, which the armored doughs took care of with the .50-caliber machine gun mounted atop the halftrack.

At 10:00 P.M. we stopped for the night at Willenberg, after traveling seventy-five miles for the day, and then moved out early the next morning. Near Kirchborchen, Task Force Richardson ran into elements of an SS panzer training regiment. And the battle was on.

The big story was the death of Maj. Gen. Maurice Rose, commanding general, 3rd Armored Division, March 30, the day of the tank battle, and I couldn't get the news back to the paper. The general was killed by a nervous German tanker who fired his machine pistol from the turret of a Tiger tank while Rose was surrendering his weapon.

The general's driver, T/5 Glen Shaunce of Albert Lea, Minnesota, said Rose was killed after he complied with an order to put his hands in the air.

As soon as I learned the news, I located a sergeant in public relations who had just finished writing a release for VII Corps and the 1st Army. He provided me with the facts and, ironically, his version was in the newspaper back in Liege under another *Stripes* reporter's byline the day I returned to work.

Richardson set up his command post in a house on the outskirts of Paderborn, and I walked in just as two German women were filing downstairs to the cellar. They had left a fire in the wood-burning range in the kitchen, and a large flat cake was cooling on the table. Alongside the cake was a basket of eggs, perhaps three or four dozen. None of us had eaten, and the food sure looked good to me.

The colonel and his men were firing at Germans out of the windows and, although we couldn't see it until later, American Thunderbolts were dropping their own eggs on a covey of German tanks on a bluff just above and behind us.

There wasn't much I could do, since I was unarmed, so I started to fry some eggs in a pan. When I finished with an egg — over-easy, the way I like it — I would cut off a big piece of the white cake, park the egg on top, and hand it to an officer or GI as he moved in and out of the house. Sugar was scarce, so the cake wasn't too sweet, but there were no complaints.

After the war ended, I received a note from Lieutenant Colonel Richardson, then stationed at Gross Umstadt prior to returning to the States, and it said in part: "Those fried eggs were pretty good that day, even though it was a little hot," he wrote. The colonel was pretty good too, I thought. I later learned that he had been wounded four times and never missed a day of action.

Brig. Gen. Doyle O. Hickey, commander of Combat Command A, took over the division following the death of Rose, and he was replaced by Col. Leander L. Doan of the 32nd Armored Regiment.

When Hickey flew back to Marburg on April 1 (Easter Sunday) in the division's liaison plane (L4), he took me along. I spent the night in Marburg and the next day caught a ride in a jeep to Liege. I had been away nine days, and Larsen wasn't amused.

"You've had it, Zumwalt." he said. "Don't you know when you're well off? You could have gotten your ass shot off. You could have been killed."

★   ★   ★

The day before I left Liege to see the war, Bob Moora and four others took off from Paris in a C-47 of the 9th Troop Carrier Command and landed at a temporary field near Mainz on the east bank of the Rhine. The four were Ben Price, Ed Clark, Jack Raymond, and Carl Konzelman. Their jeep was put on board and, after landing, the five of them piled in along with a shortwave radio, two portable typewriters, a box of pencils, their sleeping bags, and a case of 10 and 1 rations, and drove over the nearest pontoon bridge and headed for Frankfurt.

Clark, an old hand in the battle zones and the one with the map, got them pointed in the right direction. Soon they could see a smoking Frankfurt and, as they drew nearer, they could hear the gunfire. They decided to remain in the suburbs and bedded down for the night near the racetrack.

The next day they entered the city and for three days searched for a newspaper plant, but to no avail. They did learn that the *Frankfurter Zeitung* was being printed at a secret plant, and with a bit of luck and a lot of searching they found it April 1 in the little town of Pfungstadt, thirty miles south and just off the Frankfurt-Heidelberg autobahn.

Two days later, James McGowan, who knew about presses, linotypes, and things mechanical, showed up, as did Paul Elliott, an editor from the Nancy edition, and Martin Harris, a photographer. A four-page newspaper came off that auxiliary press April 6, the first *Stripes* to be published on German soil, the first free newspaper since the rise of Adolf Hitler.

An editorial writer in the ivory tower in Paris came up with one of his best, entitled "Gutenberg Is Smiling Today." It was published in Pfungstadt's first issue.

> With the publication of this free newspaper in Germany, another prop is knocked out from under the civilization Adolf Hitler promised would last a thousand years.
>
> Had the German people been told the truth, National Socialism would have died within a decade. For Hitlerism and truth don't mix. One would have to go. Truth went for a while. But in the end Hitler will exit.
>
> *The Stars and Stripes,* an Army paper, draws its news from many sources. Some is official, most is not. Much is written by its own staff, loyal to the tradition of a free press. Much comes from the rank and file of the Army.
>
> In B-Bag the soldier speaks his mind with the gusto of a free man. That's how Ike Eisenhower wants it. His order that *The Stars and Stripes* be free is based on the belief that soldiers old enough to fight the war are old enough to face the facts.
>
> To draw their own conclusions, freely reached, that in the end can be counted on to be correct. At times indiscreet. At times unfortunate. But the end product is an informed people. And an informed people doesn't goosestep to a dictator's tune.

Truth has kept America free. Freedom has made America strong. Strong in many ways of peace. And when threatened, strong in the ways of war.

Perhaps this free newspaper of a freedom-loving Army will, along with our bombs and bullets, make an impression on German hearts and minds. The Germans have what it takes to win back their freedom. Good machinery. Good ink. Good paper and an heritage of good printing that goes back to Gutenberg.

All they need is the truth. Perhaps someday the truth will make them free.

★   ★   ★

The war continued to heat up. The British shelled Bremen, and the Canadians overran a V2 site in a forest near Hellendoora in northeast Holland. It was the first such facility. The American 1st Army tanks advanced to within sixty miles of the Elbe River while the 9th took Hanover. The U.S. 17th Airborne captured Essen, the Reich's sixth largest city.

Gen. Henry H. Arnold, chief of the U.S. Air Forces, told a group of war correspondents, including *Stripes*'s Bud Hutton, that Germany still had plenty of aircraft but was short of pilots and fuel. That same day Allied air forces destroyed 245 German planes in attacks on seven airfields to set a record. On the other side of the world, the U.S. Marines captured a naval base on Okinawa — more bad news for what was left of the Axis.

Whatever news was planned for the April 13 edition in Liege was yanked out of the page when the teletype belled out a bulletin that President Roosevelt had died of a cerebral hemorrhage at Warm Springs, Georgia. Some of the papers were on the trucks when Pfc Art Force, who was in charge that night, stopped the presses. It was about 11:00 P.M. in Belgium and some of us were typing letters. Force put us to work writing fillers from the world almanac and the encyclopedia while we waited for the rest of the story to move on the machine. Our largest type said: FDR DEAD.

The next few days the paper was filled with news and photographs of the fallen leader and about Harry S. Truman, the seventh vice-president to become chief executive through the death of a president.

Five days after the death of Franklin Roosevelt, the Liege edition rolled off the presses for the last time. The paper that had started January 21 and had published eighty-eight issues closed down with its April 17 issue.

It was a sad note for the staff of the gutsy little paper, but the war news was good. The 7th Army's 45th Infantry Division entered Nuremberg, second largest city in Bavaria and the shrine of the Nazi party. The 9th's 83rd Infantry Division continued to beat off counterattacks in the Battle of the Elbe River, and the Russians were twenty-eight miles from Berlin.

The Pfungstadt edition just south of Frankfurt, which printed its first paper April 6, would now pick up our circulation. We said goodbye to Art Force, Seymour Sharnik, Dick Jones, and Frank Waters as they left for Pfungstadt to beef up its staff. The rest of us piled into six-by-sixes for the long haul to Paris for a rest and reassignment to other *Stripes* editions. With me were Jim Eathorne and Joe Cotton.

Just as we were leaving, we were told that the new blankets for the press had just arrived. "Save them for the next war," someone yelled as we drove off.

★　★　★

It was good to be back in Paris with its wide avenues, green grass and trees, and beautiful flowers. The pretty girls were out in their short spring frocks, walking along with those great legs, their open-toed shoes with cork heels built like a wedge beating springtime on the pavement. In Liege, when we left, the streets and sidewalks were still covered with mud, as they had been all winter.

This was the Paris of Bud Kane, a *Stripes* reporter who came into the city with the French 2nd Armored early on August 25, the day of liberation. He got so many kisses from grateful Parisiennes the headline on his story in the Continental edition was: KANE BECOMES REAL CITIZEN, PLAYS "POST OFFICE" IN PARIS.

Bill Estoff owned a piece of Paris too; but then Bill, a former nightclub owner in Syracuse, New York, also owned a piece of London, Algiers, Palermo, Naples, and Nancy. He was recruited for a circulation job on the London edition when a lieutenant noted that Pvt. William D. Estoff had listed his civilian occupation as "bookmaker." Maker of books? Books, newspapers — all the same thing. Why not?

When I knew Bill Estoff in Paris, he was the expediter for the Strasbourg, Dijon, and Marseille editions. Each night he would read, or try to read, despite poor connections, the news bulletins over the telephone to their editors. This meant three calls repeating the same news file in the same loud voice. Sometimes we wondered why he bothered — all he had to do was open the window.

Bill, according to his pal Herb Mitgang, who later joined the *New York Times Magazine,* was responsible for the watchword of all *Stripes* and *Yank* staffers who were trying to impress a doubtful young lady, *"Je ne suis pas simple soldat, je suis un correspondent de guerre."* That was the Bill Estoff I knew.

Upon arrival in Paris, we refugees from Belgium learned that we were on orders for Nice. We were crazy with joy. After the cold and wetness of Liege, what we needed was the sun and the beaches of the French Riviera, or so we reasoned. The Nice-Marseille edition was being published for soldiers waiting in the staging areas near Marseille to be shipped to the Pacific and for combat troops visiting the United States Riviera Recreational Area — enlisted men in Nice, Wacs and nurses at Juan les Pins, and officers billeted in Cannes.

The Nice paper was an offspring of the Rome edition and first appeared in the French resort city September 19, 1944. It was shifted to Marseille a month later and then returned to Nice on March 12, 1945. Due to expand to eight pages on May 1, the paper needed more desk help, and that was where we came in. Some of the Liege and Nancy staffers already were in Pfungstadt, others were destined for London, and the rest would remain in Paris.

It was like old times to be back in the *Herald-Tribune* building. Sid Gans was there, although he was on orders to London. Abe Cohen was still on makeup, wearing his orange *Seattle Post-Intelligencer* canvas apron. Les David was back on the desk after a brief stay in Pfungstadt, which he didn't think much of. "You can have Pfunghole and all of Germany for that matter," he said.

Thanks but no thanks, Les, we were going to Nice, the playground of the rich. We went to the Pom Pom, a Champs Élysées bistro, to toast our good fortune. On our second or third cognac someone came in to say that he had heard a rumor that some orders were being changed and that not all of us would be going to Nice; some would go to London instead. We agreed right there that since we already had orders for Nice we would leave immediately. And that's what we did — we drank up, hurried to our billet, then grabbed our duffle bags and a couple of taxis to the Gare de Lyon.

First-class tickets were no problem, and we took over a large compartment — six of us with our duffle bags but still plenty of room to spread out and try to sleep on the overnight trip. Or so we thought.

The train was hardly out of the switching yards when a number of French civilians who had tickets but no seats started to gather in front of the glass windows and door of our compartment, a couple of them pointing to the vacant seats, all of them glaring at us. The conductor, who punched our tickets, refused to let them in, since they did not have first-class fare, but that didn't stop them.

A few minutes later there was a frantic rapping on the glass and a very pregnant woman stood there patting her stomach and pointing to a seat by me. I let her in. We also let in an old lady with a battered suitcase and somewhere near Lyons another pregnant woman squeezed in. By then we were pretty crowded. A couple of us placed the duffle bags on the floor and tried to sleep on top of them. But sleeping, whether sitting up or lying on the floor, was nearly impossible, and we were a somewhat scruffy bunch when we disembarked with our two pregnant women at the huge railroad station at Nice.

3

Nice

What impressed me about southern France was its climate, which I found to be similar to that of southern California. After the cold and mud of Belgium, it was as the sign near the railroad station said: "It's Nice in Nice." Another sign greeted us: "No saluting required by restees in area."

There were plenty of restees — capless and tieless GIs — window-shopping and sitting at tables in sidewalk cafes. The city was clean and pastel bright, trees lined the streets and boulevards, and the shops were filled with more customers than merchandise.

We were met at the station by 1st/Lt. Fred Van Pelt, the officer in charge, and two of his staff who drove us down Avenue de la Victoire and past *La Patriote*, where the Nice-Marseille edition was published. We turned onto boulevard Victor-Hugo and pulled up in front of the Francia Hotel, a five-story building.

Van Pelt, an Ohio newspaperman before the war, prided himself in living the good life and saw to it that his troops did too. He outdid himself at the Francia, where the owner (everyone called him Mr. Paul), his wife and her mother also lived. The dining room was just off the lobby and the food was great. The chef, a Frenchman who had once run the kitchen of the Sands Point Bath Club on Long Island, and whom everyone called "Red," spoke English; the three pretty waitresses — Rosie, Paulette, and Hugette — did not, but no one cared.

We were each assigned a private room. Mine was small and without a bath, but it did have a bidet, which I later discovered was a great beer cooler. The bath and toilet were down the hall. For the first time in my army life I had a private room.

At lunch we met the editorial and production staff and were told that Bud Hutton, who was due the next day, would take over as managing editor. I was delighted because Hutton had "hired" me several months earlier in Paris. He also needed the change and a rest, having flown seventeen air combat missions, worked on both the London and Paris editions, as well as covered ground action in the 1st and 9th Army areas.

Hutton was to replace Leonard Giblin, a Boston newspaperman, who, like most on the staff, had come up from the Rome edition. If he resented the invasion of the Paris crowd, he never said so, although others let us know that they were fully capable of putting out a newspaper. Van Pelt was cordial, but then there was no reason for him not to be; he wasn't being replaced, at least not for the time being.

As soon as we could we took off for the beach, which turned out to be great except there wasn't any sand. I learned later that the officers had sand at Cannes, as did the nurses and Wacs at Juan les Pins. We had only rocks and large pebbles between the blue Mediterranean and the two-and-a-half-mile-long Promenade des Anglais. Located on the promenade was the former gambling casino, the Palais de la Mediterranee, which had been turned into a Red Cross club; several beautiful hotels; and the Jardin Albert, ablaze with flowers, shrubs, and trees. The only traces of war were the camouflaged walls and bunkers the Germans had ordered built in front of key buildings and street intersections. The Germans were fooled, however; the Allied landings the previous August 15 were at St. Tropez, St. Raphael, and St. Maxime farther west between Cannes and Toulon.

The luxury hotels included the Negresco and the Ruhl and were open to vacationing GIs. At its peak the U.S. Riviera Recreational Area had 120 hotels in operation with as many as 14,000 enlisted personnel vacationing in Nice weekly. The enlisted Wacs were billeted in the Alhambra and Londres hotels.

★   ★   ★

The first *Stars and Stripes* in southern France appeared in Grenoble on August 25, ten days after the invasion. Ed Hill, one of the ten staffers who flew in from Italy, remembers:

> We begged a weapons carrier from the 7th Army at St. Tropez and whipped up the Route Napoleon to Grenoble the day after we reached French soil. We established the first southern France edition in the plant of the *Les Allobrogges*, formerly the facility of *Le Petit Dauphinois*, a provincial paper with a daily circulation of 300,000 before the war.
>
> The Germans were six miles up the road toward Lyons the night we rolled No. 1. Nothing was between us and them but a roadblock maintained by the 180th Regt. of the 45th Inf. Div. Jerry was concerned only with joining his brothers coming up the Rhone Valley, and we were not molested.

Hill recalls that in its first days the Grenoble edition had no news source except a "beat-up radio which we all but locked on BBC's wave length." He said the staff's early labors were frequently interrupted by street-corner killings of collaborators by Maquis (French underground) but they still were able to produce thirteen issues of a four-page daily without missing an edition. Hill adds:

> Gen. Patch's front moved so rapidly that after three days we were no longer delivering our papers "back" to combat troops, but scratching around for transportation to reach the front which was running away. [Lt. Gen. Alexander M. Patch, Jr., was the overall commander of the landing forces in southern France.]
>
> Failing to get jeeps or trucks, we picked up the paper and took it to Besancon, where the first issue came out September 14 on the presses of *Les Neuvelles de Besancon*, and after a couple of weeks there the operation was shifted to *La République de Franche-Comte Besancon*. [The Besancon edition closed December 1, 1944, and the staff moved up to Strasbourg and Dijon.]

Hill, who after the war worked for the *New York World-Telegram*, didn't stay long in Besancon but returned to Rome. Others in Grenoble and Besancon were Bill Mauldin, Irv Levinson, Don Williams, Peter Furst, Hugh Conway, Ralph Martin, Milton Lehman, John Willig, and Paul Green.

★   ★   ★

The first *Stars and Stripes* on the French Riviera appeared September 29, 1944, in Nice, but it lasted only about two weeks before it shifted to Marseille because, as someone later wrote, "a general there wanted his paper delivered to his billet before breakfast." Although the distance between the two coastal cities was not that great, it did take a six-by-six approximately four hours to make the haul.

Vic Dallaire was managing editor then, and he recalled that the paper stayed in Marseille from October 16 until the following March 12 when "another general up north in Paris ordered the paper back to Nice." Dallaire moved back to Besancon, where he had once been assigned, and Jack Raymond took over the managing editor job. Staff members included lst/Lt. Bill Brinkley, the officer in charge, John Radosta, George Hakin, Ed Vebell, Bill Estoff, Vic Sanford, Wade Jones, Charles Hogan, and Harry Watson, who later became managing editor at Dijon.

When Raymond was transferred to Paris to be editor of a new *Stripes* magazine, Sanford took over as managing editor, and when he became ill, Leonard Giblin assumed the duties and launched the "second" Nice paper. His staff included Hugh McInteer, James Harrigan, Fred Unwin, John P. Judge, George Dorsey, and Charles Hogan. It still took four hours to truck the papers to Marseille.

★　　★　　★

Hutton's first issue was dated April 26, and the headline read: REDS' BERLIN TRAP CLOSED; NAZI ARMY BROKEN; BRITISH IN BREMEN.

The page, like that of Liege, was short and stubby and the headline type was different from what we were used to. There was plenty of Roman type but no italic, so we used Karnak, which had a slant effect but was just as black as the Roman. As a result there wasn't much contrast in our page layouts.

The following day, Hutton ordered an extra when the Yanks and the Russians linked up on the Elbe River. A feature story from Andy Rooney datelined "With Koniev's Ukrainian Army" came in on the teletype telling how the Americans swapped K rations with the Reds for vodka.

Benito Mussolini's death made Page 1 on April 30 when the bulletin arrived stating that he had been executed and his bullet-ridden body was on view in a Milan square. The headline said the U.S. 7th Army had entered Munich.

Bob Neville, Phil Kline, Bob Christenson, and Tony Iannacio

of the Rome edition were in Bologna when they learned that Milan had fallen to the partisans. They set out the next morning in a two-jeep caravan for the drive north up the leg of Italy and were within forty kilometers of Milan when they ran out of daylight.

"Pull up at that hotel. We'll bed down and get an early start tomorrow. I don't want us killed by trigger-happy partisans," Neville ordered Iannacio.

"We bitched but Bob had major's leaves on his collar and had been through the Spanish Civil War, so he knew all about partisans," Iannacio remembered.

"While we were sleeping in a lousy bed in a lousy little town whose name I never knew, the partisans captured old Mussolini and his girlfriend, Clara Petacci. They shot them near Dongo, a small village about twenty-seven miles from Milano."

Tony recalled that they were halted the following morning at a partisan roadblock on the outskirts of Milan.

This clown asked me if I was English. I told him, "Hell no, American." He about pulled me out of the driver's seat and started kissing me.

They gave us an escort into Milano and to the gas station where we saw the bodies of "Mussy" and Clara — who sure didn't look twenty-five years old — hanging by their feet. Talk about a madhouse, a bunch of crazy paisanos, screaming and firing rifles in the air! Finally they took down the bodies and, with sixteen of his Black Shirt henchmen, threw them in a truck like sacks of coal and away they went.

Iannacio said they then drove to the Continental, the best hotel in Milan, and met Bill Mauldin and Stan Swinton, also of the Rome edition.

A brunette and a redhead spotted Phil and me in the bar and told us how happy they were to see us and how they had suffered under those swine. That was some day — first old "Mussy" and Clara and then these two broads.

Two weeks later I was having a drink in the Rome Press Club when a British spook asked me if I knew that the brunette I was with in Milan was Rita Zucca, the Fascist Axis Sally. He said they had just locked her up in the jug. I had been listening for two and a half years while she played my favorite records. Now she had to face the music.

★　　★　　★

The promised eight-page paper — the reason why several of us were in Nice — rolled off the press May 1, and its expanded news looked great. It was topped the next day by a headline that took up nearly one-half the page: HITLER DEAD.

The news came from the German Radio, which also reported that Adm. Karl Doenitz, former commander of the German Navy, had succeeded Hitler as ruler of the Reich. The following day Hutton put out his second extra in a week: GERMANS IN ITALY QUIT; BERLIN FALLS TO REDS; GOEBBELS DEAD; "WORLD PEACE" ASKED BY NAZIS.

The news continued to be bad for the Nazis and then Doenitz announced that effective May 8 Germany had surrendered unconditionally to the Western Allies and to the Soviet Union. There was no official announcement from the Allied governments or from headquarters of the Allied or Russian armies, but the British Ministry of Information issued a statement in London declaring that May 8 would be treated as "Victory in Europe Day" in Britain.

There was no strolling along the beach the next day; instead, everyone was in the office early. The teletype bell began to ring, and Wally Smith got up from the copy desk to see what was being sent by the Paris news bureau. He tore the copy off and handed it to Hutton. "It's over," he said.

HOLD FOR RELEASE EXPECTED ANY MINUTE. RHEIMS, FRANCE, MAY 7 — THE UNCONDITIONAL SURRENDER OF GERMANY TO THE WESTERN ALLIES WAS SIGNED AT 0241 HOURS THIS MORNING AT GEN. EISENHOWER'S HEADQUARTERS.

The teletype continued:

EDITORS: FOLLOWING COPY BEING SENT YOU FOR PREPARATION OF EXTRAS BUT MUST NOT BE PUBLISHED UNTIL OFFICIAL RELEASE, WHICH WE WILL FLASH MOMENTARILY IN VIEW ED KENNEDY OF ASSOCIATED PRESS HAS BROKEN STORY PREMATURELY — PARIS.

Wally handed over the instructions and watched the machine tick on.

THE NEGOTIATIONS THAT PRECEDED THE SIGNING HAD

And then the machine went dead. Willy Benoit, a French teenager who worked in communications, did everything he could to get it working, but to no avail.

Wally grabbed a telephone. "Get me Paris right away," he told the operator at the Nice switchboard.

"Sorry," said the operator, "but all the lines to Paris are busy."

"Listen," said Wally, "this is *The Stars and Stripes*. The war's over. We got the story but we don't know whether we can print it. You've got to get us through to Paris."

"Wait a minute," the operator said. A few minutes later Wally was asking the news bureau editor in Paris about the surrender story. "Don't know yet," said he. "We may get a break soon but it might not be until tomorrow afternoon. We'll call you back."

"The hell you will," Wally said. "The operator down here has got us through to you by way of New York."

The teletype was out most of the afternoon, but Wally took the rest of the story over the telephone so that it could be set in type. Finally, the clearance came and the page looked great: ALLIES PROCLAIM: IT'S OVER.

The second line, in big type, was in red and the words "V-E Day" were overprinted in blue on the lower part of the page. Alton Jones, who had worked in the *Detroit News* pressroom before the war, came up with the colored ink at the last minute. The Frenchmen on his crew had been saving it for such an occasion.

Meantime in Rheims, where the surrender was signed at General Eisenhower's forward headquarters, S/Sgt. Charles F. Kiley was the only news correspondent present. He represented the world press as well as *The Stars and Stripes* and would do so the following day in Berlin when the surrender was ratified by the Russians.

Kiley had worked on the London, Paris, and Liege editions and after the war was assistant city editor of the *New York Herald-Tribune*.

The Paris edition used one word, "Victory," the Pfungstadt paper said it in two, "Nazis Quit," London used "Germany Quits," while Altdorf edition, in its first issue, told it in three lines, "ETO War Ends." None of them in color, Alton pointed out.

We left the newsroom after checking the paper and joined the thousands of happy French on the Avenue de la Victoire. We heard music in the distance and when we got to the Place Massena there were thousands of French men and women dancing in the square. Many were drinking from bottles of wine and beer, and that went on into the next day. There weren't enough girls to go around, so some GIs jitterbugged with other GIs. It was that kind of happiness; one war down and another to go.

★   ★   ★

The winding down of the war was good news for Pfc Thomas Hoge, the only *Stripes* reporter to have been captured by the Germans. He was taken prisoner the previous September when the plane he was in was shot down over Holland. Hoge and about 300 American prisoners escaped near Kustrin on the Oder River during a tank ambush by the Russian Army.

The Bayville, New York, newspaperman had covered the 3rd Army up to the Mosélle front and then went on the Arnhem airborne invasion. His plane was shot down September 17, and he and three others parachuted to safety only to be taken prisoner. Tom spent the first six months in a prison camp at Limburg after being herded across Holland, Belgium, and Germany, during which time his group was strafed by American planes, raked by British artillery, and virtually starved to death by their captors. They were being moved westward at the time of their escape.

After his release he and the other freed prisoners — Americans, French, British, and Italians — made their way through Poland and eventually to Odessa, where they contacted American and British units. A series of articles detailing his life as a POW and his escape was mailed to the Rome edition of *Stripes,* where it was relayed to Paris for release to the other papers.

★   ★   ★

Ernie Leiser's eyewitness account from Berlin appeared over the flag on Page 1 the next day. He described the German capital as a charred, stinking, broken skeleton of a city: "It is impossible to imagine what it looked like before. It is impossible to believe that the miles of disembowelled buildings, crater-pocked streets and shattered masonry once could have been the capital of Greater Germany and the home of 4,000,000 people."

He added that the Russians were everywhere and that a torn Red flag was flying from the Reichstag's hole-filled dome.

Kiley's report from Berlin of the formal ratification of the unconditional surrender was the lead, and next to it was a picture of Reichmarshal Hermann Goering and a story reporting his capture in Kitsbuhl, Austria, by the U.S. 7th Army.

At the bottom of the page Ed Clark wrote that his friend Bill Mauldin of "Willie and Joe" fame had won the Pulitzer Prize for the best newspaper cartoon. The judges cited Mauldin's ironic "fresh spirited American troops, flushed with victory bringing in thousands of battle-weary prisoners," as an outstanding example of his distinguished service in interpreting the life of the GI.

Clark said the award was "very fair." We knew it, and our readers knew it all the time.

Mauldin joined *The Stars and Stripes* in November 1943 in Naples after a couple of years in the States, North Africa, Sicily, and Italy with his Oklahoma-bred 45th Infantry Division.

The late Ernie Pyle, who was fond of the twenty-four-year-old cartoonist, called him the best in this or any other war and helped him get his work syndicated at home. Some of the editors at the syndicate thought the title "Up Front With Mauldin" should be changed to "Up Front By Mauldin," but the Oklahoman balked at the change in preposition on the grounds that he was only a time-to-time visitor, not a steady customer at the front. Mauldin did know about the front and combat, having been wounded while with Company K of the 45th Division's 180th Regiment.

Mauldin's cartoons chided the brass and poked fun at troop-training programs. Although he was based in Rome and spent most of his time at the 5th Army front, he did venture north to see what the other armies were doing. His cartoons appeared several times a week in all *Stripes* editions, having been relayed from Rome via New York.

On one trip he kidded one Lt. Gen. George S. Patton's signs in a cartoon that depicted Joe and Willie stopping before it in their jeep.

Headed "YOU ARE ENTERING THIRD ARMY AREA," the sign was a list of offenses with their fines. Mauldin added a few of his own.

No helmet	$25
No tie	25
No shine	12.50
No buttons	10
No shampoo	25
No shave	10
Windshields up	25
Trousers down	50

Enforced
By Order of
Old Blood and Guts

Willie was saying to Joe in the caption: "Radio the old man we'll be late on account of a thousand-mile detour."

A couple of cartoons later, Mauldin got a call to appear before Patton himself. The general just wanted to "talk with the sergeant."

Patton told Mauldin he did not appreciate Willie and Joe and thought they were not typical of the American soldier in the 3rd Army. Mauldin presented his view and departed. Soon after, Mauldin returned to Italy, where he had a little more freedom to draw what he saw.

★   ★   ★

Now that the war in Europe was over, the chief topic wherever GIs gathered was: When do we go home? There was a good chance that many would be shipped to the Pacific through the Marseille-Arles staging area, but it was highly unlikely that all of the ETO troops would be needed to fight the Japanese.

The question was partly answered May 11 with this headline: 85 POINTS NEEDED TO GET OUT.

In order to determine eligibility, one point was given for each month served in the United States, two points for each month served overseas, five points for each combat award, and twelve points if one had a dependent under eighteen years of age.

The same total applied to both enlisted men and officers. Wacs had to have forty-four points. Although I had been in the army since December 1942 and overseas since June 1944, I knew that I wasn't going anywhere. Hutton, Rooney, Giblin, Bert Marsh, and several others on the staff had well over 100 points.

That same day the War Department revealed that it would take at least a year to redeploy, and that meant 400,000 potential readers for *Stripes*.

★   ★   ★

How did it feel to get out of the army? T/5 Charley "Trooper" White, a gray-haired veteran of *The Stars and Stripes*, happened to be in New York on rotation when the point scheme came out and just happened to have 85 points. They twisted his arm and he finally consented to take his discharge. He headed home to Indiana.

Trooper's full name was Charles Worthington White and before the war he worked on the *Bean Blossom Bugle*, a weekly newspaper covering Brown County in Indiana. I never heard why Charley enlisted in the Essex Scottish Infantry Regiment of the Royal

Canadian Army, but he did, and when the Canadians reached England Charley transferred to the Calgary Tanks.

When the American army arrived in England, Charley sought another transfer and this time landed in General Eisenhower's headquarters as a clerk. He worked for Capt. Harry Butcher, Ike's naval aide. When *Stripes* began publication as a daily, Charley got the itch to get back to newspaper work and transferred to the London edition. There he worked on rewrite, wrote features, and did a stint in the Northern Ireland bureau.

Sgt. Dick Wingert, who was also a Hoosier, modeled his rolypoly cartoon character Hubert after Charley. Hubert's dialogue was remarkably similar to that of White's dry Indiana philosophy.

One Wingert cartoon will always be remembered. It showed two well-dressed and shapely Parisian women seated at a table in a sidewalk cafe. A tin-helmeted Hubert with a bewildered look stood nearby. One lovely said to the other: "Don't look now, but there's old 'Coushay Awvec' back in town."

Hutton, who like White was a transferee from the Canadian army, recalled a meeting with General Eisenhower when the commander, after their greetings were exchanged, said, "Well, how's White doing these days?"

"White? You mean Colonel Egbert White?"

"No. Private Charley White. How is he?"

Told later that the supreme commander had inquired about him, Charley observed, "That was sure nice of him. How's he doing these days?"

★　　★　　★

The first Pacific edition of *The Stars and Stripes* rolled off the press in Honolulu May 14, and we announced its birth on Page 1. Those of us with few discharge points agreed that a transfer to the Hawaiian Islands wouldn't be too hard to take. Being a Californian, I would be able to visit home before reporting for duty. Well, we talked about it.

The Stars and Stripes in Honolulu replaced the *Mid-Pacifican*, a weekly established in February 1942. Copies of the eight-page *Stripes* were flown forward from Honolulu at first, but other editions were expected to be set up later.

The Middle Pacific *Stripes* only lasted eight and a half months, but it boasted the largest paper route in the world, its copies reaching south from Honolulu to New Caledonia and Australia, north to the Aleutians, and as far west as Chungking and the China-Burma-India Theater.

Managing editor was M/Sgt. Charles Avedon of Los Angeles; the officer in charge was Capt. George Chaplin, former city editor of the *Greenville* [South Carolina] *Piedmont.*

We didn't know it at the time, but Lt. Col. Arthur Goodfriend had been transferred from Paris to the Pacific and sometime later opened the Shanghai edition of *Stripes* as publications officer. Replacing him as editor was Lt. Col. Fred Eldridge, who had been in the China-Burma-India Theater with Gen. Joseph W. Stilwell. Eldridge had been a reporter for the *Los Angeles Times* and returned to its staff after the war ended. Later, Col. Paul Zimmerman, also on Stilwell's staff, joined the Information and Education Division in Paris. After the war, Zimmerman returned to his job as sports editor of the *Los Angeles Times.*

Another change in the Information and Education structure in Paris was the departure of Brig. Gen. O. N. Solbert as chief, Special Services Office. He was replaced by Brig. Gen. Paul W. Thompson, who had been wounded on D-Day when he led the 6th Engineer Special Brigade onto Omaha Beach in support of the 1st Infantry Division. After the war Thompson joined the staff of *Reader's Digest.*

On May 16, a week and a day after the war in Europe ended, SHAEF cracked down on Associated Press bureau chief Edward Kennedy, who had broken the news of the German surrender twenty-four hours in advance of the SHAEF-set release time. He was disaccredited as a war correspondent and ordered returned to the United States.

Also disaccredited and ordered out of the theater was Morton Gudebrod, AP editor in charge of servicing the French newspapers, because it was said he passed the story to the French press. Kennedy had telephoned his version to London from his room at the Scribe Hotel in Paris. Robert Bunnelle, AP executive director, who transmitted the story from London to the United States, was ordered reinstated.

SHAEF Public Relations Division said Kennedy "deliberately violated the trust reposed in him by prematurely releasing, through unauthorized channels, and deliberately evading military censorship" on a news story concerning which "he was pledged to secrecy."

Kennedy had been in a group of correspondents taken to Rheims when the Germans surrendered. He telephoned the story after telling SHAEF censors he could see no security violation and accused SHAEF of withholding the announcement for political reasons, saying "my conscience is clear in this matter. I did what I considered to be my duty and informed SHAEF Public Relations Div. in advance that I intended to do it."

SHAEF said Kennedy had been suspended once before following a jeep trip through southern France.

The army wasn't through. The next day it disaccredited and ordered four more war correspondents to return to the United States because of an unauthorized trip to Berlin. They were: Seymour Freidin, *New York Herald-Tribune;* John Groth, *American Legion Monthly* artist; Margaret Irwin, *St. Louis Post-Dispatch;* and Andrew Tully, *Boston Traveler.*

SHAEF Public Relations Division said the trips violated regulations prohibiting correspondents from leaving army areas without orders.

★   ★   ★

Something bitter and something sweet happened to me during my stay in Nice. I lost my mother, Frances Mae Husted, shortly after I arrived and a month before the war in Europe ended. My sister-in-law wired me through the American Red Cross that Mother was failing, and I put in for emergency leave to California but she died of cancer before my request could be processed. My brother, a corporal with the 5th Marine Division in the Pacific, had his request approved and was at her bedside the day she died.

The something sweet was Paulette, a beautiful French girl whom I had been dating. Despite a difference in faith and the fact that neither could speak the other's language, we somehow managed. Before I left the Riviera, I met her parents, one of her two sisters, and her two little brothers. Her father, Paul Albin, vinted a great wine and something powerful called *eau de vie;* her mother, Francoise, was a fabulous cook.

The Albin family lived in Sospel, a little village tucked in the hills above Menton and near the Italian border. Sospel had seen much of the war. First, the Italians forced the villagers out, and they no sooner were allowed to return when the Germans arrived. The Germans confiscated the farm animals and much of the food, although the villagers saved some nonperishables such as wine and olive oil by burying it in the fields. The Germans stayed around until the Americans showed up, and then the battle really started.

Elements of Maj. Gen. Robert T. Frederick's 1st Airborne Task Force chased the Germans into Italy but had to use artillery to dislodge them from the village. Many of the buildings in Sospel took direct hits. The Germans had earlier blasted the eleventh-century bridge over the Bevera River. Paulette's family home still shows shell marks on its southern walls.

★   ★   ★

Meanwhile, the war in the Pacific continued to be headline news in *The Stars and Stripes* and there was plenty of it in the May 25 edition: 700,000 fire bombs from 550 Superfortresses kindling blazes in Tokyo and heavy fighting on Okinawa by the 6th Marine Division and the 77th and 96th infantry divisions.

The off-play story that day was the suicide death of Heinrich Himmler, the head of the Nazi Gestapo. British 2nd Army headquarters said Himmler took his life to avoid trial before an international bar of justice by biting open a vial of potassium cyanide which he had secreted behind his gums.

That day it was also announced that Julius Streicher, number-one Nazi Jew-baiter, was captured by a patrol of the 502nd Parachute Infantry Regiment of the 111th Airborne Division. That left only Joachim von Ribbentrop, Hitler's expert on diplomatic intrigue and the last of the old-line Nazis unaccounted for. He was captured three weeks later in Hamburg, where he was hiding under the name Reise.

★   ★   ★

Interest in the Pacific war was high in the staging areas because the troops there were being shipped out of the port of Marseille through the Suez Canal to the Indian Ocean and finally to the Philippines.

Johnny Brown, who had been with us in Liege, was the bureau chief in Marseille and was assisted by Joe Diehl and Dan Regan. Regan had seen much of the war covering the 1st Army; later he transferred to the Nice staff.

Other front-line reporters checked in for the good life in Nice. Among them were Andy Rooney and Ernie Leiser. Pete Lisagore, the managing editor at London, transferred to our staff and worked a few weeks before shipping back to the States. Ed Vebell, a talented artist who had been on the staff of the original Nice-Marseille edition and later with the magazine in Paris, spent several weeks with us sketching GIs and pretty French girls. Jean Baird, the British artist from the Paris staff, stopped over for a time before moving on to Pfungstadt.

Rooney stayed long hours in his hotel room, and we learned later that he and Hutton were writing a book. They had co-authored *Air Gunner* while in London and now were working on *The Story of the Stars and Stripes*, which was published the following year by Farrar & Rinehart.

Hutton pulled one last rabbit out of his journalistic hat before he redeployed: He launched the Blue Coast Final, a replate of Page 1 to include late bulletins for distribution to hotels in Nice, Juan les Pins, and Cannes. It continued after he left June 8 for his home in Bucks County, Pennsylvania, but was abandoned when Alton Jones ran out of blue ink a few weeks later. Then it was back to basic black.

Rooney took off for the States too, but in the opposite direction. A few days later we received one of his features datelined Iran. After his return to the States and his discharge from the army, Andy became a writer for Arthur Godfrey, later reaching stardom on CBS' "60 Minutes." A graduate of Colgate, he had worked briefly on the *Albany* [New York] *Knickerbocker News* and had joined the London edition from a field artillery outfit in which he served as battery clerk.

Hutton's departure left the managing editor's job open, and Capt. Stan Baitz, a Washington, D.C., newsman before the war, arrived in Nice just in time to name the replacement. Baitz had taken over from 1st/Lt. Fred Van Pelt, who later moved on to Pfungstadt.

My debut as managing editor occurred on a good news day. The headline: SHIPS SHELL JAP HOMELAND; 1,000 PLANES JOIN IN RENEWED ASSAULT.

The off-play story reported that the Allied nonfraternization policy in Germany was being modified by orders of General Eisenhower and Field Marshal Sir Bernard L. Montgomery. Under the new rules, American and British soldiers would be permitted to associate with adult Germans on the streets and "in public places." Previously, the fraternization ban had been relaxed to permit contact with small children. Enlisted men and officers were fined $65 and sometimes more for any contact with Germans.

We sent reporter Jim Thomas out on the boulevards of Nice to get reaction from the GIs. "When you start telling a Yank who to speak with and who not to speak with, you've got a job on your hands," M/Sgt. Charles P. Misevich of the 83rd Reconnaissance Battalion told him.

Cpl. David L. Mitts, FA radio operator and holder of the Silver Star, said: "Don't say the soldiers should get down and kiss the Jerries, but I do think that it's a good way to help the Germans by letting GIs talk to them."

★   ★   ★

President Truman arrived in Berlin July 18 to confer with Prime Minister Churchill and Generalissimo Stalin at Potsdam, and Ernie Leiser was there for *The Stars and Stripes*. Before the Big Three talks ended, Churchill had lost an election in England and was replaced at Potsdam by Labor Party leader Clement R. Attlee.

Truman also met with Capt. Max Gilstrap and Sgt. Paul Elliott of the Pfungstadt edition. Gilstrap, the officer in charge, and Elliott, the managing editor, presented Mr. Truman with a leatherbound volume of the Pfungstadt paper. The president said it would make a fine addition to the White House Library.

★   ★   ★

In mid-July, on orders from Paris, the name Nice-Marseille edition was dropped in favor of Southern France edition.

Circulation was booming. Four pages of color comics featuring "Moon Mullins" on the front and "Blondie," "Li'l Abner," and "The Gumps" were added to the paper. Printed in Paris, they were shipped to Nice by rail. The presses at *La Patriote* were turning out 95,000 copies daily, most of them shipped on six-by-sixes to the staging areas.

The long haul to Marseille and the staging areas took its toll. One of the French drivers overturned his vehicle and smothered to death under the bundles of newspapers. It was the second such fatality that we knew of, but there were probably others because the French, during the war, had trouble driving trucks.

Jack Melcher, who ran the transportation office in Paris, lost an assistant driver in May when a weapons carrier overturned near Pfungstadt. The driver righted the vehicle, piled the body of his dead companion in the back, and drove back to Paris. It was a two-day trip.

He pulled into the garage, parked the truck, and went home to sleep. He was not due to work again until 6:00 A.M. the following day. When he reported to Melcher he asked, "What shall I do with Monsieur Renaud?"

"What do you mean what should you do with him?" Melcher replied. "Take him with you. Assistant driver, isn't he?"

"Yes, but — "

"Goddamn it, I have more trouble with you Frenchmen than you're worth. What's the trouble with Renaud?"

"Monsieur Renaud is dead," the driver said. "I had a little accident in Germany and I thought — "

"Dead?" Melcher said. "Where is he?"

"He is in the back of the truck, sir."

Melcher had heard everything, but that did it. The body had been lying in the truck four days. It was another three days before Monsieur Renaud was buried, what with government red tape and a price tag of 12,000 francs for the funeral. Melcher passed a note through the editorial offices asking for donations for a "flower fund." The French Labor Ministry allowed 1,000 francs.

★   ★   ★

Thanks to Wally Smith and Larry Griffing, the Nice edition wasn't caught napping when the Army Air Force's Superfortress *Enola Gay* dropped an atomic bomb on Hiroshima. Smith went to work with his encyclopedia and fleshed out what otherwise was a terse news story. Griffing's headline that August 7: ATOMIC BOMB HITS JAPS; YANKS DROP NEW SUPER MISSILE; EQUALS 20,000 DYNAMITE TONS.

The Paris edition also gave top billing to the bombing of the Japanese city of 318,000 on southwestern Honshu Island. Pfungstadt and Altdorf editions displayed the story under a two-column head, one of the makeup editors placing it at the bottom of the page. The two French editions had an hour jump on the papers in Germany, so that could have been a deciding factor.

Two days later we trotted out more big headline type, the last few thousand copies done up in bright red ink: RUSSIA ENTERS PACIFIC WAR.

A second atomic bomb was dropped on Japan August 9, this time on Nagasaki. Approximately 253,000 lived in the port and industrial city on the southwestern Kyushu Island.

The next day we published nearly a page of reaction to the two big news events from servicemen, Wacs, and sailors.

lst/Lt. Lillian Eis, 165th General Hospital, told reporter Bob Sontag at Cannes: "I believe the psychology of having both the United States and Russia against her will force Japan to surrender."

Lt. Col. E. D. Kay of Kerrville, Texas, who was a medical officer at Pearl Harbor at the time of the Japanese attack, summed it up: "The atom bomb overshadows the entry of Russia into the war."

Then finally, on August 14, the official announcement came from Washington, Moscow, and Chungking. It was all over, and we put out an extra with our biggest type: JAPAN QUITS.

The war in the Pacific was officially over, and we said so with the last extra we would ever put out, since the Nice edition's days were numbered: SURRENDER IS OFFICIAL.

For us the war was officially over at 1:00 A.M. August 15, one year to the day when three American infantry divisions invaded southern France. Pete Lisagore wrote that veterans of the U.S. 3rd, 36th, and 45th divisions, which comprised the assault force, would be honored by the French government while the U.S. destroyers *Memphis* and *Gridley,* in remembrance of the navy's role, would stand offshore. The program was scheduled at Dramont, near St. Raphael, where a monument erected by the 36th, which landed there, was to be dedicated.

V-J Day was officially celebrated August 17, but it wasn't a holiday for us. We still had work and didn't mind a bit, since the lead story from Robert J. Donovan in Paris reported that 200,000 soldiers, most of them from the 3rd and 7th armies and the XVI Corps, were due to be shipped home in September.

The Japanese didn't get around to signing the surrender documents until September 2, when they stood before General of the Armies Douglas MacArthur and other Allied officers on board the USS *Missouri* in Tokyo Bay. After that flurry of news we settled down to a steady diet of stories about redeployment. Enlisted men over thirty-eight years of age were to be discharged immediately, and the points were dropped from 85 to 80.

We lost more old-timers. Sports editor James J. Harrigan returned to Buffalo, New York, and artist Bert E. Marsh, who had been with me in Cologne, went back to Renton, Washington. Others leaving were Walter Romany, Charles Watson, and Norman Todd.

Capt. Stan Baitz took off for Paris and later to Washington, D.C., where he went into public relations. He was replaced by Capt. Robert Dumper, a former *Time* writer, who brought the news that the Southern France edition would cease operation with its September 30 issue. He also told me that I was headed for Pfungstadt to replace Paul Elliott as managing editor. Elliott's high points rated him a ride home. I also got a T/4 stripe out of the deal, important to me since I had been a corporal for thirty months.

The high pointers weren't our only loss. We were kicked out of the Hotel Francia, the posh downtown billet, and were moved to La Colline, a one-time sanitorium in the hills west of Nice. It was about a five-mile ride and we were shuttled back and forth in a GI truck driven by a Frenchman we called "old Tomato Puss."

"He didn't get that red face from wearing tight shoes," someone observed.

La Colline, built on a beautiful hillside in a carnation-growing area, was quiet and peaceful. It even had a few padded cells in the basement, which seemed appropriate to us.

★   ★   ★

Being an organ of the Information and Education Division of the army, we printed a lot of news about education. It was important because most of the men in the ETO at this period were low pointers and it would be some time before they could return home.

To fill that time period, the army established two universities where students could take courses and get full college credit — Shrivenham, England, and Biarritz, on the southwestern coast of France. Professors were brought over from the States to teach most of the classes. Army officers who had been educators before joining the service filled the rest of the teaching positions.

The Sorbonne in Paris opened its doors to the American military and on September 9 graduated 750 enlisted and officer personnel who had taken 180 hours of French. A technical school was operating at Warton, England.

If the soldier didn't wish to go to school and wanted a change from his regular routine, he could check out a jeep from the motor pool and with two or three others go on a camping trip. Tents and cooking gear were available, and gasoline was free. What a way to see Europe.

Certain places on the Riviera were off-limits to us. Although we were newspapermen in uniform and had roamed the front lines and attended briefings given by generals, we didn't mind the restrictions. If the officers were restricted to Cannes and the nurses and Wacs to Juan les Pins, that meant they couldn't bother us in Nice. We often drove through Juan les Pins and Cannes en route to Marseille but we never stopped. There was no need to. We had everything in Nice — weather, pretty girls, the beach.

What made no sense were the off-limits signs at Monaco and Monte Carlo — the gambling capital of Europe, the playground of kings. That's what we really wanted to see, but we were told it was for political reasons, that although Monaco was surrounded by France and the Mediterranean, it was a principality, a separate country, and therefore off-limits.

French and Monegasque soldiers were on duty at both entrances to Monaco on the Cornich du Littoral, the busy street that skirts the Mediterranean. The French-Italian border just east of Menton was also closed to us, and soldiers from both nations guarded the crossing. From time to time 5th U.S. Army soldiers from Italy were permitted to visit Nice on leave, so there was some American traffic.

Some years later I learned why Monte Carlo was off-limits to American troops. Robert H. Adleman and Col. George Walton, in their book *The Champagne Campaign*, wrote that Maj. Gen. Robert T. Frederick, commander of the 1st Airborne Task Force, closed the principality to American troops. They said that during the war the German army used the enclave as a recreation center for their men and as a listening post for spies and that the roulette wheels in the Monte Carlo casino never stopped spinning.

After the 7th U.S. Army landed and the 1st Airborne Task Force began moving east along the coast, the businessmen, collaborators, and Axis officers paid their bills and left for Italy, leaving behind 300 soldiers in the Mt. Agel fortress overlooking Monaco. On September 3 a jeep with four American soldiers stopped in front of the Place d'Armes and one asked: "Hey bud, where the hell are we?"

Frederick's first inclination was to set up canteens, clubs, and PXs, turning the principality into a leave center for his 10,000 men. But Prince Louis, Rainier's grandfather, prevailed on him to preserve his little country's neutrality. The general agreed, announcing that Monte Carlo and Monaco would be off-limits to all Allied personnel, regardless of rank. That order was respected by General

Eisenhower when, in the summer of 1945, he arrived on the Riviera and stayed at Eden Roc.

★　★　★

As the days of September dwindled down, we lost more high pointers and also more readers. Circulation was dropping as troop movement to the States was stepped up. From a top of 95,000 on July 15, the press run the final week in Nice averaged 64,000.

There were several ways to get back to the States. Most went by regular troop ship, but there just weren't that many in service. The British government had made the *Queen Mary* and the *Queen Elizabeth* available through the Allied War Shipping Pool, and each made several trips carrying approximately 15,000 passengers each. That averaged out to three army divisions each month. However, the British withdrew the Queens when the U.S. Congress dropped Lend Lease and caused former Prime Minister Churchill to call the action "rough and harsh." His successor, Clement Attlee, said the step put Britain in a "very serious financial position."

The United States still had the French liners *Ile de France* and the *Aquitania* and ordered repairs at Bremerhaven on the former German luxury liner *Europa*, which could carry 10,000 passengers. U.S. Navy aircraft carriers were also pressed into troop-carrying duty.

The Green Project was the quickest way to get home if you could qualify for space. A fleet of 30 four-engine C-54s flew from Istres-Casablanca to the United States, carrying personnel on emergency leave and soldiers needed in vital jobs back home. For a time that summer, if you had prewar experience working on railroads, you had a sure ticket home. But the Green Project lost most of its planes when the Pacific war ended, and the C-54s were needed to fly liberated prisoners back to the States.

Also returning to the States was G. K. Hodenfield, otherwise known as Gaylord Kenneth to his parents, first lieutenant on his pay book, and "Hod" to his friends. He was one of the founders of the weekly *Stripes* in 1942, as well as a member of the London group sent later that year to North Africa to set up a paper. Hodenfield was best known for the stories he wrote about his pre-invasion assignment with the 2nd and 5th Ranger battalions that knocked out the German's coastal guns overlooking Omaha and Utah beaches.

An Iowan who had worked for the United Press before the war, Hodenfield switched to the Associated Press after his discharge from the army and became its education writer. He is now retired and living in Mesa, Arizona.

★   ★   ★

Much of the news those last few weeks had to do with entertainment, as Hollywood stars, singers, and dancers kept the troops happy and their minds off redeployment. Some stars even got to the Riviera.

Bob Hope and his sidekick, Jerry Colonna, did their thing in the Nice Velodrome and were followed by singer Betty Hutton. T/5 Mickey Rooney and T/5 Bobby Breen, a singer on the Eddie Cantor radio show, tried out their Jeep Shows act at the Arles Staging Area before going on to Berlin.

Actress Madeline Carroll and singer Grace Moore appeared on stage in Paris. Miss Moore, who was touring with Nino Martino, later visited in Nice to inspect property she owned. Frank Sinatra sang for the troops in Italy and then on a stopover in Paris blasted the conduct of the Special Services officer who handled his tour. Jack Benny was also critical of Special Services for the handling of his arrangements.

Benny and Larry Adler, the harmonica virtuoso, shared the same bill, while actress Ingrid Bergman signed autographs on her visit to Berchtesgaden, Germany. Glenn Miller's band made several trips to the Riviera with different musicians fronting for its famed leader, who was lost when the small plane he was in went down in the English Channel the year before. Johnnie Desmond did the singing for the big band, which returned to the States in September.

★   ★   ★

As the Southern France edition bowed into history, another *Stars and Stripes* on the other side of the world commenced publication — the Shanghai edition. Lt. Col. Arthur Goodfriend served as publications officer. The new edition made its debut September 29; the story of its birth appeared in our final issue.

Sgt. Edmund Hogan of Albany, New York, was managing editor and Sgt. John Clift of Denison, Texas, sports editor. Both had been on the staff of the Mediterranean edition.

★   ★   ★

Leonard P. Giblin, who had the points to get out but stayed to the bitter end, wrote the obituary for the Southern France edition's 201st issue. There were no big headlines that day, but there was a touching picture of President Truman receiving a kiss from his ninety-two-year-old mother, Mrs. Martha E. Truman, before he left Grandview, Missouri, to return to Washington.

Giblin's story said the Paris edition would serve the readers on the Riviera, with papers arriving daily by plane at Marignan Airport at Marseille and an hour and a half later at the Nice Airport. He later returned to his job with the Associated Press in Boston.

★   ★   ★

We had a party for the French employees on October 1, and then a couple of days later photographer Joe Brignola and I loaded the editorial jeep with a case of C rations, two portable typewriters, his cameras, two cardboard boxes containing the photo and clipping files, our duffle bags, and two jerrycans of gasoline.

We had orders for Germany. The logical route was north to Grenoble, then northeast to Strasbourg, where we could cross the Rhine River and continue to Pfungstadt, midway between Heidelberg and Frankfurt. That was the logical and most direct route, also covered by the appropriate orders.

The other was to brazen our way across the French-Italian border at Menton, drive south to Leghorn, turn east to Milan, and then hightail it northeast to the Brenner Pass and into Germany. That was also complicated by the fact that our orders didn't say anything about Italy, which also just happened to be in another theater of operations.

Joe and I discussed the itinerary at length and decided we wanted to see the country. I kissed Paulette goodbye, told her I would return (a promise I knew she didn't believe), and we drove off toward Italy.

4

Pfungstadt

As we left the Heidelberg-Frankfurt autobahn and saw Pfungstadt in the distance, I was not impressed. Later, though, I was impressed by the draft beer that flowed into the *Stripes* mess hall direct from the brewery across the street.

The Stars and Stripes had taken over the auxiliary press facilities of the *Frankfurter Zeitung,* and on April 5 had printed its first issue. *Stripes* had also requisitioned about half of the town: the Hotel Strauss, which housed the mess hall downstairs and bedrooms on the second floor for the displaced persons who worked as cooks, waitresses, and housemaids; a building for the dispensary; another for administration and circulation; a service station and garage for the motor pool; and several large houses for billets.

Soon after Joe Brignola parked our jeep in front of the administration building on Eberstadter Strasse, he and I were sitting in the mess hall talking to Joe Landau, who was filling in for Paul Elliott, the managing editor whom I was to replace. Elliott, who had worked on Pittsburgh, Pennsylvania, newspapers before the war, had already left for the States to be discharged.

"What's your staff situation? Do you have enough people?" I asked as I drank from a stein of Pfungstadter beer.

"These days we never have enough help, but we're getting

some of your Nice staff, so that should do it. Of course, we are losing a few of the old-timers."

"What about yourself? When are you due for discharge?"

"I've got some time before I go home, but I would like to take some leave here in Europe, and I will, after Captain Dowell gets back from Denmark. He's the officer in charge and his furlough is up in a week or ten days."

I had a reason for asking because I needed to let him know that I wasn't quite ready to go to work. When we left Nice, Brignola and I had orders to proceed to the 82nd Airborne Division in Berlin and then report to Pfungstadt. I told him the problem and said we would leave the next day and drive to Berlin, where I would stay a couple of days and then fly back. Brignola would remain in Berlin to shoot a picture story for the *Stripes* magazine in Paris.

"The question is, do you mind holding down the ME's job for another week while I take a look at Berlin?" I asked.

"No problem. We'll be okay," Landau said.

I was pretty certain that there would be none; he gave me the impression that he liked what he was doing and probably hoped that I would stay in Berlin for good. He was certainly qualified, having been a copy editor for the *Louisville Courier-Journal* before joining the army. I didn't really have to go, but since Dowell was away and since I had the orders, I felt it was my only chance to see Germany's fallen capital.

"Who's in charge while the captain is away?" I asked.

"Lieutenant Margolin. He's probably in his billets now. Let's go and I'll introduce you and then I've got to get to work."

The three of us walked up the street to the officers' billets and met 1st/Lt. Nathan J. Margolin. He was a New Yorker, I later found out, who had taken journalism classes at the University of Alabama but who had never worked on a daily newspaper. Margolin made an instant hit with me when he brought out a bottle of scotch from his officer's liquor ration. Enlisted men weren't entitled to liquor rations, and I hadn't tasted scotch since I had left England the year before.

I told Margolin about Berlin and that I would be back in a few days. He had no objection, since I had valid orders. Landau had to get out a paper, so Brignola and I left with him for the editorial offices, which were located in a two-story building next to the composing room and across a courtyard from the press.

Seymour Sharnik and Bill Frye, who were on the Liege edition, were the only editorial people I knew other than Bill Ahlberg, who had just arrived from Nice. Sharnik had been on the Riviera to cover a tennis match just a month before when he and I made a sortie into Italy and Monaco.

After dinner and a good night's sleep in a three-story mansion owned by the brewery family, Brignola and I took off after breakfast for Berlin.

★   ★   ★

We spent the night in the *Stripes* circulation billet at Nordous near Braunschweig and then crossed into Soviet-held territory at Helmstedt. I had never seen a Russian soldier and, other than the guards at the checkpoint, the ones I saw were ill-dressed and wandered aimlessly about in the field and along the autobahn. We were waved down by one who wanted to buy our spare jerrycan of gasoline, but we told him that we needed it to get to Berlin.

"How much?" I asked. He offered 20 marks, the equivalent of $20 in the same occupation marks that we had in our pockets.

Berlin was in a shambles. Everywhere we looked there were broken buildings and piles of rubble. And everyone was helping in the cleanup — children chipping mortar off the bricks, women sweeping up with huge brooms, and men hauling rubble away in carts.

We checked into the Berlin Press Center on Sven Hedin Strasse and were given a key and address for a billet in the Zehlendorf sector. We also stopped at the nearby Berlin Press Club and visited with *Stripes* correspondent Joseph Fleming. Joe had been in the Paris newsroom the day I reported the year before. Although small in stature and hidden behind horn-rimmed glasses that made his small face smaller, he stood out in the room filled with reporters and rewritemen because he was wearing a steel helmet, as he sat behind his typewriter. Across the front of the almost new, certainly never-used helmet were the words "Combat Rewriteman."

★   ★   ★

Brignola and I shared connecting bedrooms in a beautiful villa on a lake in the upper-class Zehlendorf neighborhood, where there was no evidence of war.

Black-marketing was rampant in the city. Everywhere we

went we were solicited by Germans who wanted to buy cigarettes, which, I was told, they didn't smoke but used as currency to buy food. The American military police were everywhere, too, but their task was an impossible one. We did sell our extra packs of Camels for $10 each. Soap and candy bars, which we didn't have, were going for $5 each in occupation money.

"You mean you didn't bring a case of cigarettes?" Fleming said. "At least you could have brought a couple of cartons. Everyone else does."

That night we visited the Femina, a sleazy German nightclub serving weak beer, fair vodka, and bad schnapps. Most of the customers were Russian officers. The few *frauleins* there wore heavy makeup. I fully expected to see Marlene Dietrich walk through the door, but Dietrich wouldn't have been caught dead in a place like that.

★   ★   ★

The next day I decided I had better get back to Pfungstadt, and Brignola drove me to Tempelhof airport.

"Take good care of the jeep," I said, noting that the speedometer had put on 1,500 miles since we left Nice ten days earlier. That's a lot of mileage for an old war horse. We had been to Genoa, Milan, Trento, Bolzano, over the Brenner Pass, through Innsbruck to Worgel, then to beautiful Altdorf before reaching Pfungstadt.

I thought about our jeep trip and those few days in Berlin as I traveled on the C-47 flight from Tempelhof to Rhine-Main Air Base, southwest of Frankfurt. There I was lucky to catch a *Stripes* circulation jeep bound for Pfungstadt and was in the office that night to work on my first paper, dated October 17.

★   ★   ★

Pfungstadt's most famous citizen was Chaim Weizmann, a Russian-born scientist and Israel's first president, who taught in a Jewish boarding school there in 1894. In addition to instructing evening classes, Weizmann attended the University of Darmstadt during the day, an hour's ride by train.

A friend of Weizmann's, who had a son attending the Pfungstadt school, learned that there was a vacancy on the staff for a junior teacher of Hebrew and Russian and he recommended Weizmann. The position was offered to Weizmann, and he accepted. For his work he received board, lodging, and 300 marks (about $75) a month in exchange for two hours daily of teaching.

Weizmann, who was nineteen at the time, didn't think much of the school, its director, the food (which he called wretched), or for that matter the town of Pfungstadt. Years later he wrote: "I left Pfungstadt without regrets, and remember it without pleasure. I have not retained a single permanent relationship as a result of my stay there, which is a rare experience for me."

In his autobiography, *Trial and Error*, published in 1949 by Harper & Brothers, he said: "I stuck it out for two semesters and had something approaching a breakdown. My Pfungstadt experience left a permanent mark on my health; fifty years later a doctor traced a lung hemorrhage to the effects of my first eight months in Germany."

Weizmann wrote that Pfungstadt was famous all over Germany for its brewery and among the German Jews for its Jewish boarding school. The brewery was still there, but the townspeople I talked with had never heard of the school; some had never heard of Weizmann.

★ ★ ★

Capt. Edwin E. Dowell, a United Press reporter in Canada before the war, and I returned to Pfungstadt about the same time. It was good to get back to work. I had been on the road for three weeks and was often out of touch with the news, but the lead story that day was still redeployment and the trans-Atlantic shipping schedules. The news rated only a one-column headline. One thing I did notice was that a new command was in place. USFET (United States Forces European Theater) had replaced SHAEF, but the boss was still Ike. I also noted that I had received another stripe: I was now a T/3.

Landau introduced me to the copyreaders — Stoddard White, Robert Sontag, and Curt Weinberg — and to sports editor Paul Parris and picture editor Homer Cable. Some of the others I knew, among them Lawrence (Larry) Stone, a Kentucky newspaperman, who had been with us in Nice. When that edition closed he returned to the 66th Infantry Division and obtained another transfer to *Stripes*, this time at Pfungstadt. A few weeks later he left for the States and rejoined the staff of his family's newspaper, the *Times-Argus* in Central City.

The next afternoon I met with Dowell and Margolin to discuss policy, and I quickly learned that the job of managing editor was not going to be easy. We were putting out a newspaper twenty-five miles from USFET headquarters in Frankfurt, right under the noses of the army command. I doubt if any of the top brass ever saw our paper on the Riviera unless they happened to read it while getting a suntan on the beach at Cannes.

Dowell had spent the morning at Information and Education Division headquarters in Hochst, a suburb of Frankfurt, and he said the army was irked because of the four-column headline "Patton Fired" in the October 3 paper. The Associated Press story plainly said the four-star general "had been relieved of his command by Gen. Eisenhower." We both knew that "fired" was a great headline word, but it was fairly difficult to defend its use at this late date. The captain said the army also objected to the October 13 headline: WITHDRAWAL OF *AQUITANIA, ELIZABETH* SETS BACK REDEPLOYMENT SCHEDULE. Robert J. Donovan, staff writer for the Paris edition, had quoted Alfred J. Barnes, British minister of war transport, as saying that the *Aquitania* and the *Queen Elizabeth* had been withdrawn from American troop transport service and would be used instead to haul only British servicemen. The *Queen Mary* would remain at the disposal of the Americans for the present but would be replaced later by a number of smaller vessels, Barnes said.

At a meeting a short time later in the I. G. Farben building in Frankfurt, which housed USFET, Lt. Gen. Walter Bedell Smith, Ike's chief of staff, told a gathering of *Stripes* officers and the managing editors of *Stripes* editions at London, Paris, Altdorf, and Pfungstadt that the army was partly at fault for the situation involving the *Aquitania* and the *Elizabeth*. The army knew that the two ships would return to the British and had made arrangements to replace them with U.S. Navy aircraft carriers. Sure enough, three days after Donovan's original story, this was the headline: 12 WARSHIPS WILL BEGIN REDEPLOYING TROOPS HOME FROM ETO NEXT MONTH.

★   ★   ★

Whether *The Stars and Stripes* was an official or unofficial publication of the U.S. Army was discussed at another meeting in late 1945. Since many readers, organizations, and even some foreign governments considered the newspaper an official voice of the army and even of the United States, it was agreed that the word "unofficial" would be used under the flag on Page 1 and in the masthead on an inside page.

Attending the meeting in the Lurgi Haus in Frankfurt were Brig. Gen. Paul Thompson; Lt. Col. John Ulmer; Maj. Neil Regan; Larry Griffing, chief of the *Stripes* news bureau in Paris; Art Force, managing editor at Altdorf; and myself.

Griffing later returned to the *Lincoln* [Nebraska] *Journal,* while Force joined a public relations firm in Las Vegas.

★　　★　　★

Redeployment continued to dominate the news the first few days I was on the job in Pfungstadt, but on October 19 I had a chance to use my first five-column headline: ALLIES INDICT 24 NAZI LEADERS.

The story by Joseph Fleming was datelined Berlin and was accompanied by mug shots of Hermann Goering and Rudolf Hess. It said the trial was expected to start within thirty days at Nuremberg. The case against the Nazis opened with a meeting of the Nuremberg war crimes court, officially designated the "International Military Tribunal," at which the forty-three-page indictment was presented by the prosecutors of the United States, Russia, France, and Great Britain. The indictment was drawn to cover all criminal acts committed by the twenty-four defendants both at home and abroad. Charges ranged from seizure of totalitarian control in Germany and the destruction of Reich trade unions to the invasion of neighboring nations.

Six days after the indictments, the list of twenty-four Nazis was reduced by one when Robert Ley, who cracked the whip over German labor, committed suicide in the Nuremberg city jail. The former Labor Front boss strangled himself with a towel while sitting on the toilet in his bare cell.

★　　★　　★

Another major story during my first week had to do with currency control, but I failed to recognize its significance and placed it on the back page. In an attempt to prevent large sums of money being sent out of the ETO, all military personnel except general officers would have to declare their cash holdings and each individual would be issued a "currency exchange control book" to account for all receipts and withdrawals of money.

The program probably was a success, but I'm sure the army didn't count on "lost" books. It wasn't too difficult to get a replacement. I knew one GI in Paris who had a pocketful of "lost" books.

★　　★　　★

The Pfungstadt edition had printed its first issue April 5, and two weeks later the Liege and Nancy editions had closed. Six months and 196 issues had passed as I became the ME in the little Hessian beer town in October.

The London edition shut down on October 15, and that left only Paris, Pfungstadt, and Altdorf in operation. Sidney Gans, who joined the Paris paper soon after I did, was the last managing editor in London. He was there only a few months, having replaced Peter Lisagore, who had since returned to the States for discharge.

Gans printed a message from President Truman to the London staff on Page 1 of that final paper: "I salute you on upholding a fine tradition and rendering a service to your comrades." General Eisenhower, Prime Minister Clement Attlee, Secretary of War Robert P. Patterson, and U.S. Ambassador John G. Winant also sent messages.

The London edition, born April 17, 1942, as a weekly, became a daily six months later. After three and one-half years, when its circulation dipped below 50,000, it died a noisy death. Many of its readers those final weeks were English war brides seeking answers to the question: "When do we join our Yanks?"

Gans wrote of that last issue:

> The small staff had gone down to the composing room to watch the last edition go to press. Jim Frost, our composing room foreman on loan from the *London Times*, locked up Page One and sent it off. A whistle blew to signal the "starter" (because the last page on the press starts it rolling) as it did every night for the three years past. But the whistle this night was also the signal to the hundreds of men at work on issue No. 50,273 of the *Times* to stop work and join in creating a din that must have resounded clear across the Thames and down to the houses of Parliament. It was the English printers' custom of "banging out," reserved for New Year's Eve and rare and important occasions.

★   ★   ★

Pfungstadt couldn't match its sister on the Thames in history and tradition, but it had a bit of its own, for after all it had the first free newspaper in Hitler's Germany and it was still going strong.

Carl Konzelman, one of the five staffers from Paris who located the printing plant in the small town south of Frankfurt, remembered:

> American tanks had passed through Pfungstadt, but we were

the only Americans in town. We just stormed in, located the plant and took over.

We rounded up five tons of news print, somebody located some ink, dug up an engraver, rounded up some Germans to run the linotypes and the presses and got enough coal on hand to operate the sterotype.

Meanwhile we were running the town of Pfungstadt. At least the Germans thought we were. They queued up every day outside our quarters to make requests, such as permission to bury their dead.

We started putting the first paper together about noon. We didn't have a line to Paris nor a teletype, so we switched on the short wave and swiped anything we could get. With type shortages, language difficulties and mechanical breakdowns, we didn't get the presses rolling until 5 o'clock the next morning. Our first edition was four pages and we ran off 10,000 copies.

Capt. Rader Winget, who set up communications in Paris, recalls his role in providing teletype service:

Fighting was still going on near Pfungstadt and we couldn't even get a field line. I jeeped to Frankfurt and led a Signal Corps intelligence team to Europe's biggest underground repeater station, still smoking from the German sabotage bombs.

Signal Corps guys are appreciative. They gave me a line to Paris. A line from Frankfurt to Darmstadt was a little harder. It took two barrels of Pfungstader beer — one light, one dark. Then we got stuck. From Darmstadt to Pfungstadt, a few miles, there wasn't a line working. So the Signal Corps put a line through Nancy and Mannheim which we tested with a headset in Pfungstadt and all we got was the command post of a Puerto Rican outfit. We got them off and the line settled down. Just as we were about to hook in to the Paris teletype, it went dead.

Later we found out why. Some German children were shooting off insulators and wires near Worms. The Signal Corps Joes put us back in business again and chastised the little saboteurs. We were ready to go ahead and the wire went dead again. Later we found other children had been playing with a Teller mine and blew down a house to which our line was attached.

This time the Signal Corps said they would string a whole new line for us. Bright and early they started out unreeling their line from a truck, mile after mile. And what happened? A salvage outfit spotted the wire, proclaimed it salvage and started reeling it in, mile after mile. The Signal Corps told us to string our own wire.

So I rounded up a couple of guys and started from Darmstadt at the end of our old Paris-Frankfurt-Darmstadt line. We hooked that to a line to Griesheim, kicked the door off the telephone office there and found the other end of the wire. I spent endless hours searching through phone company frame rooms for those wires. The Germans didn't need their phones. They hadn't rung for months anyhow.

On the last leg into Pfungstadt we got a heavy maintenance Signal Corps company to set poles. We couldn't work it through channels so we just rolled out the barrels — one light, one dark. At last it was done. The Paris-Pfungstadt circuit was operating. In the newsroom, the teletype kept up its steady 60-words-a-minute clip, a warm and comforting thing. It was a real newspaper the guys put to bed that night.

★   ★   ★

The barrels of beer Winget used as work incentives soon ran out since the brewery was not operating and hadn't been for some time. The flow of draft to the mess hall had also stopped.

One day an administrative officer searched a dank basement under the brewery for hidden barrels of the foamy stuff but also to check out a rumor he had heard. When he kicked at a door at the end of a dark passageway it slowly opened, disclosing a vast underground factory filled with Opel automobile engines. Further exploration revealed room after room which lay underneath the *Stripes* editorial offices, the mess hall, and the billets.

Capt. Max Gilstrap, the officer in charge, had this to say about the find in an article he later wrote for the *Christian Science Monitor* magazine:

This startling discovery helped to break the reserve of the timid Pfungstadters, who, excepting the children, had kept pretty much to themselves. With their big secret out, they gradually came forward to lend assistance, hoping to obtain food in return.

Cobblers, with leather from Offenbach, offered to make boots for the staff; bookbinders in Eberstadt bound the newspaper's files. A family of bakers at Seeheim, using GI rations, turned out tasty German bread, hard rolls, and pastry for the mess. An ice cream shop, with considerable coaching, supplied some delicious desserts. Even a greenhouse proprietor insisted on donating fresh flowers for the offices and mess hall.

To make sure the GIs took advantage of every opportunity for comfortable living, professed anti-Nazis eagerly pointed out

the houses of former Nazi Party members with sly suggestions
that if a radio or car was needed, well . . .

I, for one, benefited by this action and later moved into one
such house.

The few Germans I came in contact with were the linotype operators and pressmen, and a little old man who trimmed my hair,
for which service I gave him three cigarettes. There were German
civilians on the cobblestone streets of Pfungstadt and in nearby
rubble-strewn Darmstadt, but our paths never crossed.

Once in a while the transportation and circulation GIs
brought German girls to the Saturday night dance in the dayroom
behind the mess hall, but the Polish girls, who waited on tables or
cleaned the billets, gave the *frauleins* a hard time. I recall one or two
incidents of bumping and shoving.

Because of the nonfraternization policy set in motion before
the Allies invaded Germany, GIs and officers had been fined $65
for just talking to a German. This was later amended to exclude
children, and after the war ended it was dropped altogether — not,
however, before a lot of money changed hands. I recall reading that
one warrant officer in V Corps had been fined $390 after being
found guilty of failure to obey nonfraternization orders of SHAEF
and the 1st Army. He was accused of visiting a German family.

Fraternization was the subject of General Eisenhower's third
monthly military government report, which was our lead story November 1. In it he cited sporadic nonfraternization activity and
hatred for displaced persons as a sign of an "increasingly restless
state of mind" among German youths, whose ranks were being
swelled by the discharge of prisoners of war. There had been instances of physical attacks on American soldiers, the report said.
The general was concerned that the campaign against fraternization and displaced persons might "serve as a rallying point for the
idle youth and young discharged soldiers." This type of "resistance
activity," he said, "was only one step removed from organized resistance directed against the occupation forces."

The general said the chief source of unrest and lawlessness was
displaced persons "who have stirred up the civilian populace by
their maraudings." He charged displaced persons with "cases of
murder and organized looting," which, he said, occurred at "an
unpleasant rate."

We didn't have any trouble with displaced persons. If it hadn't been for the DPs in Pfungstadt, we wouldn't have been able to function. Ours was an international settlement in the true sense of the word. We had two German-speaking U.S. Army sergeants; four pretty French *mademoiselles*, two who came from other *Stripes* editions to help out the Americans; Dutch and Polish DPs in the kitchen; as well as more Polish, Czech, Latvian, Estonian, Russian, French, and Luxembourgeois workers in the dining room and the billets.

Rinus and Harm Huberts, brothers from Holland, had been in the forced labor program in Germany and were released by the Americans. Rinus, who spoke English, worked for supply and production, buying newsprint and other paper products on the German market. Harm was a printer.

Reiner van Abshoven was also a Dutchman. His home had been looted by the Germans and his brother killed while in the Netherlands navy in the Pacific. He married a German girl he met while both were political prisoners. "Reiney" drove the ration truck and always got to the head of the Quartermaster Depot line in Darmstadt by distributing *Stripes* to the other drivers waiting for rations. He also roamed the countryside trading Spam and other GI food for fresh fruit and vegetables, which cook John Borcx, a fellow Hollander, prepared in the kitchen. The other cook, Marie Blomkwist, the German wife of a Dutch patriot, was rescued by the Americans two days before she and her husband were scheduled to be sent to Dachau.

One of the dishwashers was Lina Baku, a former ballet dancer who still bore the scars of beatings by SS troopers. Later she switched to working in the circulation billets. Stefanie Janetchko also worked in the kitchen and later moved to a less strenuous job cleaning the billets.

The head waitress was Leonarea Swideruwna, whom everyone called "Mama," although she was only nineteen. In turn she called each GI customer "Baby." She looked older due to a poor posture caused by long days in a Nazi slave labor gang, carrying bags of dirt and sand to build Hitler's autobahn.

Maria Cisielska, who spent two years in a Nazi concentration camp, managed the editorial billets. She had help from Bronya Krakowianka, Alfreda Stucnskaite, and others. Alexander Lewicki kept the yard clean, and he did it as well as the son of a former Polish consul might be expected. Sophia Bednavska, twenty-one-year-old daughter of a well-to-do Polish lawyer, did her fair share of work. She and her husband had been imprisoned by the Germans and later sent to a labor camp.

Helena Anna Gustowska had been taken from her home in Dubno, Poland, in May 1942 to a labor camp in Vienna. She ran away after three weeks and was caught in Frankfurt. After a few weeks in prison she was put to work in an airplane factory and in 1945 was reunited with her father and brother in the Darmstadt displaced persons camp. Her father and brother later attended her wedding October 16, 1945, when she married T/5 Charles W. Hessler, of Indianapolis, Indiana.

Estonians Kamilla Voolar and Eliu Poldre worked in the editorial and circulation offices, respectively. There were others, probably twenty or so, whose names I never knew, but all contributed to our well-being and to getting out a daily newspaper for the Joes on occupation duty.

Jeanette Augusta Kieffer, whose nickname was "Gussie," first came in contact with *Stripes* when she led a group of Alsatian girls to the editorial offices in Strasbourg. She acted as interpreter and invited Victor Dallaire, the managing editor, to cover their musical event. Impressed with her fluent English (she had lived in the United States for a time), he hired her as his secretary. In Pfungstadt she worked in the business office, handling correspondence and answering questions of the Pfungstadters. In those days the officer in charge of the army newspaper was also the military governor of Pfungstadt, and she was his interpreter and adviser in dealing with the *burgomeister*. The townspeople recognized and respected her authority.

Marie-Odile Schreiner was employed in circulation, a job she had learned while working on the Nancy edition. She had done office work in Paris for three years and then lived in Dijon for a short time while working for the French government. She had sought to return to Paris and got as far as Nancy, where she found no further transportation for civilians. Casting about for a job, she was sent to *Stripes* by the prefecture, and after being interviewed she joined the paper January 9, 1945. She worked with another French woman, Suzanne Pons of Lyons, in circulation and with Simone Offner of Metz in production and editorial.

Boss of the mess hall was S/Sgt. Robert F. Mazur, thirty-three-year-old former mess sergeant in the 83rd Infantry Division. Mazur spoke German, Polish, Russian, and Hungarian as the result of five years in a Polish grade school in Monessen, Pennsylvania.

Sgt. Hans Kraatz spoke German fluently, and when the fraternization ban was lifted he sought out and visited with relatives who lived nearby.

★   ★   ★

The building that housed the editorial billets was called the Chateau Moe because its occupants all went by the nickname Moe. Jeanette, Suzanne, and Simone, at a party one night, thought the name following the word *chateau* should have the French spelling and cited the small city of Meaux, just east of Paris, as an example. From that night the name was spelled Chateau Meaux.

When I arrived in Pfungstadt the nickname solved a problem for me: If I didn't know a person's name I called him Moe and got his attention. Of course, four or five others on the copy desk also looked up. While our readers and most GIs were called Joe, editorial personnel at Pfungstadt were called Moe. I still don't know why.

★   ★   ★

I thought I was doing pretty well in my job as managing editor; at least, I hadn't received any complaints. Captain Dowell met a couple of times a week with the Information and Education Division brass in Hochst and fielded a few telephone calls which he didn't bother to tell me about. Outside of losing copyreaders to redeployment, things were pretty quiet until the morning of November 10. That's when the stuff hit the fan. Later we called it the "Egbert White" flap.

Egbert White, a former colonel and editor of *Yank* magazine and the Mediterranean edition of *The Stars and Stripes,* made a speech the day before to the American Legion in New York, charging that the army had "failed dismally" to meet the needs of the soldiers overseas by blocking the publication in the soldier press of adequate and impartial U.S. and world news.

Redeployed to his former civilian job as an executive of an advertising firm in New York, White particularly criticized the activities of the Information and Education Division and its commanding officer, Maj. Gen. Frederick H. Osborn. White said, "We had wonderful backing from General Eisenhower but we had plenty of trouble from General Osborn and his staff in Washington."

White's charges appeared in a story in the European edition of the *New York Herald-Tribune* in Paris. The *Tribune,* the story said, interpreted White's blast as the "opening gun" fired at officers who interfered with the soldier press during the war.

We placed the story, which was sent to us by teletype from our Paris news bureau, on the lower part of Page 1. Sure enough, before the day was over, Dowell's telephone rang and it was the I&E brass in Hochst wanting to know why *Stripes* was printing stories critical of our parent organization. The captain got the caller cooled down by pointing out that since the story was in the Paris newspaper — that would be read a day later in Germany — we had no choice but to use it.

"But did you have to put the damn thing on Page 1?" the protester said. Dowell agreed that it didn't have to be out front, and I had to admit that it wasn't a Page 1 story. Despite a Paris dateline, it could have been inside with the domestic news.

I'll never forget the Egbert White flap. It was the first of more to come.

★   ★   ★

The opening of the Nuremberg trials brought out our large type, and for the occasion we dispatched Stoddard White to that Bavarian city to cover the proceedings. The Paris edition sent Lester Bernstein, while Altdorf's correspondent was Arthur Noyes.

Of the twenty-four top Nazis accused of trying to destroy the world, only twenty actually appeared in the Nuremberg Palace of Justice when the trial began. Of the remaining four, Robert Ley had committed suicide a month earlier; Martin Bormann was still at large; Ernst Kaltenbrunner was ill and in a Nuremberg hospital; and Gustav Krupp von Bohlen und Halbach was too ill to be tried.

White wrote that the entire first day was spent in reading the indictment. Lord Justice Sir Geoffrey Laurence, the British member and presiding judge, opened with a brief statement citing the history and authority of the court.

Bernstein's accompanying story said the defendants had "the appearance of an oversized jury of businessmen." He said Hermann Goering mugged repeatedly to indicate his agreement or disagreement with various points raised in the long indictment. All wore neckties except Rudolf Hess, who sat there in a shirt with a collar that was much too large. Standing behind the defendants were eight tall GIs, part of the trial's security detail furnished by the 18th and 26th infantry regiments of the 1st Infantry Division.

The trial was to continue for a year, long after Stod White was discharged from the army and returned home to work on the *Detroit News*.

★　　★　　★

We got a new boss about this time. Eisenhower was nominated by President Truman to succeed Gen. George C. Marshall as army chief of staff. Gen. Joseph T. McNarney, former deputy chief of staff, took over all of Eisenhower's jobs — commander of the U.S. forces in the European Theater, commander in chief of U.S. occupation forces in Germany, and U.S. representative on the Allied Control Council for Germany. McNarney also retained control of U.S. forces in the Mediterranean Theater, which a month later would be combined with the European forces.

Our biggest scoop was about another general. The telephone on my desk was ringing as I walked into the newsroom a few minutes after noon on December 9. The caller was Pvt. Ed Seney, who said he was a driver for a colonel who had told him that Gen. George S. Patton, Jr., had been injured in an auto-truck collision near Mannheim. The general had just been admitted to the 130th Station Hospital in Heidelberg, he said.

I told him to hold a minute, and I turned to Bob Sontag, who had just walked through the door. "Grab a jeep and get to the 130th Hospital in Heidelberg. Old 'Blood and Guts' has been hurt in a car crash," I said.

Back on the line, I asked Seney if he was certain the injured man was Patton and he said yes, that he was in the hospital parking lot and had seen the general on a stretcher just before he was admitted to the emergency room. I asked Seney to get back to me because I wanted to have a letter of commendation written for his 201 file.

Patton, commanding general of the 15th Army, and his chief of staff, Maj. Gen. Hobart R. Gay, were en route from their headquarters at Bad Nauheim to hunt pheasants near Mannheim. Just outside the city limits of Mannheim, their sedan collided with a two-and-one-half-ton truck belonging to a Signal Corps outfit that was coming in the opposite direction. Witnesses said the truck turned in front of Patton's car. Gay, the driver, and the general's dog, Willie, were unhurt. The driver of the truck was also not injured.

Both drivers were held to be careless, but no charges were

filed. The general was heard to say to the soldiers taking him to the hospital, "This is a hell of a way to die."

Patton received "a simple fracture of the third cervical vertebra, a posterior dislocation of the fourth cervical vertebra and complete paralysis below the level of the third cervical vertebra." His condition was listed as critical. Twelve days later he died after incurring a pulmonary infection. He was sixty years old.

★   ★   ★

We only had one photographer in those days, and when the report of the Patton accident came in, Bob Merritt, on loan from the U.S. Signal Corps, was on another assignment. We printed an Associated Press photo of the general's wrecked sedan the following day.

Merritt's assignment was to cruise the Frankfurt-Wiesbaden-Heidelberg area asking questions and taking pictures. We had his jeep painted white with a big sign that read "Inquiring Photographer" along the side of the cab. The words *The Stars and Stripes* in red, white, and blue were below the windshield.

The Inquiring Photographer feature started December 8 on Page 1 with the question: "Do you favor peacetime conscription in the U.S.?" Three said no and two said yes. The question the next day — "Should U.S. soldiers be allowed to marry German girls?" — again brought three to say no and two to say yes.

"No, even though the soldier may love the girl, evidences of her Nazi teaching will crop up to cause trouble between them," Pvt. Roger H. Bolmey said.

Pfc Charles Lende said: "Yes, Germans as people are human like anyone else. The war was fought against an evil system set up by force and brutality."

"No, the thinking of Germans and Americans is too vastly different to warrant such a step," Pfc Otto Bor said.

The Inquiring Photographer feature continued for several weeks and finally was dropped, not because of lack of questions or interest but because someone in the high command decided that changing the color of government equipment was illegal. *The Stars and Stripes* was ordered to have the jeep restored to its original OD tint. That seemed a good reason to drop a popular feature.

★   ★   ★

I had my own jeep problems, but it had nothing to do with the color of the vehicle. I drew one out of the motor pool every Thurs-

day to negotiate the often wet and foggy autobahn between Pfungstadt and Frankfurt, where I went to take religious instruction from
Capt. Berwin R. Sikora, a Catholic chaplain with the 29th Infantry
Regiment. I hadn't told Paulette, whom I left in Nice, what I was
doing because I was not certain the Catholic church would accept
me — a divorced Protestant. Finally, I was baptized with Tommy
Sheil, a *Stripes* printer, as my sponsor. After his discharge, Sheil returned to Boston to work in the *Herald-Traveler* composing room.

I had taken the first step toward getting married. The next
was to get army permission to wed. The third was to return to Nice
and see if she still wanted to go through with the ceremony and
eventually live in the States.

Meantime, Christmas was upon us and we began to lose more
people. Curt Weinberg was one of the first to go; he returned to
New York, where he was a publicist for a number of Broadway entertainment figures. Homer Cable was returning to his prewar job
as picture editor of *Look* magazine, and we were hard put to fill his
position, not so much as *Stripes*'s photo expert but as the house pi-
anist. It turned out all right because Jack Browne, a proofreader,
joined the editorial staff and took over the piano, playing duets with
Cable well into the morning, with Sharnik accompanying them on
the violin.

Nathan J. Margolin, the assistant officer in charge who had
just made captain, told me one evening that he would like to learn
copy desk work and offered to help out after his administrative
chores were over.

"What do you think about Margolin's offer?" I asked Joe Landau, the slotman. "Can you use him? Do you have time to teach
him to write heads?"

"Listen. I've had pimps, drunks, and queers on my desks. I
guess I can work with an officer," Landau said. Landau and Margolin got along fine. In fact, a few years later Landau recommended Nate for a job on Joe's paper, the *Louisville Courier-Journal*.

It was that kind of an end to the year 1945 in a wintry land
whose people had either lost their home to Allied bombs or to U.S.
Army requisition officers. In nearby Darmstadt, a prewar city of
115,000 which was 60 percent destroyed in a single, one-night, 300-
plane RAF raid September 11, 1944, Christmas wreaths were laid
on piles of rubble still claiming the dead. The wreaths were exchanged for spring flowers a few months later.

★   ★   ★

Six days into 1946, we got out our big type and got ourselves into big trouble over still another of those redeployment stories. This time it was Joe Harvey's report that redeployment had ended as far as the point scores were concerned and that military necessity henceforth would determine the rate at which men would be returned home. The story quoted General McNarney, and I used a two-column picture of him from our morgue along with a quote "There are no replacements" taken from the story.

The uproar over the quote and the picture, which unfortunately showed him smiling, rattled the windows of the I. G. Farben building that housed USFET, shook up the Information and Education Division headquarters in Hochst, and it sure as hell didn't make things too pleasant in Pfungstadt.

Brig. Gen. Paul W. Thompson, I&E chief, fired off a memorandum to the officer in charge of *Stripes*, Lt. Col. William G. Proctor, which said the quote was inaccurate and objectionable. "What Gen. McNarney really said was that replacements have not come in as fast as anticipated. The title under the picture represents a sacrifice of accuracy in the interests, apparently, of putting a punch in something." He liked the picture, but General McNarney's staff thought it poor taste to use one of him smiling to illustrate a serious story that said 50-pointers would have to stay in Germany three additional months. In the next few days the Signal Corps delivered a half dozen preferred photos of the general, none of them showing him smiling.

Although we were scolded in one paragraph of General Thompson's memorandum, the Paris edition was lambasted on three accounts, while Altdorf escaped unscathed. Of Paris, the I&E chief said: "I find objectionable the series of scare headlines which have featured the stories from Litchfield. Analysis of the various editions shows that Paris is spreading these headlines banner-wise across two or three or four columns whereas the other editions are playing them more conservatively and, in my opinion, more soundly."

The story concerned trials going on at Litchfield, England, about mistreatment of prisoners at the 10th Reinforcement Depot during the war. It was true that Paris displayed the Litchfield story more prominently than Pfungstadt and Altdorf, but it was also a fact that it was the Paris paper that was being distributed in England for the troops still stationed there.

Thompson didn't like the headline in the January 4 Paris edition that read "Mom Thinks Two-Headed Girl Is Twins, Thinks Up Names." He wrote: "This is too facetious a treatment for a story that involves a great personal tragedy for someone."

He also faulted another Paris story about some missing chorus girls which contained a passing reference to a New Year's Eve party given by a U.S. Army general: "There is absolutely nothing in the story to show that the party was in any way connected with the alleged AWOLs. Yet the innuendo is that such was the case. Of all things in the business, I dislike innuendo the most. It is almost always a recourse of those who wish to put over a point regardless of the availability of facts. Innuendo has absolutely no place in the columns of *The Stars and Stripes*."

Before a month was over — February 1, to be exact — the Paris edition was no more. It had a seventeen-month career, was read by more fighting men than any newspaper in history, at its peak printed 800,000 copies daily, and became the last edition of *The Stars and Stripes* to be printed on Allied soil.

Jacob (Jack) Badiner, who joined the staff at war's end and who later went to work on the *New York Times* copy desk, was its last managing editor. The official reason for the closing was that declining troop strength in France no longer warranted a separate edition in Paris. Some thought that if it hadn't been for Litchfield, the Paris edition might have lasted longer.

★   ★   ★

Across the world in Honolulu, the Mid-Pacific edition of *The Stars and Stripes* also was in trouble with the army. It lost and, before the month was over, it too closed down. Its reporters had interviewed Secretary of War Robert P. Patterson on Oahu and Guam during his Pacific tour and demanded to know what was being done about getting the troops home. Unprepared, or perhaps uninformed, Patterson's answers irked GIs all over the Pacific.

In Manila, 10,000 soldiers, angered by the slowdown in getting home, booed their commander and someone called Patterson "No. 1 enemy." They called for an avalanche of political pressure on Congress to get them back to the States. The demonstrating GIs carried placards in front of the Philippine legislative building and the city hall. One sign read, "We are tired of false promises, double-talk and double-crossing." Another said, "We want Ike."

International News Service carried the Manila story on its wires and it was given big play in the States. Newspapers there followed up with editorials criticizing both sides. The *New York Times* gave a verbal spanking to the soldiers who demonstrated in Manila and lambasted Congress, charging it with the responsibility for the furor. The newspaper *PM* gave a sympathetic hearing to the protesting troops under a headline which read "GIs Have Blown Their Tops."

We published the INS story as our lead on January 8, along with a one-column picture of the secretary of war under the caption "Labeled 'No. 1 Enemy' " and never received a complaint. Not so in Honolulu, where the army struck back at the protesters. Lt. Gen. Robert C. Richardson, Jr., U.S. commander in the mid-Pacific, cautioned *The Stars and Stripes* not to make any discourteous reference to the president, secretary of war, chief of staff, and others in army authority.

The Associated Press story, dated January 10, said although this immediately was termed military censorship by some in Honolulu, it was pointed out that Richardson was only calling attention to the Articles of War which provide severe penalties for such criticism. Richardson ordered the paper not to publish soldier letters which could be construed as discourteous or derogatory to authority. Twenty-six members of the staff immediately charged that the Pacific edition had been converted into a "house organ for the War Department" and that the officer in charge of the paper "broke faith with them."

"From the moment of its inception, the Pacific edition of *The Stars and Stripes* has never enjoyed the privilege of a free press, even by Army standards," the statement said. "It has, through open and implied pressure on it, been forced to delete, destroy and play down news to serve personal and professional interests of the Army hierarchy, and in many instances officers generally."

The editorial board of five men, which had control of the paper and its policies, voted to carry out Richardson's order. The letters to the editor column went out. All local news was eliminated, and editorials and editorial cartoons were replaced by wire service copy. The wire services noted the change and told the world about it.

The next day General Richardson summoned to a conference M/Sgt. Charles Avedon, the managing editor; T/Sgt. Aaron Buckwach, city editor; and Capt. Joel Irwin, the officer in charge. The general explained that his order had been misunderstood and that it was intended to prevent "name calling" against individual officers not to stop criticism of the army, the government, or public policies.

The meeting was followed by a press conference at which Richardson told civilian correspondents that "although the men of my command may disagree with the policies of the government and express themselves freely thereon, it is improper while we are in uniform to attack our leaders as individuals. There is no other restriction placed upon the freedom of expression of men of this command."

The statement over Richardson's signature was published in the second edition of the "sterile" *Stripes*, and the next day the paper was its old self again.

The War Department in Washington put in a final word when it announced January 11 that General Richardson did not ban criticism of army policies or methods in the Mid-Pacific *Stripes* as personnel of the paper charged but warned the staff that the Articles of War prohibited disrespect to army authorities. Denying any censorship, the department described the circumstances attending Richardson's directive as follows:

> Gen. Richardson, following publication of articles in *The Stars and Stripes*, including one which termed the Secretary of War Public Enemy Number One, issued a directive to the editorial staff of *The Stars and Stripes* calling their attention to the fact that they are in military service, that they are publishing a newspaper under the auspices of the United States Army with authority of the Secretary of War and that their actions are governed by the Articles of War.
>
> Gen. Richardson did not prohibit publication of news received or criticism of policy or method. He did prohibit initiation of disrespectful action against officers as individuals. No censorship whatever has been placed upon *The Stars and Stripes*.

That same day in Washington, General Eisenhower, the army's chief of staff, authorized theater commanders to speed home all "surplus" men not needed for occupation duties. The announcement that the army was redrafting its demobilization program came less than a week after the War Department ordered a slow-down that touched off the GI demonstrations. A week later the general told congressmen that demobilization had been slowed down to prevent a collapse of the army and that since September the army had been releasing approximately 1.2 million men monthly, and if that rate had been continued there would be no army left after July 1. He pledged nevertheless that the army would meet its goal of reducing to 1.5 million by that date.

Three weeks later, as Russell J. Jandoli, its last wire editor, remembers, he and other key personnel on the Mid-Pacific edition of *The Stars and Stripes* became eligible for discharge. Demobilization struck its final, fatal blow. The newspaper closed January 30 on a few days' notice.

Born six days after the war in Europe ended, it lasted 222 issues, or just about eight and a half months.

★   ★   ★

The Honolulu-based newspaper wasn't the only one in the area having problems early in 1946. The Pacific edition in Tokyo came under fire with charges of communism leveled at two of its staff members. General MacArthur approved on March 2 the removal of Sgt. Kenneth Pettus of Chicago, the managing editor, and Cpl. Barnard Rubin of Waterbury, Connecticut, a columnist, after the inspector general reported their "discretion and integrity" questionable. They were ordered sent to the Yokohama Reinforcement Depot.

Col. E. J. Dwan, the IG, reported that an "abundance of evidence reflects adversely on the discretion and integrity of each. It was evidenced that each held membership in the Communist Party and at times flavored writing with Communist thought."

Pettus and Rubin denied they were Communist, although Rubin said he had been a party member for four years but resigned before he was inducted. Rubin also said he served a year with the International Brigade in the Spanish Civil War.

A few days later four members of the staff requested a transfer from the paper as a protest to the removal of Pettus and Rubin. T/3 Arthur R. Davidson of Houston said in his request that he found it "impossible to reconcile my professional ethics with the type of editorial work desired by the officers in charge of this paper."

Maj. Gen. Charles A. Willoughby, intelligence officer on

MacArthur's staff, speaking later in Honolulu, expressed concern at the "wholesale infiltration of Communists into key Army positions, especially on Army newspapers." The United Press quoted Willoughby as saying that the assignments of such individuals as Pettus and Rubin to the Tokyo edition of *The Stars and Stripes* "started in Washington and went all the way down."

"How and where they were placed was part of a prearranged plan. We both know Pettus and Rubin are labor agitators belonging to the most radical of Communist organizations," Willoughby said.

The *Daily Worker*, the Communist Party newspaper, added a final word to the Pettus-Rubin matter in an editorial March 7 entitled "Brass Hats Versus Free Press":

> The kind of mentality brass hats want to impose on GIs was clearly stated by Brig. Gen. Charles T. Lanham, chief of the Army's Information and Education Section.
>
> Lanham compared the soldier press to Scripps-Howard and Hearst and asserted that the soldier publication should not be allowed to criticize the War Department or high officers.
>
> This is the man in charge of informing and educating American soldiers.

That was the last we read about Pettus and Rubin, although for years to come charges were aired by others, including congressmen, that *The Stars and Stripes* had Communists on its staff.

★ ★ ★

The Rome edition came in for its share of postwar problems with censorship and friction between the brass and the enlisted staff. The United Press reported March 8 that Lt. Gen. John C. H. Lee, commander of U.S. forces in the Mediterranean Theater, confirmed a report that he was censoring all GI "gripe letters" sent to the Rome edition of *The Stars and Stripes* and threatened to dismiss any Communists found on the paper.

Lee told a press conference, in which three GIs from the paper's staff attended, that he already had signed a censorship directive and intended to enforce it. He pointed out that the future American army in his theater would be a "professional" force of volunteers rather than a "democratic army" which existed during the war, and that members would be subject to a different type of discipline. Lee acknowledged that he had seen no harmful letters published in the paper but intimated strongly that he regarded it as potentially dangerous to army morale.

Lee's remarks raised the hackles on Egbert White's back, and the former editor of the Mediterranean *Stripes*, who had made earlier charges of censorship against the army, was soon contacting General Eisenhower. In a telegram to the chief of staff, White declared: "News reports of military censorship of *The Stars and Stripes* at Rome represent such a drastic departure from policies you established and supported that I am prompted to ask your continued interest in maintaining an honest, competent and objective Army press."

White, a former colonel and now an executive with a New York advertising firm, told the Associated Press that final selection of news should be made only on the "basis of news values."

"The military mind, like any other lay mind," he said, "will think in terms of what he wishes news to be or what he thinks readers should know. Such thinking applied to a newspaper in or out of the Army results in vicious angling of news and is certain to destroy reader confidence."

The *New York Times* commented editorially that news and comments of a political nature or critical of command policy had no place in an army newspaper. The editorial pointed out that "*The Stars and Stripes* is accepted outside the service as an official publication."

As a matter of interest, the Pfungstadt and Altdorf editions in Germany noted at the top of Page 1 that the paper was an "unofficial publication of the U.S. Armed Forces in Europe."

The *New York Times* wasn't through. A couple of days later Hanson W. Baldwin, its military analyst, castigated "some soldier" newspapers for spreading discontent and lowering morale among GIs, particularly since V-J Day. "The editors failed to realize," Baldwin wrote, "their duty was not merely to reflect the views of readers but to lead them — too often some papers showed an amazing lack of responsibility."

He cited the Mid-Pacific edition's article calling Secretary of War Patterson "public enemy No. 1." He said this was not freedom of the press but was an invitation to disaffection and breakdown of discipline.

★   ★   ★

The Mid-Pacific and the Paris editions of *The Stars and*

Stripes both folded January 30, but the pot was still boiling in Rome. United Press there reported that strict censorship had been imposed on the Mediterranean edition, and its staff of fifty-five men planned to resign unless the restrictions were lifted. The paper said it had been "muzzled" by Lieutenant General Lee through an activation of an order giving Lee and other officers of his staff supervision over letters written to its popular Mail Call column.

"The Mail Call column is being discontinued rather than submit to Lee's supervision," the paper said and added that the staff of four officers and fifty-one enlisted men "chooses to continue on duty with *The Stars and Stripes* only if the current affront to their judgment is withdrawn." The paper's announcement was printed in the form of an editorial set in five columns across the top of the front page and did not mention Lee by name but referred to his censorship directive of three weeks ago.

The paper also said that its publication officer, Maj. Hal C. Kestler, had cabled protests to President Truman, Secretary of War Patterson, and General Eisenhower, asking, "How much of their constitutional liberty must members of the U.S. armed forces sacrifice?"

Ten days later Lee relieved Major Kestler from his job as publications officer and brought in Lt. Col. A. D. Clark to take his place. Kestler had worked on the *Des Moines Register* before the war, Clark on the *New York Times*.

Then on April 2, Clark, with a new title of officer in charge, announced that Lieutenant General Lee had formally rescinded his order of March 13 requiring censorship of the GI letters and that Major Kestler and the staff of four officers and fifty-one enlisted men had agreed to continue in their jobs. Clark said the policies existing prior to Lee's order would continue: no anonymous letters published, although the writer's name would be withheld on request; letters thrown out only on grounds of decency or lack of news interest; and copies of all grievances to be sent to the commanders involved for priority action.

Clark added that staff members still desiring reassignment would be relieved individually on renewal of their request, "without prejudice," since "no enterprise involving creative effort can be a success if men are unhappy."

Old-timers on the London edition of *Stripes* recall an order to the paper sent by Lee in March 1944 to stop referring to President

Roosevelt as FDR. Lee said it wasn't dignified and said CINC, the abbreviation for commander in chief, should be used instead. The substitution was never made because a few days later Lee's order was withdrawn.

John Clifford Hodges Lee was from Junction City, Kansas. Mostly, GIs called him "Courthouse" Lee, but others said the initials stood for "Jesus Christ Himself."

Lee's problems were solved two months later when the Rome edition closed.

We in Pfungstadt didn't get off scot-free from the charges. Victor Bernstein, writing for the New York newspaper *PM* out of Berlin, declared that *The Stars and Stripes* has "now become spiritless and a censor-ridden house organ of the Army brass and the War Department." Asserting that the present-day *Stars and Stripes* no longer belongs to the GIs "but to the generals," Bernstein said that "the new turn has left more than 500,000 GIs in the ETO without a single newspaper, periodical or other publication which they can call their own, or use as an instrument for the inalienable American right of free speech."

Bernstein's item was rebutted two days later by Maj. Neil T. Regan, executive editor, who called the *PM* reporter's charge untruthful and then set about to restate the editorial policy for the two Germany editions as set forth in a letter from Maj. Gen. H. R. Bull, USFET chief of staff, dated February 1, 1946.

Regan closed by saying that "in many cases, it has been a tough job for *The Stars and Stripes* to withstand the onslaught, but as of this writing, and backed up by policy, the fort is still being held."

Bernstein had the last word. He said Regan's response to his story "wasn't a very good editorial" and reiterated his charges that the European editions of *The Stars and Stripes* had "passed into the hands of the brass." Bernstein said that he was surprised to see Regan sign his editorial with both his name and rank and admitted that he might have exaggerated in his statement that *The Stars and Stripes* was only for generals.

"Majors," he wrote, "seem to play a big role too."

Brig. Gen. Paul W. Thompson, Regan's boss, didn't think the major's reply was a "very good editorial" either, Regan later recalled:

> I was alone in the Hochst office when the Bernstein story came over the wire; Proctor was in Bavaria, so I wrote my reply,

put it on the teletype and called Zumwalt in Pfungstadt to alert him. The next morning the general phoned from Paris, and I could tell right away that he was displeased.

Before he could say too much, another telephone rang on his desk and he asked me to hold on. I could hear him saying to the other party: 'Yes, sir, general. Yes sir, general. We thought it a good reply too.' He came back on the phone, asked me how I was doing and then told me to carry on. No mention of the Bernstein flap or my answer. I never heard another word about it, not even from Proctor.

Once a reporter for the *New York Daily News,* Regan later worked for a public relations firm before entering the army in February 1942 as a second lieutenant in the infantry. He left the service in April 1946 as a lieutenant colonel and returned to the firm's Chicago office, where he worked until his retirement in 1978. He now lives in San Diego, California.

★   ★   ★

I began to give serious thought to my own redeployment, and although I liked my work it wasn't getting any easier with more of the staff leaving every week. I was long overdue for discharge, having more than enough points. I had put in my request to marry, and my thinking was that as soon as the wedding took place I would get in line for transportation to the States. The problem was that I would be returned to California, where I had been inducted at the Presidio of Monterey in 1942, while my new wife would probably be sent to New York.

While other persons' redeployment made headlines, we did take time out January 9 to report a story that should have shocked us more than it did. The banner read: NEW ATOM BOMB REPORTED BUILT BY RUSSIA. It was an Associated Press story out of Londonderry, Northern Ireland, quoting Dr. Raphael E. G. Armattoe, director of the Lomeshie Research Center. The director said the Russian bomb "renders the Anglo-American bomb almost obsolete" and that it was developed with the help of German scientists captured by the Russians. He identified them as Voller and Hertz but didn't know their first names.

★   ★   ★

Finally, I learned that my request to marry had been approved and that I might pick up the papers in Paris en route to Nice. My last day of work in Pfungstadt was January 17, and that night I turned over the desk to Stoddard White. The next morning I caught a C-47 to Paris, where Major Regan handed me the papers. Regan was more than helpful, said he would try to arrange a trip to the States, as he had done for other staffers, but told me not to get my hopes up too much since there were fewer ships crossing the Atlantic these days. Some *Stripes* people had gone home on the Queens, aircraft carriers, and at least one on a ship filled with war brides. All that was expected was that the staffer write a story about his trip. Regan also held out the possibility of my working in the New York news bureau while awaiting the arrival of my new wife and then perhaps taking my discharge on the East Coast. I gave all this much thought on the train trip from Paris to Nice.

Mademoiselle Paulette Albin and I were married January 24 in the city hall in Nice and later at St. Pierre d'Arene Church. Mademoiselle Rosette Olagnier was the maid of honor, while 1st/Lt. Hal Boes, the U.S. Riviera Recreational Area's public relations officer, stood up for me. Boes, whom I had met only the day before the ceremony, threw in a Signal Corps photographer and a staff car for the ride from city hall to a restaurant where I popped for the champagne. We had a bridal suite in the Hotel Negresco.

Six days later, I kissed my bride goodbye at the railroad station in Nice and boarded a train for Germany.

"I'll probably see you in New York," I said. "I'll let you know what's going to happen to us just as soon as I know." I hoped she would understand my mixture of French and English. The train pulled out, and two days later I was back in Pfungstadt.

I helped out on the copy desk and gave Stod a hand with his administration duties, but he was doing fine in the ME post. One of the stories that intrigued me concerned a War Department directive that dependents of all ranks would be permitted to come overseas effective April 1, contingent upon the availability of housing, food, and medical care and provided that the soldier would agree to remain overseas for at least a year after the dependent's arrival. I didn't mind staying in the army another year because I had just received another stripe; I was now a technical sergeant and making more money.

Major Regan was still working in my behalf because one day he called to ask if I would like to work in London while awaiting transportation home. I jumped at the chance because the thought occurred that I might be able to take Paulette with me. Sure enough, a few days later we were both in the British Embassy in Paris, where I showed an officer my travel orders and our marriage certificate. He issued her a visa.

That afternoon we caught the boat train to Dieppe and the Isle of Guernsey to Newhaven, and the next stop was Victoria Station in London.

★   ★   ★

I worked in the Associated Press office on Fleet Street relaying wire service copy from New York to Germany. We had our own line and moved several thousand words daily. I shared the job with Arthur White, with whom I had worked in Paris.

It was good to be back in London, the city I had left seventeen months earlier. Paulette and I had a room on Upper Cheyne Row in Chelsea. Our landlady, Mrs. Anna Elizabeth Baker, who had worked in the Washington American Red Cross Club before it closed, provided bed and breakfast. We had the rest of our meals out. Although Paulette qualified for food ration stamps, we weren't in London long enough for her to apply.

I rode the bus to Fleet Street and the next day took her along so she could see how to transfer and where to get off. Since she spoke little English, I gave her a slip of paper with my name and Fleet Street telephone number on it in the event she got lost. She never had to use it. We spent a lot of our free time taking in shows, visiting Westminster Abbey, and making trips to Hampton Court palace and Richmond.

One day Creed Black, who came to the Pfungstadt paper from the 100th Infantry Division, stopped off at the AP office. At dinner that night he told me that *Stripes* was now hiring civilians since the army could no longer find qualified enlisted men. He said William Weinstein, the ME at Altdorf, had signed a contract, so I decided to write a letter applying for a position.

When Creed stopped in Paris en route to Germany, he gave Major Regan my letter. It worked out fine, too, because a couple of days later I received a message over the teletype from Regan offering me a job as the civilian managing editor at Pfungstadt until that edition closed and then as slotman in Altdorf. The job had a CAF 12 rating, which was in the neighborhood of about $6,000 a year — a pretty good neighborhood for someone who was making less than half that when I left my newspaper job to join the army in 1942.

I sent off my acceptance and ten days later was back at my old desk as managing editor of the Pfungstadt edition.

★ ★ ★

Upon arrival in Paris I had found out that a jeep needed to be returned to Pfungstadt, so I loaded my two duffle bags and Paulette's suitcase in the back and we took off for Germany. I decided to go by way of Strasbourg — not the direct route — because I thought it might be easier to enter Germany, since my orders didn't call for a married couple to cross the border into an occupied country. I intended to try anyhow, and if I was unsuccessful Paulette could get a room in Strasbourg until I could make arrangements for her to enter as a dependent. But luck was with us, mostly because it was midnight and freezing cold.

I drove up to the checkpoint on the west bank of the Rhine River and a young French soldier stepped out of the sentry shack. When he saw what looked like two American soldiers, one with a hooded GI field jacket covering her long black hair, he ducked back to the warmth of the red-hot stove I could see through the window.

An American GI emerged and I met him in front of the jeep. After taking a quick look at my orders, he too made a hasty exit. So did we, across the bridge to Kehl and up Highway 36 to Karlsruhe, where we picked up the autobahn to Pfungstadt. When we arrived there almost frozen in the topless jeep, the dining room at the Hotel Strauss was open and we fell to the hot coffee. I like to say that Paulette was the first dependent to arrive in Germany, but there were probably others. Her March 27 arrival date preceded the official dependent's entry to Germany by one month and a day.

★ ★ ★

The timing was perfect. I walked in to reclaim my old job as managing editor at Pfungstadt the day Stod White left for the States. I had turned the desk over to him late in January when I went off to get married. Nothing had changed. We were still desperately short of copyreaders, and the manpower situation was so critical at both Germany editions that a June 30 closing of Pfungstadt was moved up to April 18. Maj. Richard E. Knorr, the business manager, and Capt. Edwin E. Dowell, the executive editor, were interviewing anyone who had ever worked on a newspaper and were advertising in New York newspapers for help.

We were so short-handed that I was unable to take time off to

get my discharge and start making that big money I had heard
about. A technical sergeant's pay was good but not all that great. I
did drive to Frankfurt in the mornings and take part of my physical
examination at the hospital, but I would have to go back several
times to complete it. It wasn't until the day after our final edition
that I was able to pick up the discharge papers making me a civilian again after three years and five months in the army, one year
and ten months overseas.

★   ★   ★

Redeployment was no longer the lead story those last couple of
weeks. Instead, it was the trials — the Nazi big shots at Nuremberg, the ones responsible for the Dachau atrocities at Landsberg
and the SS men accused of killing Americans at Malmedy, Belgium, during the Battle of the Bulge. There were also the trials of
the Americans accused of mistreating their own prisoners at Litchfield, but the scene of these proceedings was scheduled to move to
Bad Nauheim, Germany.

★   ★   ★

Brig. Gen. Paul W. Thompson, chief of the Information and
Education Division, retired and was replaced by Col. Edwin P.
Lock. Thompson later went to work for *Reader's Digest,* heading up
its international editions. With a new boss at the top, we also got a
new directive from the War Department which stated that news
supplied to *The Stars and Stripes* and other service newspapers must
be impartial and should not feature unjustified "inflammatory material." The April 12 statement also advised that "permitting the newspaper to become the mouthpiece of the Army, theater, or other command or of any individual or group should be avoided." Military
commanders were made responsible for assuring that the papers were
staffed by qualified personnel and would conform to policy.

★   ★   ★

Soon after our arrival, Paulette and I were assigned the upstairs half of a house on Thalmann Strasse overlooking the brewery. The lower half was occupied by Mr. and Mrs. Clyde Jack
Browne, also newlyweds. Mrs. Browne was the former Beatrice A.
Dahl of Minneapolis, who had worked as a War Department secretary in Wiesbaden. Browne, an ex-GI from Los Angeles and now
a civilian, was production manager of *Stripes.*

We weren't the only honeymooners in Pfungstadt that spring.
T/Sgt. Joseph S. Burzinski of Throop, Pennsylvania, and Noma

Sakowiez of Tulkov, Poland, were wed in the Catholic church in Pfungstadt on February 16. Burzinski worked in administration. Harm Huberts, the Dutch DP from Nyeveen, Holland, who worked as a printer, took Maria Drewniak, a Polish DP, for his bride ten days earlier.

We had post exchange cards but no commissary privileges because Pfungstadt wasn't recognized as a dependent community. Such facilities were available in nearby Darmstadt, but since we were to leave soon for Bavaria, no attempt was made to secure cards that would enable us to buy food.

Spring was in the air, the fruit trees were blossoming in the Odenwald, and the storks were settling down in the wood and thatch nests atop the city hall. The farmers were out in the field ladling the contents of their "honey carts" onto the soil. The odor was powerful, like something out of a cesspool — which is what it was.

After the final edition on April 18, we packed our bags and set off by jeep for Altdorf, where I was to be one of two assistant managing editors of the Southern Germany edition. The day after we closed, that edition took a new name — the European edition.

5

Altdorf

One of the advantages of a transfer to Altdorf, the little Bavarian town where the last remaining European edition of *Stripes* was published, was its proximity to the big story — the trials of the Nazi bigwigs in the Palace of Justice at nearby Nuremberg.

My bride and I spent the first two or three of my days off in the remodeled Nuremberg courtroom which contained the figure of the Jew Moses holding the Ten Commandments. We sat in the press section that looked down on an often smiling, often mugging Hermann Goering and the other defendants. We had a good view of the once pompous former Reichsmarshal, who wore a pale gray uniform stripped of insignia, and of Rudolf Hess, who sat stoically next to him. Also in the front row were Joachim von Ribbentrop and Wilheim Keitel.

We were able to follow the proceedings with headphones, I in English, Paulette in French. A twist of the dial and we could hear the Russian and German translations. The first day we heard Walter Funk complain that he had never been more than a second-rater in Hitler's power structure. The former economics minister portrayed his role in party and state affairs as "insignificant." Five months later Funk was given a life sentence. On another visit to the courtroom, we watched as the contents of bank vaults were entered as exhibits and placed on tables in front of the four justices and their alternates. Displayed were mounds of gold teeth and piles of gold-rimmed spectacles taken from Jews.

The tribunal attracted several hundred of the world press who sent out millions of words from the press center at Stein Castle. Schloss Stein, which was built by Baron Lothar Faber in 1850 and added to fifty years later by Count Alexander von Faber-Castell, is on property of the A. W. Faber pencil factory in the Nuremberg suburb of Stein. It seemed fitting to house a bunch of pencil pushers in a pencil maker's enormous, rambling Bavarian village.

There were certainly Faber pencils in abundance in the quarters occupied by the press center, but there were also typewriters, teletype machines, and radio equipment — everything that was needed to get the story of the trials out to the public. Allan Dreyfuss, a former newspaperman in Boston and Chicago, was the *Stripes* reporter at that time.

The trials continued through the spring and summer, and finally, on October 1, the verdicts were returned. Hermann Goering and eleven of his cohorts were sentenced to death by hanging for their parts in crimes against peace and humanity and for the participation in plans made for war during the twelve years of Hitler's rule of Germany. Seven of the original twenty-one defendants, including Rudolf Hess, were given prison sentences ranging from ten years to life. Three others — Franz von Papen, Hjalmar Schacht, and Hans Fritzsche — were set free.

Fifteen days later, less than an hour before he was scheduled to die, Goering cheated the gallows by committing suicide. Despite a heavy guard, he managed to swallow a vial containing cyanide of potassium. The hangings proceeded with Von Ribbentrop, Hitler's adviser on foreign affairs, leading the parade of death up the stairs of the gallows, which were set up in a small gymnasium building inside the yards of the Nuremberg city jail.

★   ★   ★

The hangings at Nuremberg and the suicide of Hermann Goering rated the headlines, but there were other important proceedings going on too. Fourteen of the Dachau killers were hanged at the Landsberg prison May 28, and another fourteen met their death at the end of a rope the following day. On both days seven died in the morning and seven in the afternoon. Irving Dilliard, who was there for *The Stars and Stripes*, reported.

In another trial at Dachau all seventy-three defendants were found guilty. On July 11 an American military court charged that those defendants murdered American prisoners of war captured at Malmedy, Belgium, during the Battle of the Bulge. They were also accused of slaying Belgium citizens, a total of 900 persons.

Forty-three were given death sentences, among them Joaquin Peiper, commander of the 1st SS Panzer Regiment whose "Task Force Peiper," an armored formation which included his own regiment, participated in the massacre of the unarmed prisoners of war. Among those given life terms was Gen. Josef "Sepp" Dietrich, veteran of Hitler's beerhall putsch in Munich and commander of the 6th Panzer Army which spearheaded Germany's counteroffensive in the Ardennes in December 1944.

On the American side of the court docket, in a trial held at Bad Nauheim, Col. James A. Kilian of Highland Park, Illinois, the former commander of the U.S. Army's Replacement Depot at Litchfield, England, was convicted August 29 of permitting cruel and unusual punishment of American soldiers imprisoned in the depot's guardhouse. Kilian was fined $500 and reprimanded by the seven-officer military court, which found him guilty after two hours of deliberation at the end of a ten-week trial.

The court acquitted Kilian of "aiding, authorizing and abetting" the cruelties for which nine enlisted guards and three subordinate officers were previously convicted. The Litchfield trials finally ended September 7 with the acquittal of the former commander of a guard company. He was the last of six officers accused. The final score: nine enlisted guards and four officers convicted, one EM and two officers acquitted.

★   ★   ★

Although my job was assistant managing editor, I spent the first month on the copy desk. William Weinstein, the ME and a former newspaperman from Cleveland, Ohio, put out the daily paper. Edward Pye Chamberlain, who worked for the *New York Herald-Tribune* before the war, was the slotman. Altdorf had enough chiefs; it even had enough Indians.

One of the newcomers to the staff was John W. Livingood, an old pro who had worked on the *Baltimore Sun,* the *Evening Ledger* and the *Record* in Philadelphia, and the *New York Daily News.* He had joined the staff from the Office of War Information after serving in

London, Luxembourg, and Vienna, and when that agency phased out at the close of the war Livingood hired on with *Stripes*.

The paper also published *Weekend*, a twelve-page magazine edited by James McLean, formerly of the *Miami Daily News*. It contained mostly staff-written features and cartoons, and despite its one-color limitation *Weekend* was a very attractive addition to the Sunday paper.

★   ★   ★

The Southern Germany edition (called the European edition when Pfungstadt closed) was born the day the war in Europe ended. It was an auspicious start for the last of the combat-spawned newspapers. The headline on May 8, 1945, told it all: ETO WAR ENDS.

With the flag at the top, the headline took over most of the tabloid page. The paper was printed in the plant of *Der Stuermer*, Julius Streicher's violently anti-Semitic and pornographic weekly. The facilities were specially built to house *Der Stuermer*, which also means The Stormer or Battler, after Allied air raids had driven it from the center of Nuremberg's old walled city.

Capt. Frederic S. Schouman and S/Sgt. Harry Watson were with the 45th Infantry Division of the 7th Army when it entered Nuremberg. After asking around, they learned of the plant in Altdorf. They then drove the twenty-five kilometers to the little town and decided it would do. Posting signs stating that the buildings were confiscated property of *The Stars and Stripes*, they immediately got in touch with headquarters in Paris.

Five days later, James McGowen, Carl Konzelman, and Moe Mulligan arrived to direct the reconditioning of the plant. Jim, who had worked for the *New York Herald-Tribune* before the war, scoured the nearby towns and what was left of Nuremberg for printing equipment. Mulligan's task was to locate Germans who could run the press and operate the linotype machines.

John Radosta, formerly managing editor at Marseille, Nancy, and Pfungstadt, assembled his staff and put out a dry run on May 6. The teletype line was out of operation, so Konzelman used radio copy and some staff-written features. Then on May 8, with the teletype in service, the big news story broke: the war in Europe was over. The press turned out 245,000 four-page copies of Volume 1, Number 1, which were trucked throughout southern Germany and into Austria and Czechoslovakia.

Four weeks later, on June 13, Radosta's crew upped the pages to six; three days later they cranked out the first eight-page paper. Arthur Force, a veteran of Liege and Pfungstadt, took over as managing editor on June 26, when Radosta shipped out for the States and his discharge from the army.

When the war in the Pacific ended, Altdorf was printing 265,000 papers and for that occasion published its first color plus an eight-page victory supplement. T/4 Frank Waters took over as ME when Force left, and Waters in turn was replaced by Sgt. William Weinstein.

★　　★　　★

Paulette and I shared a three-story house with Jack and Bea Browne, whom we had lived with in Pfungstadt. The house, like all those requisitioned for use by the Americans, was owned by a member of the Nazi Party. We took our meals at the Balzar House, where editorial and production personnel ate. Circulation and transportation crews shared the Goldener Hirsch, both under the supervision of Mess Sgt. John Wacker, who before the war had worked for the Eppley Hotels, a large Midwest chain.

While at Pfungstadt I never really got to know Lt. Col. William G. Proctor, the officer in charge, who had taken over from Lt. Col. Fred Eldridge during Christmas week of 1945. It was Proctor who had approved my assignment to the London bureau and later my request for a civilian job. A native of Hillsboro, New Hampshire, and a West Pointer, he had served on General Marshall's briefing team in the Pentagon during the war. Although he had no previous experience on newspapers, he brought to the organization a good business sense and college-boy enthusiasm. However, he was strictly military and went by the book, as we were soon to find out.

George Higuchi, who was assigned to the fiscal department in 1946 and who has recently been with Radio Corporation of America at Cherry Hill, New Jersey, well remembers his Altdorf days:

> I lived in the GI billet called the MacArthur House and we always had Coke and a keg of beer in the cellar and what was left of the 10-bottle liquor ration. Three of the bottles were hard stuff and that went first and fast.
>
> We stored small arms ammo in the attic and under the sofa in the living room for our weekend deer hunts. We had the Military Government on our tail after a few outings because we all

shot up a storm. We did bag one deer and hid it out at the home of one of the fellow's German girl friends. The venison steaks were great.

On occasion I would cook rice or noodles on a portable gasoline stove in the MacArthur kitchen to satisfy my craving for something close to Japanese food. There were always a lot of guests and we had to wait for them to get out of the bathroom the next morning so we could get in, clean up and go to work. MacArthur was quite a billet.

In addition to MacArthur, named for the general, there were the Roosevelt, Truman, Eisenhower, Jefferson, Lincoln, Churchill, and Clark houses. We were assigned to Clark, named after Gen. Mark Clark.

★   ★   ★

On our return from the Nuremberg trials May 4, I had just driven the jeep to the motor pool when I heard loud explosions off to the west and could see flashes of light and billows of smoke. The Rotherback ammunition dump at nearby Feucht had blown. It burned all night and well into the next day, destroying 29,000 tons of small-arms ammo. Windows shattered in homes as far as eight miles away, and fire blackened the dense forest that surrounded the facility, but poison gas stored in concrete bunkers survived the inferno.

There was one death, and it happened to a member of the *Stripes* staff. T/4 Kenneth E. Faller was one of ten *Stripes* drivers who responded to a military government plea for volunteers to help evacuate German families from the vicinity of the fire. Faller's command car had skidded on the wet pavement and turned over. The Canova, South Dakota, native was buried in France after memorial services in Altdorf.

The death of Faller was followed three days later by a fatal shooting of two other *Stripes* enlisted men in a residential area in north Nuremberg. S/Sgt. William R. Timmons, twenty-one, of West Haven, Connecticut, and T/4 Paul R. Skelton, twenty-one, of McKinney, Texas, were killed while riding in a jeep with four others. Timmons and Skelton, as well as three of the passengers, worked in the *Stripes* fiscal department.

A week later Pvt. James C. DeVone, twenty-six, of Sampson County, North Carolina, confessed that he fired the shots after drinking "beer and schnapps all day." Later that year, on August

17, a nine-man general court-martial in a unanimous verdict found DeVone guilty of murder and sentenced him to hang. A member of the 3757th Quartermaster Truck Company, he later beat the death sentence for the dual slaying, instead drawing a long-term prison sentence.

Rose I. Korb of Hammond, Indiana, Kathleen Gass of London, England, Kathleen O'Farrell of Limerick, Eire, and T/5 Elmer Holdway of Cambraia, Virginia, were the others in the jeep. The six had been to the Stork Club, a popular enlisted man's hangout, and were taking Miss Korb, an American civilian employed by the office of the chief counsel in Nuremberg, to her quarters. As they drove down Moericke Strasse, a quiet, tree-lined street, three shots were heard, one of them killing Skelton, who was in the back seat, and Timmons, the driver. It was brought out later that the same bullet from an American carbine killed both men.

Miss Gass, whom we called Kay, told military police that an open jeep filled with GIs just ahead of them was not fired on. The *Stripes* vehicle was winterized, complete with top and side curtains, and might have been thought to contain officers or VIPs.

"The first two shots were faint, like pops of a carbine. One of them killed my companion instantly," Miss Gass said. "Then there was a deafening blast from a weapon close at hand or a high-powered rifle. Bill put on the brake, halted the jeep, stepped out into the roadway, and fell dead. We ran a few yards to a sentry post. Soldiers and military policemen poured out and searched the woods on both sides of the road but found no one."

Timmons was formerly a student at The University of Texas. Skelton was on orders to return to the States for discharge. The memorial services were held May 14 in the Protestant church in Altdorf.

★ ★ ★

A month later some of us on the staff made news, in the States as well as in our own newspaper. Actually, it was a confrontation between Proctor and Weinstein, but several of us got caught in the fallout.

Proctor's office in Hochst had sent word of a new USFET directive ordering *Stripes* to pay civilian employees from its nonappropriated fund rather than on a civil service basis. This meant, explained Maj. Richard E. Knorr, the business manager, that $4,000 would have to be slashed from the editorial segment of the $1 million annual budget. Weinstein was told that he and key personnel would have to take pay cuts of approximately $500 per year each.

I wasn't too surprised at Weinstein's anger, since I was being paid the same salary he was getting and I wasn't even doing the work of an assistant ME. Of course, I didn't like it. I had been a civilian for only a month and had just received my first paycheck. I was just beginning to feel secure, and then this had to happen.

Weinstein said it was a move to tighten army control of the newspaper and called a meeting of the editorial staff. He said Proctor was due in Altdorf later that day, and he proposed that we stick together and if need be go on strike rather than accept the pay reductions. He ordered me specifically not to talk, stating that it was best that he handle the negotiations. I found it difficult to remain silent, but I did as I was told. The others must have been so informed because Weinstein and Proctor were the only ones doing the talking. After making their points, Proctor told Weinstein in effect to take it or leave it. Weinstein replied, "We quit," and left the room; the rest of us followed.

Livingood and I walked out together. He had just switched over from OWI and now would probably have to pay his own way back to the States. I, who had recently married, would have to come up with money for two fares.

"Geez, that's the fastest shuffle I've ever seen. I've never been blown out of a job that quick in my life," Livingood said.

In a few hours, the Associated Press, United Press, and International News Service, operating out of Stein Castle in nearby Nuremberg, had the story on the wires.

Weinstein was quoted by the UP as saying: "The Army claimed it was canceling our old contracts and offering us new contracts at lower salaries to save money under a new financing scheme. But the real reason is to give the Army tighter control over the publication. The Army knew we would quit. There was no other motive in the move."

Proctor denied that pay cuts were in store for the staff, except in one case (the story didn't name the person but I knew who it was) and he said the others were scheduled to get more money. He said he had "no criticism" of their work.

Later, when I got home, Jack Browne, the production manager, told me I was foolish to have quit. He proposed that I reconsider. Capt. Edwin E. Dowell, the executive editor, told me much the same thing when he arrived from Hochst, and when I learned that Livingood and James McLean were having second thoughts I agreed to the pay cut and to return to work. Weinstein, Chamberlain, and Robert Sheldon refused and left Altdorf immediately. Later that afternoon, I took over the news desk, Livingood sat in the slot, and the paper came out on time. Sometime later Sterling Lord took his discharge from the army and became a civilian member of the staff.

As soon as he learned of the walkout, Sgt. Ed Seney, who was a general assignment reporter and the ranking noncom in editorial, offered his services as managing editor, and Proctor put him in charge despite the fact that Seney had no desk experience. He was the young soldier who had tipped us off in Pfungstadt about General Patton's auto accident and who eventually was transferred to the staff. The appointment of Seney solved a problem for me because I didn't wish to be accused of undermining Weinstein.

As soon as Weinstein and the rest of us walked out, Proctor put out a call to all bureaus to have the reporters come immediately to Altdorf for duty on the desk. He also let it be known that *Stripes* would be hiring civilians with newspaper experience.

Lt. Col. Irving Dilliard, who had held key positions on the *St. Louis Post-Dispatch* before the war and who returned there later as an editorial writer, arrived and was a settling influence in the post-strike period. Also there as an adviser was Capt. H. Peter Hart of New York City.

Dilliard took Seney under his wing when the young man decided, or was advised by one of the administrative officers, that he should be the active news editor as well as managing editor. I came in one noon to read the news file and to start laying out the inside pages and found Seney sitting in the news editor's chair. He refused to budge, and everything halted until Dilliard was able to change his mind.

Ten days after the "strike," June 13, Proctor appointed me managing editor. Livingood shortly afterward took over as assistant ME, and Seney returned to the States for discharge from the army.

Because I returned to work my paycheck was not affected; however, the flap over the walkout prompted reaction from some readers.

One unsigned letter, which included a funzig pfennig, said:

Dear B-Bag:

Enclosed please find one-half mark to start a voluntary fund to pay Zumwalt the difference between $6,789.16 and the mere pittance of $5,700 on which he will have to subsist for the next year.

My heart bleeds over such injustice.
A Lt. Col. in the A.C.
Sans flight pay

The short-lived strike over, we settled down to put out the eight-page paper. We lost more GIs to redeployment but, meanwhile, others had accepted civilian jobs. Among those were Harold McConnell of Long Beach, California, and Joseph Rabinovich of New York City, both top-notch copy editors. McConnell, who had joined *Stripes* before the strike and was called back from the Paris news bureau to work on the copy desk, retired in 1985 from *The San Diego Union*. Rabinovich is now an assistant managing editor of the *New York Post*.

It wasn't to be an eight-page paper long, because on August 16 we launched a twelve-page edition without an increase in staff. It wasn't easy, but it came out nevertheless. There were two additional pages of stateside news, an augmented sports section, a picture page, and a solid page of comics, including "Li'l Abner," "Dick Tracy," "Blondie," "Moon Mullins," "Gasoline Alley," "Joe Palooka," and "Terry and the Pirates."

★   ★   ★

While we were expanding and looking to the future, it was not all roses with our sister publication in Rome. There was still friction between the Rome edition of *The Stars and Stripes* and Lt. Gen. John C. H. Lee, the theater commander. The general ordered the paper closed for good as of June 1, but then he sent word that he wanted to personally decorate two members of the staff: M/Sgt. John S. Mason of Oakland, California, then managing editor, and T/Sgt. William Bradshaw, a journeyman printer from Michigan and a veteran of the Algiers edition. The general had in mind a bronze star, a token that would show the army's appreciation for the fine work the editorial and production departments had performed.

Mason would have none of it and wrote the general through channels "if dropped on my desk it would not ring true, and I ask to be relieved of the embarrassment of accepting it." The award ceremony never came off. The rejection was part of the staff's pro-

test against Lee's "censorship and control efforts against the newspaper," and Lee's putting another officer over Maj. Hal Kestler,
publications officer.

★ ★ ★

The Italian theater wasn't to be without a newspaper for long.
Major Knorr, Captain Dowell, and Earl Ericson, the circulation
manager, traveled to Italy to meet with Lee. The general was gra-
cious and gave them permission to circulate the European edition
in Italy with special emphasis in Trieste, where the 88th Infantry
Division was stationed.

However, when Knorr sought to buy the linotype machines
and other equipment used by the recently closed Rome edition, Lee
turned him down. We didn't know it until later, but the general had
given the machinery away — yes, gave the entire stock of equipment to former members of the Rome *Stripes* staff, who then started
their own paper, the *Rome Daily American*.

Circulation of the *Stripes* in Italy began two months later, and
we sent Arthur Noyes to Trieste to open a news bureau. He later
was replaced by Ernie Reed.

A distant cousin — the *Daily Pacifican*, published in Manila —
had problems. The army fired its entire twenty-two-man staff after
accusing it of distorting the news. The staff, including 1st/Lt.
George W. Cornell of Oklahoma City, the officer in charge, was
transferred to the 86th Infantry Division. "They'll make soldiers of
you at the 86th and that's what you all need," Brig. Gen. E. J.
McGraw was quoted by Cornell as saying.

A week later an army court-martial convicted T/5 Clair Miller
on charges of publishing false information detrimental to the service in connection with "snipe" letters written to the *Daily Pacifican*.

Miller, who was busted to private, was accused of writing a
letter protesting too frequent guard duty. He signed his own name
but added the words "and eight others." He did not sign their
names but said that the eight had verbally agreed with him. The
case against him hinged on whether he had the authority to speak
for his comrades. A group of soldiers pooled their funds and tele-
graphed Sen. Claude Pepper, D-Fla., protesting Miller's conviction.

The wire to Senator Pepper brought a response from the War
Department, which said that the twenty-two soldiers were relieved
because "they failed in their responsibilities as soldiers and news-

papermen." Pepper's office made public a lengthy letter of explanation from Brig. Gen. Miles M. Reber, War Department legislative and liaison officer, which stated that the twenty-two staff members had shown they did not possess "maturity, good judgment and the qualifications required by War Department Circular 103," government publication of the army.

★   ★   ★

With a twelve-page paper it now became necessary to have more wire copy — more stories than Associated Press, United Press, and International News Service deemed profitable to file to European clients. Up until now we were getting the same news that was being sent to the *Paris Herald-Tribune,* the only other English-language daily on the Continent. Of course, French, German, and other European newspapers were receiving AP, UP, and INS copy but in the translated version.

We depended heavily on features and photographs sent once a week by air freight from our New York office, which consisted of a couple of desks in the AP bureau in Rockefeller Center. This was most helpful, but in order to sustain the appetite of a twelve-page daily, what we needed was news from every state in the nation because our readers came from every one of those states.

Proctor sent Knorr to New York with instructions to expand the operation and hire a civilian bureau chief. Knorr found the space with AP inadequate for what he had in mind, so he leased larger quarters on Broad Street in the financial district. He also hired Sidney Gans, a New York newspaperman and veteran of the Paris and London editions, to be bureau chief.

Knorr and Gans started interviewing applicants for jobs in Altdorf and hired Joseph Fleming, Ernest Leiser, and John Sharnik, all ex-*Stripers.* Knorr also signed up Morton Gudebrod and Bill Boni, former AP war correspondents, and Henry Matteo, who had worked with OWI during the war in Europe.

Matteo, copy editor on the *Schenectady* [New York] *Union-Star,* said, "I went to see Sid Gans and he asked some very penetrating questions about copy editing in a very thorough manner. He wanted to make sure that the person he recommended for the overseas assignment knew his job. We agreed on a salary and I was told by him that my family could join me about six months later."

Matteo returned to Schenectady to await clearance. Gans

summoned him to New York early in October to meet Knorr and discuss his contract.

"Knorr overruled Sid on the salary I was to get, setting it at a lower figure, and I had to accept it or give up going overseas. Nothing was said about my family joining me and I didn't bring up the subject," Matteo remembered.

I knew nothing of this dialogue, but I do recall that Matteo was originally offered $4,500 a year and came over at $4,100. Because of his good work we had him up to $4,500 within six months. But pay was not Henry's real problem with *Stripes*; it was the matter of his dependents.

"When I arrived in Altdorf and put in the necessary application to bring my wife, Dorothy, and daughter, Marcia, over, I was told by personnel that I didn't qualify," Matteo said. "I then called Hochst and asked to talk to Lt. Col. Proctor. After some wait he got on the phone. He was very curt, told me that I could not have my family over."

Matteo then turned to the army's judge advocate, and a few days later we learned that *Stripes* had been overruled.

"Proctor telephoned me that he had decided to let me have my family join me but after the year was over, back home we had to go," said Matteo. "I stymied him, however, by getting in touch with a former OWI co-worker who was editor of the Military Government publication, *The Information Journal,* and accepted a job in Berlin."

At the end of his contract in September 1947, Matteo and his family moved to Berlin. When that job expired six years later, we rehired him for a two-year contract that terminated in March 1955.

Henry Matteo was definitely one of our best copy editors — a methodical, reliable worker and a good influence on office morale. He returned to Renssalaer, New York, and is now retired.

★   ★   ★

I was delighted to get Matteo and the others because we were desperate for help, but I was sure surprised when Morton Gudebrod walked in the door. He had been kicked out of the theater sixteen months earlier by the army when he assisted his AP co-worker, Ed Kennedy, in breaking the news embargo on the German surrender at Rheims, and here he was working on the army's newspaper. It didn't make much sense, but Mort, being a gifted writer and a good editor, was a big help.

Bill Boni had been in the southwest Pacific and the China-Burma-India theater, and then late in 1944 he was sent to Europe. At the end of the war he was chief of the AP's Amsterdam bureau, but when he was reassigned to New York he quit the wire service and joined *Stripes*. We were glad he did and gave him the sports editor's title, for which he was well qualified. His daily column, "Slants on Sports," was very popular.

Fleming was assigned to the Berlin bureau, Leiser to Vienna, and Sharnik joined the staff of *Weekend*. Leiser brought along his fiancée, Carolyn Camp, who as a Wac was also on the wartime *Stripes*. They were married in Vienna.

While in New York, Knorr ran into Henry Epstein, who had worked with him in Paris as a teletype operator. Since Henry was footloose and spoke fluent French, Knorr hired him for a circulation job in France. Epstein remained with the paper for thirty-six years, the last few as chief of distribution.

Meanwhile, Gans was busy hiring a civilian staff and signed up Russell Jones, Philip Bucknell, Joseph McBride, and Sidney Shapiro, all *Stripes* veterans. Jones, one of the founders of the first edition in 1942, later covered the 1st Army. Bucknell jumped on D-Day with the 82nd Airborne Division and broke an ankle when he dropped in Normandy. After he was evacuated to England, he dictated his story to a medic, and a lieutenant attached to the hospital staff was ordered by the colonel in the operating room to hop on a motorcycle and rush Buck's story to the *Stripes* Fleet Street office. McBride had worked on both the London and Paris papers, and Shapiro on the London edition.

★   ★   ★

A major story for our expanded paper — and it was a good thing we had the extra pages — was the introduction of military payment certificates, commonly called scrip. These were to replace the old Allied military currency and to end black-market activities. It was an exclusive story, and one in which *The Stars and Stripes* participated.

The paper's performance in the reporting of C-Day might have saved its life, because there was reason to believe that some high-ranking officers wanted to shut down the paper for good. We had heard rumors of a plan to retire *The Stars and Stripes* name. One suggestion was to change it to the *Occupation Chronicle*. This had a precedent: the World War I *Stripes* closed down in Paris at the end of hostilities and was replaced by the *Amaroc News,* a four-page daily published at Coblenz for troops of the American Army of Occupation.

The name *Chronicle* came easy for the proponents of the idea to abandon the *Stripes* name because that is what the weekly published by the Frankfurt Military Post was called. Its staff members, when asked about the rumor, said they'd be damned if they would give up their name.

We also learned that some of our own I&E officers were all for the change in names, pointing out the problems that forced the early closure of the Paris edition, the troubles that Lieutenant General Lee was having in Rome, and even our own personnel situation in Altdorf in which the managing editor and two of his staff quit the paper.

The scrip story was written by Ed Dowell, the executive editor. The army flew him in a liaison plane from Frankfurt to a little field near our headquarters. He stepped into my office and closed the door, saying, "Here's your lead story for tomorrow. Also we're going to need two or three pages inside."

"What the hell is going on?" is all I could say.

"The War Department has ordered a change in the money system, and McNarney has declared a moratorium suspending all sales for three days. It's an effort to kill off the black market," Dowell said, "and it's all top secret. The old Allied Military currency is out and a new type of bills called scrip is in, and we've got an exclusive."

Using my telephone, he called Gordon Skean, the assistant production manager, and told him to come at once while I rounded up John Livingood, the assistant ME, and Nate Margolin, the cable editor.

"The less people here at the plant that know about this the better. I have my orders," Dowell said. "If the word gets out, a lot of money could change hands real quick. So mum's the word."

When Skean arrived, Dowell asked him if he had a good German linotype operator who could not speak or understand English.

"None of them can speak or read much English but all of them know how to follow copy," Skean said.

"Give this to your best man," Dowell said, handing him a dozen pages of War Department Circular #256 which detailed the regulations that fiscal officers in the field needed in order to recall the old money and issue the new. Later, when the type was set, we found that the text took up two and one-half pages.

The story, which Livingood and Margolin edited, was positioned over the masthead on Page 1. The headline: WAR DEPT. ORDERS USE OF SCRIP IN THEATER; McNARNEY SUSPENDS ARMY SALES FOR 3 DAYS.

Three planes took off at dawn with the September 14, 1946, edition of *The Stars and Stripes* for Berlin, Vienna, and Paris to supplement the trucks and trains that normally hauled the newspaper. The following day the paper was filled with C-Day news, as well as praise from General McNarney.

"Despite mechanical difficulties which were solved on short notice, *The Stars and Stripes* completed its phase of the top secret operation with great cooperation," he said. "The columns of *The Stars and Stripes* supplanted Army methods of communication in the emergency plan to broadcast the complicated details fully and widely."

A top finance officer said, "The theater could not have met its C-Day deadline without the cooperation of its unofficial paper."

Joe Fleming reported from Berlin that Americans there "admitted that the lush old days were indeed gone forever and Berliners bewailed the demise of a market that supplied them with their principal medium of exchange, tobacco."

Robert R. Rodgers, writing from Frankfurt, said the top-secret plan had been under consideration for five months and that shipments of the new money arrived by water on August 23 and 26.

Arthur White, our man in London, said the introduction of scrip in Germany passed almost unnoticed in London and rated only a five-line paragraph in an early edition of the *Daily Mirror*, the only London paper to carry the news.

The new scrip "is bad for us but good for the government," a GI told correspondent Gene Levin in Paris. In Munich, reporter Julia Edwards was told by one soldier that "the fast operators will find a way."

Win Fanning, checking in from Stuttgart, was told by GIs that they felt it would be "only a matter of time before some new market method of beating the new supply of control would be devised."

Because of the moratorium suspending all sales, with the exception of charge accounts at mess halls and commissaries, *Stripes* provided free copies to its readers for the three days, but on the fourth the paper started charging five cents for each copy payable not in pfennigs, francs, groschen, or English pennies but real, honest-to-goodness, crisp GI scrip.

McNarney repeated his remarks about the success of the scrip operation and *Stripes*'s part in its execution, and nothing was ever heard again about changing the name of the paper.

"You haven't anything to worry about. *The Stars and Stripes* will be around as long as there are American troops in Europe," Col. George S. Eyster, director of USFET public relations, told Livingood and me. Eyster had recently taken over the role of directing policy guidance of *The Stars and Stripes* as well as AFN (American Forces Network). Administration control of the two organizations remained in the hands of the chief of I&E.

A fine officer and a good friend, Eyster went to bat a couple of days after his appointment when a two-star general ordered us not to print a story about the death of a baby on board a dependent ship that had just put in at Bremerhaven. When I took the matter up personally with Eyster at a cocktail party in Heidelberg that evening, he promised to look into it. The embargo was lifted the next day and we published the sad story. The general never interfered again.

★   ★   ★

Cupid and reporter Ernie Reed were busy the summer of 1946. Ernie's assignment was to arrange Paris weddings for Maj. Richard E. Knorr and Betty Luros and Capt. Edwin E. Dowell and Suzanne Berthe Pons. The double rites were held August 8 in city hall and later at St. George's Church.

When he returned from a brief honeymoon, Knorr suggested that I go to New York to familiarize myself with Gans's operation and discuss with him and others there our needs in Altdorf. Since Proctor was in the States on leave, it was decided that he and I should meet in New York with Gans.

I was delighted because I hadn't been back since June 1944, a period of two years and three months. After some delay in Paris I finally was able to get a flight on Air France. When I landed in New York, I found that Proctor was attending the World Series in Boston between the Red Sox and the St. Louis Cardinals.

"Why don't you go see a couple of games? I'll arrange for press credentials," Gans said. I was on the train that night and the next day sat with Proctor in the press box and watched the Sox beat the

Cards 3 to 2. The Cardinals would later win the series in St. Louis, 4-3. A couple of days later we met with Gans to view his operation. When I returned to Altdorf there was a new baby in our house and a Bavaria that was settling down for the winter. While I was away, the Jack Brownes had become the parents of a daughter, Roberta, born in the army hospital at Nuremberg.

Roberta was the first *Stripes* baby, but she wasn't the first baby born in the European Theater to a dependent. That honor went to Mrs. Crosby Lewis, who gave birth April 2 to a daughter at the 317th Station Hospital in Wiesbaden. The father, a U.S. civilian employed by the War Department, and Mrs. Lewis, also a former WD employee, named her Katherine Baldwin Lewis.

★   ★   ★

Living and working in rural Bavaria those closing months of 1946 was pleasant. Altdorf was a quiet hamlet surrounded by lush farmlands and forests spread over rolling hills. The only noise was the roar of the press and the clanging of the town crier's bell and his guttural announcements in German.

Personnel with dependents were issued commissary cards, and transportation was provided for the wives to travel to Furth on the other side of Nuremberg, where milk and eggs from Denmark and fresh meat and food from America were available. The groceries were put on a tab, and we paid the bill at the end of the month. The post exchange was also at Furth and it was as well stocked as any big store in the States.

While personnel in editorial, production, and administration enjoyed the good life, it wasn't all that easy for those in transportation and circulation. There were too many war-weary vehicles that broke down all too frequently and too many miles between the loading dock and the reader's billet.

We didn't like to admit it, but Altdorf was not the ideal place for a printing plant for a newspaper with as large a circulation as we had. It was soon determined that we should move to the Frankfurt area. *Stripes* was in Bavaria because it was believed in the closing days of the war that Nazi troops would hide out in the mountains of southern Germany in what Dr. Joseph Paul Goebbels, Hitler's propagandist, called the "national redoubt." Goebbels also boasted that "werewolves" would operate behind the lines and kill American troops. This did not happen, so a large Allied occupation force in that region was unnecessary. Most of the American troops were in the Frankfurt area and at Bremerhaven on the North Sea.

Proctor and Knorr, after some study, decided to reoccupy Pfungstadt, where the press was still in operation turning out color comics. Larger space for editorial and production was requisitioned from the Germans. Elmer D. Frank, a native of Pittsburg, Kansas, who came to *Stripes* from an army weekly in Berlin to be assistant production manager, was put in charge of construction. The new facility was just off Rugner Strasse, and it was necessary to carry the mats across town to the sterotype department and press on Fabrik Strasse. Editorial and production were on the ground floor; *Weekend,* the artists, communications, and the library on the second story. M/Sgt. Wattie T. St. John, a regular army combat veteran who had recently joined the administrative staff, was ordered to requisition office space and houses for billets.

I led the advance party the 160 miles northwest to Pfungstadt, where we were assigned billets and moved into our new office. John Livingood remained in Altdorf to put out the final issue (Volume 2, Number 337) dated December 5.

The new European edition (Volume 1, Number 1) was barely in the hands of the readers when I was awakened by the telephone in my billet. It was Proctor, and he was mad as hell. He had been rousted out earlier because of a story on Page 1 — a story that we held over especially to get our new edition off with a bang.

A bang is just what we got. The story, written by Phil Bucknell in the New York bureau, was printed under this headline: IKE VIEWED AS PRESIDENTIAL TIMBER. Accompanying the story, which was a well-written and balanced article, was a large photo of the general of the armies. We thought the story balanced because in the first paragraph "Buck" plainly stated that "the general considers such ideas [as his possible candidacy] embarrassing in his military duties." Whoever chewed out Proctor, and there might have been more than one, must not have read that far into the story.

Captain Dowell, the executive editor, fired off a wire to Sid Gans, chief of the New York bureau. It said: "Bucknell's Eisenhower for President feature unappreciated here effective immediately cancel all specials including features, weekly news roundup and editorial projects by our own staffers until further notice."

★　　★　　★

So ended 1946. The editorial staff took a vote to determine the top news story of the year, a year that had its beginning for me in Pfungstadt, then my wedding in Nice and honeymoon in London, the summer and fall in Bavaria, and finally the last three weeks back in Hesse.

The suicide of Hermann Goering and the execution of ten of his Nazi co-defendants was selected as the top story of the year. The Republican Party's election sweep, assuring its control of Congress for the first time since 1930, was voted second. Third was the atom-bomb tests at Bikini. Both the Associated Press and United Press selected the Republican victory as their top stories.

6

Business

Two young army captains in the Information and Education office in Hochst — Bernard J. McGuigan of Boston, Massachusetts, and James E. Bromwell of Cedar Rapids, Iowa — triggered an idea that was to put *The Stars and Stripes* in the magazine and periodical business that in turn did much to save the newspaper's hide.

Mac and Jim stopped by Lt. Col. William G. Proctor's office in the I. G. Farben building after a visit to the PX, where they picked up the *Saturday Evening Post* and a *Life* magazine.

"Will you look at the dates on these magazines? It's outrageous," McGuigan grumbled. "This one is three months old. The PX people market reading material the same way they sell toothpaste."

Proctor agreed but noted that the peacetime system had enormous logistical problems, since it had to stock and maintain stores all over Europe.

"That may be, but they still do a lousy job with dated material. Colonel, you're the boss of *Stripes*, why don't you get the PX brass to let the newspaper handle the magazines? You have the trucks and the drivers and the paper goes out every day," McGuigan said.

125

"Maybe you could talk them into letting you have newsstand space in the PXs too," Bromwell said.

"You might have something there. The markup must be pretty good and *Stripes* could use the extra revenue. I'll get to work on it," Proctor said.

Proctor did get to work on it. He called in William Pelletier, the circulation manager, and asked him for an assessment of *Stripes*'s circulation capabilities, the number of trucks being used, as well as air and rail routes. A few days later Pelletier, who had recently taken over the job from Earl Ericson and Warrant Officer Henry T. Malone, reported that it appeared *Stripes* could do the job with existing vehicles, but for better service more trucks and personnel would be needed.

A few days later, Proctor was in Lt. Gen. Clarence R. Huebner's office on one of his frequent visits. When Huebner became deputy commanding general of EUCOM, he promised Proctor his complete and wholehearted support to *The Stars and Stripes* and suggested that the colonel visit him on a regular basis.

On this occasion, Proctor told the general of the recommendation that *Stripes* take over the sale of periodicals from the PXs. Proctor said later that the general jabbed the button of his squawk box and said: "Alex, I have Proctor of *The Stars and Stripes* here in my office and he says they want to take over the sale of your magazines."

"Give him the damn magazines, sir," Maj. Gen. Alexander W. Bolling, chief of Special Services, EUCOM, said, "and they can have all we have in Europe and for free."

The Stars and Stripes was in the magazine and periodical business. Proctor and Knorr decided to hire an expediter to work in the New York office and wired Gans to start taking applications for the job. It was a key job: the individual would coordinate the purchase and arrange trucking to dockside, waterproofing, and shipping. Gans hired an old friend, Milton Adler, who was given the title of publisher's representative.

The distribution and sale of the magazines once they had arrived at Bremerhaven was routine. They were placed on the newsstands according to the date. But, to do a good sales job, it was necessary to display them well. A cabinet shop was set up and display racks with roll-top covers were built and shipped to the various PXs.

The first major problem had to do with returns. *Time, Life, Newsweek,* and the *New York Times* magazine objected to the no-return system. They and *Reader's Digest* had enjoyed a no-return situation during the war and wanted it to continue. When all but *Reader's Digest* balked at taking back unsold periodicals, Proctor informed them that *Stripes* would then progressively cut its orders until it reached some figure where returns would be at a minimum.

Brig. Gen. Paul W. Thompson, who only a few months before was chief of I&E and Proctor's boss, and was now vice-president of the European editions of *Reader's Digest,* thought otherwise. He and Don Stedman, circulation manager of Curtis Publishing Co., helped get the other magazines to accept the *Stripes* position. The returns were never a factor, since the Germans bought anything left over, especially the comics, fashion, and women's magazines.

McGuigan's and Bromwell's idea and its implementation by Proctor was a great success. Within a few years *Stripes* had over 500 newsstands, more than 400 of which carried, in addition to *The Stars and Stripes,* a full selection of stateside magazines, pocket-size books, and hard-cover best sellers. A fleet of 180 trucks logged 420,000 miles per month, while trains accounted for another half-million miles. The newspaper was sold in mess halls and at snack bars, and home delivery routes numbered 27,000 subscribers. In addition, the mailing department sent nearly 1,100 subscription copies to many parts of the world where military and embassy personnel were stationed in small numbers. The newspaper was read in twenty-four countries, including Norway, Turkey, the Soviet Union, and Greece.

And what of all the money *The Stars and Stripes* was making with this new venture into the realm of big business? Well, it paid its bills, and profits reverted to the Armed Forces General Welfare Fund, which doled out money to AFN (Armed Forces Network), Special Services, the dependent school system, and a variety of off-duty troop functions.

What happened to the three officers who started all of this? Proctor, after his tour with I&E and *Stripes,* headed the public information office at the U.S. Military Academy, West Point, then transferred to the newly formed Air Force, picked up his new blue uniform and the silver eagles of a full colonel, and later retired. He and his wife Eulalie now live in Vancouver, Washington.

McGuigan, now deceased, did transfer to *Stripes,* was its distribution chief for a number of years, and then returned to the United States, where he was active in Democratic Party politics in Michigan and for a time was closely associated with the late Adlai Stevenson. Bromwell, a successful attorney, represented the state of Iowa in Congress.

★   ★   ★

Proctor didn't spend all of his time on business matters; he kept a sharp eye on editorial too. After our return to Pfungstadt, I saw Proctor more frequently then I did when we were located in Altdorf. When Dowell wasn't available, the colonel often called me on the telephone. He got me out of bed on the third day of the new 1947 with the question: "Did you read the lead letter in today's B-Bag?"

Sleepily, I stammered that I wasn't sure which letter he meant as we worked two and three days in advance on that particular page. I asked what the letter said. That was a mistake.

"You are familiar with the staff box on the same page, I trust," he said. I answered that I was. "Well, you just change the title behind the managing editor's name to 'acting managing editor.' Got that?"

"Yes, sir," I said and he hung up.

"What was that all about?" my wife asked as I poured a cup of coffee to steady my nerves.

"That was the colonel, and he's wild this morning."

The letter in question was from a civilian who was interested in the auxiliary language Esperanto and was appealing for American support to spread the movement that had been banned by Hitler. Proctor and I never again discussed that letter, but I later learned that his objection was that it was written by a civilian attached to UNRRA (United Nations Relief and Rehabilitation Administration) and it led off the daily column. Proctor apparently felt that a serviceman's letter would have been more appropriate in a military newspaper. He had a point, but since the civilian ranks were growing I reasoned that an occasional letter from that segment was in order. My crime was not the use of the letter but in not knowing at the time which one he was referring to. The following day the word "acting" appeared in my title and remained there for the rest of the month. On January 28 I received this note:

> It gives me great pleasure to come down off my high horse and re-appoint you managing editor of *The Stars and Stripes*.

Please supervise the entire editorial function of the paper keeping apart from the mechanical end as much as possible. Give Sharnik and Livingood plenty of leeway and you, yourself, retain editorial responsibility of the paper. Mr. Dowell is to give you every assistance in editorial guidance.

/s/ WILLIAM G. PROCTOR
Lt. Col. Inf.
Officer in Charge

On January 31 my title was restored in the staff box. The reference to keeping apart from the mechanical end was an effort by Dowell and Knorr to get me to spend more time on administrative duties and less on editing and makeup.

"You are trying to do too much. You've got good people. Let them do the work. You be the managing editor," Dowell said.

I reluctantly turned over the news desk to John Livingood and spent more time on scheduling, operations reports, and answering the mail. Proctor and I never discussed the B-Bag letter or my brief demotion, but we laughed about it years later. I still have his "high-horse" note.

The staff box was changed in mid-March to reflect a new title for Proctor and the deletion of Edwin E. Dowell's name as executive editor.

On March 23, Proctor was listed as officer in charge; the next day he was editor in chief. I asked Dowell, who gave up his *Stripes* job to join the *Herald-Tribune* in Paris, what was behind the switch in Proctor's identification.

"He wasn't invited to a Frankfurt Press Club bash given by the public relations people because he wasn't an editor. He's an editor now," Dowell explained.

The title "editor in chief" still stands there forty-plus years later, but that's how it came to be.

★   ★   ★

The Stars and Stripes had taken on a major responsibility when it acquired the periodical business from the post exchange. If it were to be successful, it was necessary to purchase more vehicles, hire more people, upgrade the eight-page newspaper, and get it and the magazines out to the troops.

In late 1946, soon after the move from Altdorf back to Pfung-stadt, it was decided to publish more than one edition of the newspaper in order to get it to the outlying areas earlier and provide later news in the final run. The result was four bulldogs and a final. It necessitated bringing in editorial personnel for a 9:00 A.M. to 5:00 P.M. shift to get out the early editions and have them off the press and onto trains bound for Berlin, Bremen, and Vienna. The late desk arrived at 2:00 P.M. and went off duty at 10:00 P.M., with two copy editors working from 4:00 to midnight and another responsible for the late bulletins until 2:00.

The bulldogs were called the Berlin-Bremen, Western Europe, Austrian-Bavarian, and Italian editions. This all went well from the start on January 4, but since meaningful changes other than the name of the edition were infrequent, the decision in early May was to concentrate on one bulldog for the outlying districts. The desk setup remained the same as for the final edition. We also started to publish New York Stock Exchange closings, something unheard of for a war-born army newspaper. Senior officers, who had investments, loved it; the average GI couldn't care less.

Circulation climbed, and sales of the newspaper and the magazines jumped from $5,000 a month in October 1946 to $20,000 in February 1947 in the nine districts that made up the circulation area. This also resulted in the increased use of newsprint. *Stripes* had been buying newsprint from the States at $175 a ton, but as of the first of the year the price was increased to $190 just at the time we needed more of the big rolls. The German newsprint mills, which had been damaged during the war, had been restored to full production, and their salesmen were anxious to sell to the army newspaper for dollars. But the U.S. Military Government decided that such sales might be a threat to the German newspapers, which also were just getting into production.

Stripes was ordered by the army to try for other sources or to get stateside mills to increase their allotment. Knorr came up with an idea to subsidize the Haindl newsprint mill at Schongau in Bavaria. Haindl had plenty of woodpulp and all the ingredients, but it didn't have coal or trucks. *Stripes* had the vehicles and provided what coal it could but ran into a roadblock when its request to Military Government for additional supplies of coal was turned down. We did get some newsprint from Haindl but not much.

When General Clay inspected the *Stripes* operation in Pfungstadt, Knorr was asked to ride along in the limousine and point out the facilities. Knorr mentioned to the general that he had just received an agreement from Warsaw to buy coal to permit *The Stars and Stripes* to continue printing, since an allocation from Military Government was not being made.

"He looked at me with those piercing brown eyes and said softly and with a smile on his face that it would be unnecessary to buy coal from Poland. I didn't say anything because, after all, he was Military Government. The next day we received an allocation from MG for the coal," Knorr recalled.

A few days after Knorr spoke to General Clay, Proctor happened to be in the office of Lieutenant General Huebner, Clay's deputy, and mentioned the difficulty *Stripes* was having obtaining another source for newsprint. The general listened and then smiled and told Proctor that *Stripes* should continue planning on using German newsprint and to forget about making our own.

"Behind the scenes, General Huebner was always fighting for *The Stars and Stripes*," Proctor remembered.

The new supply of German newsprint plus what we were getting from Haindl was a big help. The stateside shipments continued to arrive at the port of Bremerhaven, and before long the Scandinavian market opened up to dollar accounts. Finland also became an important source in later years.

★　　★　　★

Proctor was faced with still another problem that took a bit of doing to resolve. This concerned *Weekend,* the magazine supplement. A first-class periodical, printed in color on good stock, it was also an expensive operation — actually a luxury. In fact, it was not really Proctor who finally resolved the matter but his successor, who cast the magazine adrift to find its own destiny. Proctor still gave it his best shot, approving the expansion to twenty-four pages, switching to rotogravure printing, and placing a ten-cent price tag on it in the hope that *Weekend* would pay or partly pay for itself. It didn't. It was increased to twenty-eight pages but continued to lose money.

Proctor's additional problem was that the wives of both Knorr, the executive manager, and McGuigan, the distribution chief, worked for *Weekend.* Betty Luros Knorr and Dorothy Gies McGuigan, were talented writers, and both drew good salaries. You just didn't talk about staff cuts in the office under those conditions, so Proctor didn't.

The extra dime didn't come near to offsetting the salaries, the cost of high-grade newsprint, special artwork, and payments to free-lance writers. It helped, but it caused extra work and more man-hours in the accounting department.

Weekend had its genesis in *Midweek*, an eight-page feature supplement to the Southern Germany edition at Altdorf. *Midweek* came out each Thursday starting August 23, 1945, four months after that edition was born. The date and name were selected so as not to conflict with the Sunday magazine then edited by the Paris edition. When the Paris paper closed and the magazine went out of business, *Midweek* then became *Weekend* and made its debut June 26, 1946, along with the Sunday paper.

When editor James V. McLean returned to the States, Dick Jones, who had been the first editor of *Midweek* as an enlisted man and now a civilian, took over as *Weekend* editor. *Weekend* shifted from Altdorf to Pfungstadt when the paper moved in December 1946.

Although a part of the *Stripes* editorial staff, *Weekend* had autonomy, and its personnel answered to Jones. However, *Weekend* used the *Stripes* photo staff, the work of some of the daily's artists, as well as reports from correspondents in New York and the European bureaus.

Weekend's articles were for the most part excellent, filling the needs of the army and air force to publicize their missions in Europe. Fiction also made its appearance in *Weekend*, most of it written by staff members often using pseudonyms. Sad Sack, the scrawny GI that was a *Yank* magazine favorite during the war, joined up early in 1947.

★   ★   ★

The magazine got stateside mention by the wire services in 1948 when Jones put a picture of Adolf Hitler on the cover. It was the first time since the war ended three years and three months earlier that the German people were able to see a photograph of their former Fuehrer on the cover of a magazine circulated in the homeland.

A year earlier, *Weekend* was in stateside wire service reports when two staff members were shot by bandits. The shooting occurred about 9:45 P.M. July 30, 1947, while staff writer Richard L. Cohen and photographer Michael A. Vaccaro were driving on the rocky Pyrenees road connecting Bilboa and Santander on the northern coast of Spain.

Cohen, who was at the wheel, was struck in the hip by a bullet and had shell splinters on his face and head. Vaccaro was shot in the wrist but took over the driving and made his way to the nearest town, where they were treated.

Although the opinion was that the shots were fired by bandits, Cohen said the secret police who interviewed him insisted that whoever fired the shots must have been "enemies of Franco," while the town police said they were "Communists."

The governor of the province of Santander apologized to the two Americans and paid Cohen's $400 hospital bill. He also sent them a huge Roquefort cheese and provided a 1928 Packard car to drive Cohen to the border to catch a train to Germany. Vaccaro continued on to Madrid in the jeep and returned later to Pfungstadt with photographs.

★   ★   ★

Hitler's picture appeared August 26, 1948, five weeks after Lt. Col. William M. Summers, the new editor in chief, decided to cancel the *Stripes* tie with *Weekend*. Dick Jones wanted to buy the rights to the name, but Summers felt it wasn't the newspaper's property to sell. The *Weekend* staff vacated the office and their billets and moved to Frankfurt, where Jones acquired office space and press time with the *Frankfurter Rundschau*.

Now able to accept paid advertising that had been denied him when *Weekend* was part of the army newspaper, Jones set out to woo potential advertisers. However, since ad schedules are made up months and sometimes a year in advance, *Weekend* wasn't able to attract the big accounts.

The Hitler cover was a circulation-building gimmick, and Jones was on the right track. What he did wrong was to underestimate the appeal that the Fuehrer still had and only printed his usual 20,000 copies for the German market. He could easily have sold two or three times that amount.

The 5,000-word story, written by Michael A. Musmanno, former Nuremberg war crimes judge, was entitled "Is Hitler Still Alive?" Jones's awareness of the eye appeal of the undraped female form and his steady use of cheesecake came into play. On the inside, under the title "Hitler's Women," were three nude photographs of Eva Braun and her sister Gretl, cavorting beside a Bavarian lake.

Musmanno later sold publication rights to German newspapers, so his story did get out to the public. His answer to the question was yes, "Hitler is dead. The evidence of his death is conclusive and absolute."

★   ★   ★

Weekend died the following year. A European magazine using the same name threatened court action, and rather than fight Jones decided to change to *Now* magazine. The first issue was January 1, 1949. Jones moved the operation to Paris with himself as editor, Sterling Lord as managing editor, and Oliver Gregg Howard as associate editor, but they still couldn't generate enough advertising revenue to make a go of it. *Stripes* continued to sell *Weekend-Now* on its newsstands, but sales dropped, so finally on February 22, 1949, Jones closed up shop and returned to the United States.

Dick Jones is now a free-lance writer living and working in the New York area. Lord is an agent in New York City and represents a number of prominent authors. Howard died in 1980 after many years with *New Yorker* magazine.

Stripes replaced *Weekend* in July 1948 by adding features to an expanded daily newspaper. Although I lobbied for a magazine, Summers said it wasn't right to drop *Weekend* and then turn around and start another.

It wasn't until January 1950 that we came up with a twelve-page section of features, called just that: *Feature Section*. It had color, sometimes full-color, and was quite handsome; not as slick as *Weekend* but also not as costly.

Howard Katzander, a Philadelphia and New York newspaperman and a *Yank* magazine writer during the war, was its first editor. He was followed by George Learned, a Santa Barbara and San Francisco newspaperman.

The *Feature Section* continued until July 1954, at which time *The Stars and Stripes* expanded to twenty-four pages and it was dropped. Material from the section was integrated into the daily.

★   ★   ★

Summers took over November 10, 1947, as editor in chief from Proctor, who had assumed command two years before from Lt. Col. Fred Eldridge. Eldridge returned to Southern California to work for the *Los Angeles Times*.

At about this same time, Knorr resigned as executive manager to enter the import-export business, and he was replaced by Maurice R. Kirkwood, of Tipton, Indiana, who had since 1946 been manager of the fiscal department. A graduate of Indiana University with a master's degree in accounting, he had served in the Quartermaster Corps as a first lieutenant and also taught accounting at Shrivenham, England, in the GI university program. Kirkwood's wife Anne, also of Tipton, who had been personnel director in Altdorf, gave up her job to become a homemaker and to raise their two daughters.

The Proctor-Knorr team put *Stripes* on a business basis, thanks to McGuigan's and Bromwell's suggestion that the newspaper get involved in the magazine distribution field, and Summers and Kirkwood kept the newspaper on a steady course and in black ink for the next few years.

★ ★ ★

All went well with Richard E. Knorr, the Union, New Jersey, major-turned-businessman, after he left *The Stars and Stripes*. He formed an import-export firm called Ampurex, had it licensed in Lichtenstein, and started selling to the U.S. Army commissaries and post exchange system. Knorr opened an office in Frankfurt, where his wife, former *Weekend* reporter Betty Luros, was accredited to the *Chicago Tribune*. Thus he became a dependent and was issued a PX card. They also had a home in France, where he operated a furniture factory.

Then in May 1953, a little more than five years after he left the newspaper, Knorr was arrested by the Germans and tossed into Hammelgasse jail in Frankfurt on a charge of nonpayment of taxes. He shared a cell with two others for a week before Earl J. Carroll, his attorney, could spring him.

The Germans claimed that Knorr owed them 250,000 marks or $59,000 in taxes on sales of furniture sold to the U.S. Army in Germany between June 1950 and October 1951.

Following his brush with German law, Knorr moved to Puerto Rico, where he started a frozen-meat business and again sold to the U.S. Army in Europe. In recent years, he has worked out of London, where he and his wife live in fashionable Lowndes Square.

Dick Knorr wasn't the only *Stripes* executive to be listed as a dependent. Henry Thompson "Hank" Malone, a warrant officer turned-civilian and the assistant circulation manager, turned up on army transportation records as his wife's son and actually traveled across the Atlantic as her dependent.

Hank had put in the necessary request for his wife Perrillah, whom everyone called Pat, to travel from their home in Georgia to Germany. That was in 1946, and the waiting list was long.

Meanwhile, Hank had combined a business and pleasure trip to the States and was visiting Pat at their home in Calhoun when she received orders to depart immediately for Germany. Her orders read "and son," which she didn't have, but Hank decided he would like to take a leisurely sea voyage so he talked a friendly sergeant at the POE into letting him accompany her.

"Last thing he said to me was, 'Have a good trip, sonny,' " Hank recalled.

Proctor met the Bremerhaven train in Frankfurt wondering what to do with a stray woman and child but was relieved to find his overdue circulation executive with her.

The Malones didn't remain long in Germany. They returned to Georgia, where Hank enrolled at Duke University and later at Emory University for graduate work. He taught high school algebra in Calhoun (one of his students was Bert Lance, President Carter's controversial budget director) and wrote a book entitled *Cherokees of the Old South,* which he brought out in 1956.

Prior to his death in 1977 of cancer, Henry T. Malone was dean of the School of General Studies and professor of history and urban life at Georgia State University.

★   ★   ★

Bernard J. McGuigan, the captain who first suggested in 1946 to his friend Lt. Col. William G. Proctor that *Stripes* take over the magazine distribution from the PX system, decided to transfer to the newspaper and eventually take a civilian job.

He obtained his discharge from the army at Frankfurt and worked for a few weeks as assistant to Proctor, learning the functions of the various departments at Pfungstadt. He wed Dorothy Gies, who came overseas with the American Red Cross and who was hired in May 1946 as a correspondent for *Weekend.* She left the paper a year later to have their son, Michael John, in the 97th General Hospital at Frankfurt.

On November 11, 1947, McGuigan was named chief of distribution services, replacing William H. Pelletier, who had held the post six months. A year later, McGuigan's title was changed to chief of distribution.

After eighteen months of service, in which sales of the newspaper and the publications steadily grew, McGuigan resigned

March 15, 1949, to go into the import-export business. He was replaced by Louis H. Brown, an ex-air force officer originally from Beaumont, Texas. The change was made the same week that the masthead on the newspaper noted that *Stripes* was now an army-air force publication.

The air force, which had long been critical of the army-sponsored publication, was now in a position of authority. It was also in a position to get "a bigger slice of the financial pie," as one Wiesbaden-based colonel put it. And it wouldn't be long before the air force assigned a major to be assistant editor in chief, and still later, just to show the army it meant business, it brought in a full colonel as editor in chief.

The Stars and Stripes was ready for takeoff.

7

Cheesecake

Readers of *The Stars and Stripes* were given generous helpings of cheesecake during the war and the immediate postwar years. Editors of the editions that sprouted like wildflowers in North Africa, Sicily, Italy, and on the Continent, used at least one picture daily of a scantily clad young woman and, when the fighting stopped and the paper expanded to twelve pages, two and sometimes three photos of an actress, starlet, model, or bathing beauty were published.

GIs loved it, and some even submitted pictures of their girlfriends for possible publication. Officers, Wacs, and nurses tolerated the practice; only the chaplains objected and not too loudly. However, in 1953, an official of the National Catholic Community Service complained to Col. Otis McCormick, chief of the Information and Education Division, Department of Army, in Washington, D.C. Included with the complaint were seven clippings from the European edition of *Stripes*, all pictures of leggy girls including Ava Gardner, Cyd Charisse, and Kathleen Hughes.

There was one of a pretty Arizona State College coed with bare midriff, wearing a baseball cap and glove. The camera caught her jumping, legs spread wide in the act of catching the ball. The caption read "hot corner," which, as baseball fans know, is a term used for third base. There was no indication she was covering any base, let alone third; we could just as well have used another caption.

I replied to Colonel McCormick that we felt that the pictures used were no different from what had been seen thousands of times in films, on beaches and tennis courts. No further word was heard from the NCCS.

A short time earlier Maj. Gen. Ivan Loveridge Bennett, chief of chaplains, visited *Stripes* at Griesheim. He expressed satisfaction with the paper and especially the three full pages of church services for all the troops in Europe that we printed each Easter, Thanksgiving, and Christmas, as well as the schedules for the Jewish holidays. No mention was made of cheesecake. The Reverend Billy Graham, on a visit to the editorial department, told us that we had probably the most important newspaper in the world, but he said he thought it would be even better if we didn't use too much cheesecake.

The following year, when the paper expanded to twenty-four pages, Archbishop Aloisius J. Muench, attached to the American mission at Bonn, wrote to Lt. Col. Arthur L. Jorgenson, the editor in chief, complaining that *The Stars and Stripes* "uses valuable space for cheesecake pictures offensive to good taste and decency." Here is part of his August 15, 1954, letter:

> Pictures of scantily clad women incite to lust and lewdness and thus get to be a cause of debasing standards of moral conduct. Beyond a question such pictures, bordering on the pornographic, degrade the fine sentiments of high regard for womanhood that it took centuries of civilization to build up; they contribute toward sexual delinquencies of youth as parents, educators, psychologists and judges of juvenile courts know only too well; they debauch the life of young men in the Armed Forces away from the finer protective influences of a good father and mother.

The Most Reverend Muench had been in Germany four years as chief of the Vatican mission and regent of the apostolic nunciature, or papal representative. One of twenty-six American archbishops, he had been sent to Germany by President Truman as a representative of Francis Cardinal Spellman and a consultant in religious affairs to the Military Government. He had jurisdiction over all the Catholic chaplains but spent most of his time working out of his Kronberg home with displaced persons, refugees, and expellees. The archbishop had served eleven years in North Dakota.

The protest from the National Catholic Community Service and the archbishop did slow down the use of cheesecake, but it didn't put a halt to the practice. While we printed a photo of Marlene Dietrich in an almost transparent dress at a Las Vegas nightclub in 1953, we did pass up another of actress Terry Moore wearing a blue beaded evening gown that the designer called a "nude souffle," and which showed much of Moore's ample upper torso.

During the war, news and feature photographs were mailed from the office of the Army News Service (ANS) and after the fighting ended the *Stripes* bureau in New York continued the practice. Word went out that the army newspaper wanted cheesecake photos, and most every press agent in New York and Hollywood obliged. When the mail bogged down and the supply dwindled right after the Battle of the Bulge, the picture editor at Liege lifted a likeness of Marie McDonald from a page in *Life* magazine. You could tell it was a reprint rather than a glossy because it was grainy, but who cared? *Life* probably never knew.

Benny Price, picture editor at Paris, came up with the idea of a Miss Cheesecake award. Polling the staff a couple of days after Christmas, he announced that actress Toni Seven was the winner. Her picture was printed January 1, 1945, and the wire services picked up the news and relayed it back home. The stateside papers gave it a good play, stating that the GIs in the foxholes had made the choice. Since the first day of the year is often a slow news day, most newspapers used the picture with the caption. The next year starlet Adele Mara was the winner, followed by model Myrna Keck in 1946.

When the staff civilianized and finally settled down to one edition at Pfungstadt and later at Griesheim, the practice was continued. Just before Christmas each year the picture editor would produce a list of all the young women who posed in strictly cheesecake situations. The one who appeared the most often was named Miss Cheesecake and her name and photo were released to the wire services with a January 1 embargo on its use.

Rita Hayworth was the 1947 winner, followed by Virginia Mayo in 1948, model Mary Collins in 1949, and Marilyn Monroe, 1950. For a couple of years Gussie Moran, of the lace-edged tennis shorts, topped the list until the sports editor reminded us that she was a sports figure. Other Miss Cheesecakes were Italian actress Franca Faldini, 1951; Kathleen Hughes, 1952; Vanessa Brown,

1953; and Marla English, 1954. The annual selection was discontinued in 1955, which just happened to be the year I left the paper to return to the States.

The young ladies usually sent notes of appreciation, although Rita and Marilyn didn't bother. Vanessa Brown, Miss Cheesecake of 1953, who was then appearing in a play on Broadway, sent a box of real cheesecake from Lindy's and it arrived in the newsroom the next day, thanks to a friendly airline pilot.

★   ★   ★

The American obsession with cheesecake was not shared by the British management of *The London Times*, where *The Stars and Stripes* was published.

In their book *The Story of the Times*, authors Oliver Woods and James Bishop had this to say:

> The Times Publishing Company was at that time printing and publishing *The Stars and Stripes*, the United States Services newspaper which had its editorial staff at Printing House Square. This newspaper was a source of anxiety to the Manager, Mr. C. S. Kent, not because we were unable to cope with the printing demands of the American journalists.
>
> On the contrary, a fairly large number of our compositors was devoted exclusively to the printing of *The Stars and Stripes*. Mr. Kent's worry was that too many pictures chosen by the Americans for publication in their paper — pictures of girls in the very nearly nude — were in his opinion too near the knuckle.

Too near the knuckle indeed. Joe McBride, who was on the London staff of *Stripes* at that time, recalls an incident in which a photo of a Vargas drawing entitled "Bundle for Britain," which featured a pretty miss, was "lost" somewhere between the picture editor Ben Price's desk and the engraving department.

"Benny handed the photo to me and I took it to the engravers. When it came time to make up the page all the other zincs were there but not the Vargas drawing. It just plain disappeared and I had a hell of a time convincing Benny that it wasn't my fault," McBride recalls.

While the editors concerned themselves with which picture of a well-proportioned girl would grace which page, Don Sheppard, a twenty-year-old GI cartoonist from San Rafael, California, created his own version of cheesecake. She was a fat, pug-nosed maiden with swastikas embroidered on her skirts and on the bows of her pigtails. Shep, who insisted he disliked German women, called her Hilda. It was Hilda who said to her Pfc date, "I heard mama and papa talking last night, *liebling*. What's a burp-gun wedding?"

On July 9, 1946, Shep gave her a new name. She became Veronica Dankeschon, with the initials VD inscribed on her handbag. The cartoon showed two soldiers and a *fraulein* seated at a table. The gag line read: "Sarge, I'd like you to meet the sweetest little girl in Deutschland — Miss Veronica Dankeschon."

The following day the surgeon general's office of the U.S. Forces, European Theater, requested permission for its preventive medicine division to reprint and distribute posters of Shep's cartoon as part of an all-out war against venereal disease.

The cartoon was cited by Capt. Ernest Drenick, epidemiology officer, as an "intelligent and effective method of warning soldiers of the danger of venereal disease."

Caught up in the glamorous aura of publicity usually associated with cover girls and pinup queens, Veronica Dankeschon received an offer to appear in a movie. The 2nd Motion Picture unit wanted to feature Veronica in a nonspeaking role in an anti-VD film trailer to be shown in Germany and Austria, but sadly Veronica's brief encounter with fame died the next day when Maj. Gen. J. M. Bevans, USFET G-1, banned any consideration of Sheppard's cartoon as an anti-venereal disease poster sponsored by the army. Col. O. B. Schreuder, Air Corps chief surgeon at Wiesbaden, advised the 2nd Motion Picture unit that its use of the hefty *fraulein* in a campaign film was not approved.

"The United States is trying to re-establish and revive the German government," said Col. George Eyster, USFET public relations officer. "If we attack German womanhood as the sole source of VD, we're raising a difficult problem for ourselves. We feel it is poor taste to use the cartoon as an Army poster, since it would seem to be directed at all of German womanhood."

Veronica's casting in the Air Corps movie "would create the impression that all German girls are infected with VD," Schreuder said. "This is obviously not the case. There are many clean-living German girls who rightfully would be shocked at any such implication." He said that he was of the opinion that selection of Shep's controversial VD cartoon would not aid the campaign.

Shep didn't give up easily. Veronica Dankeschon returned to the paper July 20, complete with swastikas on her skirt and pigtails and the initials VD on her handbag. Her boyfriend, a private in uniform, said: "Veronica, if you are not the sweetest, cleanest most honorable young thing I know — why then I'm a monkey's uncle!"

It wasn't funny, but Shep made his point. He drew more *frauleins* but none with swastikas or initials on her handbag.

Stateside magazines, including *Life,* featured Shep and his cartoons and one publication called him "the Mauldin of the occupation," a term he disliked.

For the rest of the former 66th Infantry Division soldier's time in Germany, he contributed cartoons featuring GIs on occupation duty and turned out illustrations for *Weekend* magazine. He attended the Nuremberg trials and, on October 4, we published a full page of his sketches of the defendants and their judges.

He was on board a ship heading home when his final blast at German women was published December 10. The cartoon showed an army private wading through a mud puddle heading for the ZI (Zone of Interior) and being chased by the shadow of a hefty *fraulein,* her pigtails flying in the air.

★   ★   ★

Sheppard's art left its mark on the Germans. Two years after he returned to the States, the residents of Celle were calling their British Zone community "Veronica Town" when 2,000 *frauleins* arrived to be near the 8,000 U.S. Air Force pilots and airmen stationed there during the Berlin airlift.

Time magazine reported that the girls increased the shortage of space until the people of the quiet old town of 33,000, swept along on the tide of opportunism, began renting rooms for the night only. Some mothers even sent their children into the streets to lure the GIs home: "Nice warm stube with big bed Joe."

When the airlift ended and the Americans left, the city council cracked down and summoned to court 200 people who had rented rooms to the *frauleins.* Only fifty were actually sentenced, but then the Bonn government stepped in and set them free by amnesty, explaining that it was impossible to single out "individual crimes for something of which a whole town is guilty."

8

Griesheim

Lt. Col. William M. Summers came aboard in November 1947 as editor in chief, replacing Lt. Col. William G. Proctor. Summers, who saw combat with the 104th Infantry Division, endeared himself to us right away by moving *Stripes* headquarters out of Hochst to Pfungstadt. He took over offices across the courtyard from editorial and production and was readily accessible, he shunned billets in Frankfurt (when his wife and two sons arrived, he had a house in Darmstadt ready for them), and he saw to it some of the rest of us were given better quarters.

We had received quite a scare early in the year when Proctor talked of abandoning the operation in Pfungstadt and of opening a plant in Berlin and another in the Munich area. We learned of this in a request to assist in preparing a staff study only five weeks after we had left Bavaria and moved back to Pfungstadt. The two plants would split the circulation area. His personal recommendation, however, was that editorial, production, and circulation remain in Pfungstadt and that fiscal, personnel, and all the business offices be transferred to Information and Education Division headquarters in Hochst. He suggested "that all personnel be quartered in Frankfurt with as many as possible in one location, in order that *Stars and Stripes* transportation can pick them up daily and take them to Pfungstadt and return."

If his recommendation had been approved by EUCOM "the new paper would be under the operational jurisdiction of Headquarters I&E inasmuch as many of *The Stars and Stripes* headquarter personnel will be eliminated and their duties and responsibilities taken over by headquarters."

That alone was shocking, but that wasn't all that Proctor asked in his January 16, 1947, staff study request. He sought our ideas on how the editorial policy should be rewritten, "stressing the fact that the staff feels that with the newspaper primarily set up as a soldier's publication it would very well go out of existence on V-E Day plus two years, together with some of its features, such as an over-abundance of 'cheese cake,' B-Bag and so forth."

I don't know where he came up with the "V-E Day plus two years" idea, but nothing came of the staff study. And the newspaper is still in existence, still publishing letters and an occasional cheesecake photo.

Like Proctor, it didn't take Summers long to determine that Pfungstadt wasn't really a suitable place in which to work or live. Faced with the necessity of buying a larger press to replace the small and antiquated one that had served since April 1945, he set about scouring the area for a new publication site.

I went along on some of the forays, but mostly it was Summers and Maurice R. Kirkwood, the general manager. Often Elmer D. Frank, the production manager, accompanied him, as did Kenneth Howland, the transportation supervisor. I remember looking in on the *Frankfurter Rundschau,* which had a large press but lacked office space. The trouble with Frankfurt was that the inner city had been heavily bombed, and what wasn't demolished was occupied by U.S. Army installations, none anxious to give up their space. What was needed was a site where we could start from scratch, get army approval, and then have the Germans build something for us, using occupation deutsche marks.

The deutsche marks were tax monies paid by the Germans for the occupation and protection of their homeland. The money in turn was used by the Allies to pay the Germans working for them and for construction of buildings necessary for the occupiers.

It turned out there was just such a location right under our noses — a one-time Luftwaffe auxiliary field between the village of Griesheim and the city of Darmstadt and just off the Frankfurt-Heidelberg autobahn. It had a three-story terminal building, another two-story office structure, two wooden hangars, two houses, and some smaller buildings. The larger buildings were damaged but repairable. Not only was there bomb damage but also the window framing and doors had been removed, if not for firewood then for someone else's bombed-out abode, of which there were many.

The field had a history of sorts. It was used in 1934 twice by the Graf Zeppelin on its return from U.S. trans-Atlantic flights. The landings sparked a move to make the field a world airport, but it failed because of sand storms. The Rhine-Main airport just south of Frankfurt became the Graf Zeppelin's home port. In 1943 the field was used briefly by the Luftwaffe as a base for night flights.

About this time in stepped Brig. Gen. Philip E. Gallagher, EUCOM director of military posts. When *Stripes*'s problem had been explained to him — and, of course, after he saw Pfungstadt — he advised Summers to submit the necessary paperwork to the Engineers and Logistics Branch. EUCOM would request the acquisition of the property on the airstrip, which was owned by the German federal government, and the refurbishing of the buildings. When Summers told the general that an addition would be needed to the office building to house the press, Gallagher said to include that in the request.

Summers submitted the papers early in 1949 and to our surprise it was approved almost immediately. The work came under the jurisdiction of the engineers at the Darmstadt subpost, who let out the contracts to the various German contractors. Construction started April 19, and the first sections of the newspaper started to move in the first week of September.

We never knew how much influence Gallagher had, but I for one always felt that without his support the newspaper would have been stuck in Pfungstadt probably to this day — stuck there along with the brewery.

We never knew what the project cost, since *Stripes* never received a bill, but it was probably between $150,000 and $200,000, paid for with a ten-cent deutsche mark, an artificial figure which appropriated funds used for accounting purposes. EUCOM found the money in the appropriated fund budget, actually money for occupation costs, and recommended the move.

Editorial had little to do with the move from Pfungstadt to the buildings on the airstrip near Griesheim. New furniture and a specially built copy desk, seating a slotman and eight copy editors, were in place. We brought our own typewriters and copy pencils and were in business that afternoon.

Production manager Elmer Frank and John E. Alter shouldered the load in making the shift. Frank had to move the press in sections and half the linotypes and other printing equipment in order not to skip an edition. It was necessary for Alter, the communications chief, to transfer the teletype machines, radio and telephone switchboard, which he did, without missing a page of copy or dropping a phone call. Alter borrowed a manual telephone switchboard from the Signal Corps and put it in place at Pfungstadt, while he and his crew installed the regular board at Griesheim. It was the second move for that switchboard, having been used in Altdorf and trucked to Pfungstadt three years earlier.

★   ★   ★

Editorial moved into new quarters the last week of September 1949. The first paper was dated the 26th, but it didn't look any different, since it was printed on the same old press. Two units had been installed in a new building which had been added on to the circulation office; one unit remained in Pfungstadt to print the paper those final weeks. The only noticeable difference was that the Sunday comic section appeared in black and white.

The refurbished three-story terminal housed the executive offices, editorial, and production on the ground floor. Fiscal, personnel, communications, and the photo section were located on the second floor, and the kitchen, dining room, Press Club bar, and a movie theater were on the third floor.

The newsroom was spacious, with two copy desks taking over much of the area. Each could seat eight copy editors with a slotman in the center. We soon learned that the army's inspector general found fault with this arrangement, stating that the personnel could not be expected to do effective work in such a confined area, and the report recommended that each worker be given a separate desk. We chuckled over this and promptly ignored the recommendation.

The IG also criticized the morgue (library), stating that files must be retired every two years with sensitive material shipped to an army installation in Missouri for safekeeping. We pointed out that our files were active and some of it in use daily. After much discussion and reams of paperwork, the IG finally decided that the morgue could stay but not under that name; henceforth it was to be called historical files.

★   ★   ★

Additional housing became available, and some families were moved out of Pfungstadt. Paulette and I were assigned to a two-story house in a wooded area between Darmstadt and Eberstadt. It had been occupied by an army lieutenant colonel who was transferred to Greece to train the Greek army.

As new dependents arrived, they were assigned quarters in Darmstadt and the Odenwald area to the south. Only a few families and bachelors remained in Pfungstadt. Those employees not eligible for government transportation of their dependents sometimes brought them overseas at their own expense to share their cramped quarters. The wives were not eligible for PX or commissary cards and had to make do with their husbands' post exchange rations. A lot of wives with commissary cards shopped for those who had none.

The PX at Darmstadt was enlarged and well supplied. The commissary was stocked with canned and packaged goods and frozen meat from the States, dairy products from Denmark, and vegetables from the Netherlands. Frozen foods had just come into vogue, as had the metal shopping carts. Scrip was necessary for PX purchases, but food purchased at the commissary was put on a charge account and the bill handed to the shopper at the end of the month.

We were able to buy bread, vegetables, and eggs from the Germans, but they didn't want money, certainly not deutsche marks. They insisted on cigarettes, soap, or coffee, or they wouldn't do business.

I came home the day before Thanksgiving and found my French bride busy putting away the groceries she had just purchased at the commissary.

"What goodies did you find today, *chérie?*" I asked as I embraced her.

"*O chéri, voila! La dinde!*" she beamed.

"*La dinde,*" she repeated and then opened the refrigerator,

"*La dinde,*" she repeated and then opened the refrigerator, and there on the top shelf was a twenty-pound turkey, all naked and ready for the oven.

"So that's a *dinde.* That's what we call a turkey."

Since my wife was a great cook I knew that I was in for a treat.

But hours before she started to prepare our first Thanksgiving feast I detected something amiss. There was no sign of dressing.

"What about the dressing?" I asked.

"Qu'est-ce que c'est?"

"The dressing, *chérie* — *bread crusts, onions, pork sausage, celery, sage.*"

"Je ne sais pas," was her reply.

I was at a loss for the proper words, so I grabbed the telephone and dialed M/Sgt. Wattie St. John's billet and his wife, Mary, answered. It was Mary I wanted to talk to because I knew that the Alabama native was a good cook, American-style. And that's what I wanted — typical American.

I told her my problem and added that I knew about the bread but didn't know what to do after that. She filled me in quickly. I thanked her and then, rather than try to explain in my limited French, I set about to make the dressing myself. My wife was skeptical but then became interested because of the distinctive aroma. When I finished and then started to stuff the concoction into the back end of the bird, she got the idea.

★   ★   ★

Summers received his orders in July 1950 for a new assignment as head of the ROTC department, University of Maine at Orono, and departed. He was replaced by Lt. Col. Henry J. Richter, also an infantry officer with duty in the Pacific Theater. His wife, Janet, and daughter and son soon joined him at his quarters in Darmstadt.

These were exciting times, and although we lost many readers when the Berlin Airlift ended the same month, we moved into our new location, the Korean War started, and before long we had three and one-half divisions of soldier readers in Germany.

While the shooting war was going on half a world away, the cold war was very much a part of our lives in Europe. There was a strong feeling that the Russians might invade Germany, and this caused a great deal of apprehension. Several employees gave notice that they intended to return to the States at the end of their contracts.

We had been living in the draft of the cold war for some time, and most of us joked about it. It was not really a laughing matter when the army gave each sponsor of a family a directive that he keep a supply of food, blankets, water, and a jerrycan of gasoline handy in the event of an evacuation order. We in Darmstadt and Griesheim were instructed to head west for France.

"We'll never get across the Rhine. The Rooskies will knock out all the bridges before we get to the autobahn," said John Livingood. "We will be sitting ducks."

When the editorial office was being planned, we had made arrangements for a possible evacuation. The drawers in the morgue, which contained the news clippings and photographs, were made of steel and could easily be removed to the bed of a six-by-six vehicle. Copy editors were told to grab a typewriter on their way out of the building. Of course, nothing happened, but the tension was there.

The army was prepared for any move by the Russians, as Jack Browne, supply and transportation chief, learned when he was handed requisition papers from the Ordnance Property Office of the Frankfurt Military Post.

One paper, the date left open, was for ninety-six grenades, incendiary "WP" for the demolition of eighty-two vehicles. He was instructed to send a soldier to the dump at Hedderheim for the grenades and other soldiers to the quartermaster in Darmstadt for 200 emergency rations (to supply 100 persons for two days), as well as five-gallon cans for a water supply for 100 persons.

★ ★ ★

Lieutenant Colonel Richter was a fine officer and a gentleman in every sense of the word, although he was inclined to be stubborn and took a long time to make a decision, or so it seemed to me. He was fair game for the stateside press. Arthur Noyes, a former *Stripes* reporter and at the time working for the *New York Daily News*, took Richter to task when the colonel banned bikini bathing suits at the *Stripes* swimming pool. Noyes, however, did not name Richter in his July 4, 1952, story which was printed in the *Daily News* under this headline: YANK CO IN GERMANY BANS BIKINI SUITS FOR GI'S SAKE.

The story said the unit commander of the army-operated swimming pool in Darmstadt banned women wearing bikinis because "entirely too much flesh is being shown for the good of the troops." The order applied to dependent wives of army officers, top noncoms, and army civilian employees, many of them native Germans who seemed to feel that a woman's bathing suit should be like a good short story: short enough to be interesting and just long enough to cover the subject.

A Special Services officer in Frankfurt told Noyes that the regulation was "only a whim" of the local commander and "no theaterwide order had been issued against the bikini."

Although his name wasn't mentioned, Richter was noticeably hurt by the story, which had been picked up by the wire services. It did not appear in *The Stars and Stripes*.

"That wasn't Richter's idea. Hell, he's never had an idea. That was Jan's doings," one *Stripes* veteran observed. Jan (or Janet) was Richter's wife and had been his boyhood sweetheart in Sheboygan, Wisconsin.

★ ★ ★

We continued to lose members of the staff but didn't consider it serious until Maurice R. Kirkwood, the general manager, announced that he and his family were returning to the States. Much of the credit for the financial stability and the success of *Stripes* was due to Kirkwood's five years of stewardship of the paper, first as fiscal director and since 1947 as general manager. The Kirkwoods returned to Indiana, and soon afterward he joined the American Fletcher National Bank in Indianapolis.

Kirkwood was replaced by Maj. Warren H. Scheffner, who during World War II was with a task force in the Pacific that later became the Americal Division. After his discharge he worked for a telephone company in Missouri and then was recalled to army duty in July 1951. It turned out that Scheffner had a good business head, but we knew that any army officer in that post wouldn't be with us long. He was relieved after two years and given another assignment in the Information and Education Division and, as we suspected, was replaced by a civilian.

★ ★ ★

The following year — February 16, 1953 — *Stripes* expanded its twelve pages to sixteen and welcomed a new editor in chief, Lt. Col. Arthur L. Jorgenson, who replaced Richter. A schoolteacher in civilian life, Jorgenson came to Europe with the 4th Infantry Division during the Korean buildup. He was to be with us only eighteen months.

Jorgenson reached *Stripes* about the same time the 280-millimeter guns, the so-called "atomic cannon," arrived in Europe to bolster the North Atlantic Treaty Organization's defenses. The new editor in chief soon learned that the army in Heidelberg operated on a different wavelength than the army in the States.

The issue was the thirty-five-ton gun's nickname. The Aberdeen Proving Ground, Md., called it an "atomic cannon" in its press releases. Both Daniel Z. Henkin, *Stripes* correspondent in Washington, and the wire services used the term.

Public Information Division in Heidelberg told Jorgenson that it planned to contact the Pentagon and ask that the nomenclature be changed. "There is an atom bomb and an atomic submarine, but there is no such thing as an atomic cannon. You can say that it is capable of firing atomic ammo but we prefer that *Stripes* just not use the words atom or atomic," Jorgenson was told.

Stripes obliged. It was just plain 280mm from then on, even when the 868th Field Artillery Battalion from Ft. Bragg, North Carolina, arrived in Bremerhaven with its big guns in tow — even when the troops had to test the back roads and bridges before moving and even when one overturned and was lost for two days when it lost radio contact.

Jorgenson was still there August 7, 1954, to press the button that started *Stripes*'s new $145,000 four-color letter press. His wife, Inez, broke a bottle of German champagne across its bow.

The press, built at nearby Frankenthal by Albert & Co., was a 185-ton "Super Albert 60," capable of turning out a thirty-two-page newspaper. It produced sixteen pages at the rate of 22,000 an hour, and printed twelve pages of color comics in one day; the old press took three days.

Fifteen months were required to build the press, but it was worth the long wait. Frank and Georg Hofricter, superintendent of the press room, were delighted with their new toy. The Jorgensons hosted a reception, and there was free beer all around.

The new Super Albert 60 was a wonder, the state of the art in that highly specialized field and by far the best *Stripes* had ever had. Presses, like linotype machines, were something that you requisitioned from someone else and you took what was available. This was ordered specially and paid for out of *Stripes*'s profits.

★ ★ ★

Presses were on the mind of Lt. Col. Egbert White, the *Stripes* boss in North Africa, when late in 1942 he ordered a pair of Miehles from the States. Typically, they arrived in Oran after the Americans had moved on to Sicily and Italy.

"I don't know what kind of presses they had, but a mobile unit was set up at Mostaganem in Algeria," remembered Victor J. Dallaire, a veteran of the *Stripes* edition at Strasbourg and later associate editor of *Printer's Ink*, a trade weekly.

The mobile unit consisted of a truck with a generator, another with a linotype and some hand type, and two other trucks, each mounting a press. "When the mobile unit reached Sicily, one of the presses was stolen, but the guys stole an equivalent press in return," Dallaire said.

John O'Kearney, a *Stripes* veteran and later with the Associated Press in London, was in charge of organizing the mobile unit in Italy but said it did not include the Miehles. "As far as I know they were still in crates in Oran. We had Italian equipment liberated from shops in Salerno and Naples. The equipment which I alternately prayed and cursed in 1943 was never even unpacked while there was any fighting still going on. *Stripes* turned the mobile unit over to VI Corps of the 5th Army."

What is known is that the unit functioned for a time with the 5th Army until the *Stripes* Naples edition drove them out of business. Then it moved to Anzio, where it printed a paper called the *Beachhead News*.

"It was a good paper with a circulation of about 30,000. I believe it went next to Corsica, then to France as the *VI Corps News* or some such name," Dallaire said.

"The information that the mobile unit was brought into southern France by *Stripes* personnel is faulty. It was already VI Corps property at the time of the August 15, 1944, invasion, having been handed over in Italy during the Anzio battle," O'Kearney recalled.

Both Dallaire and O'Kearney believe that mobile unit was loaned or turned over to the First French Army.

"The last I heard it was in Dijon," O'Kearney said.

★   ★   ★

Despite the Richter-Jorgenson command change and the rapid turnover of civilian personnel, sales of the newspaper, magazines, hard-cover and paperback books (especially comic books) were high. Additional air force personnel assigned to the United Kingdom, France, Spain, and North Africa opened up a new market for the Germany-based newspaper.

Adding readers in North Africa was a little like going home. *The Stars and Stripes* had been there before — Algiers, Oran, Casablanca. It also meant changing the label, or motto, at the top of the front page. *Stripes* had more labels than a traveling salesman's sample case and was about as peripatetic.

First, there was the World War I edition: "The Official Newspaper of the A.E.F." on one side of the top of Page 1, and "By and For the Soldier of the A.E.F." on the other.

In World War II the motto was "Weekly Newspaper of the U.S. Armed Forces in the British Isles." When the paper went daily a few weeks later, the words were changed.

After D-Day, *Stripes* began publishing in France and the motto read: "Daily Newspaper of the U.S. Armed Forces in the European Theater." When the war ended and EUCOM replaced USFET, which in turn had taken over ETO, the word "occupation" was substituted for "armed" on November 6, 1945.

The occupation of Germany was terminated in May 1955, and that word was retired and "armed" put back in the motto. "North Africa and the Middle East" were also added, and nearby were the words "Army, Navy, Air Force."

There was an attempt in 1952 to add the word "authorized," but nothing came of that until it made its appearance in the late 1960s. The motto today reads "Authorized Unofficial Publication of the U.S. Armed Forces."

★   ★   ★

The buildup of troops in Germany meant more readers for the daily *Stripes* and the twenty-two weekly unit publications in the command. It also meant more newsprint. The estimate at Heidelberg was that 1,500 tons would be needed for the fiscal year of 1951–52, of which 700 tons was for *Stripes*.

German newspaper publishers protested when *Stripes* requisitioned its 700 tons from German newsprint firms, but the protest was rejected by John J. McCloy, the high commissioner. HICOG sources countercharged that the German publishers were wasting newsprint, particularly because of the sensational picture magazines on the market in West Germany.

American army headquarters defended the need for newsprint, pointing out that newspapers were essential for morale purposes to keep troops informed of American objectives. *Stripes* paid from its own money; the weeklies were financed from army funds.

There was no objection initially from the German newsprint firms after the order was cleared through the British procurement office at Herford because it was assumed that payments would be in dollars. That was all the money *Stripes* had, so what was the worry?

The German Association of Paper Manufacturers (Treu-handstelle der Zellstoff und Papierindustrie) recommended that the *Stripes* order for 170 tons per month be placed with the Feldmuehle paper mill. Feldmuehle accepted the order, worked Saturdays so as not to interfere with its regular customers, but then objected when it discovered that the dollar payment was being made to the Bank Deutscher Laender, with the firm receiving deutsche marks in payment.

Fortunately, *Stripes* didn't have to depend fully on German sources. Newsprint from Sweden and Finland came on the market, but the chief supplier was United States mills, with shipment handled by the military sea transport to Bremerhaven and by rail to Darmstadt.

★   ★   ★

The newspaper's financial picture was sound, and although we had competition from the Army Times Publishing Company, which started a daily in England and later moved to Germany, we upped our pages again, this time on July 11, 1954, from sixteen to twenty-four pages and still sold for five cents. The *Feature Section,* which was launched in January 1950, was discontinued and its features were included in the new twenty-four-page paper.

Much thought was given to the feasibility of printing in the Paris area to better serve the air force readers in Western Europe and North Africa. Nothing was said about the possibility of a Russian invasion of Germany, but the thought was there.

I was appointed chairman of a committee to study the problem, which boiled down to whether we could afford a completely independent newspaper in Paris with its own staff or whether we would ship mats of the inside pages by rail the night before and transmit the news pages by the Teletype Setter System (TTS). Before we could make a judgment, it was decided to dispatch production manager Elmer Frank, along with Henry Epstein, district circulation manager in France, who spoke French, to Paris to survey possible printing sites.

Frank and Epstein surveyed ten plants in the Paris area, including the Imprimerie Richelieu on Rue Richelieu, which at one time printed the Continental edition of the *London Daily Mail;* the Imprimerie Parisienne Reunies on Faubourg Montmartre; Imprimerie Centrale du Croissant Societe Nationale on Rue Croissant; and the Imprimerie Chateaudun on Rue La Fayette, formerly the plant used to print mats of *The New York Times*.

I followed up with a visit to Orleans and Paris the following February and met with a number of generals, including our good friend Maj. Gen. Philip Gallagher. He now had another star since the days when he helped us get out of Pfungstadt and into the plant at Griesheim.

I also visited Camp Des Loges, the site of the new headquarters for EUCOM, and met with Col. Milton Rosen, Hq. Command CO, and an old friend and former commander of the Garmisch post and later the Darmstadt subpost. He told me there was plenty of land upon which to build but that the U.S. Army would not be able to use its funds to put up buildings needed for a newspaper facility. I also met with Lt. Col. B. F. Munster, in charge of property allocation, and he told me much the same. He suggested we try to obtain an unused factory or commercial-type building on the outskirts of Paris.

The proposal to move to the Paris area was a good idea, but the situation solved itself. We were unable to obtain U.S. government funds to build on requisitioned land, the use of our own money was rejected by the welfare fund council and, anyway, Gen. Charles de Gaulle made things difficult for the Americans, who tired of the hassle, pulled up stakes in France, and moved out of the country completely — back to Germany and to Brussels, Belgium.

Instead of two separate printing plants, it was back to square one: the newspaper would continue publishing at Griesheim no matter what the disposition of troops. To hell with the Russians. We gave up plans to move to the Paris area or to any other site, for that matter.

At the invitation of U.S. Navy officials in London, who had a Sixth Fleet full of potential readers in the Mediterranean, we produced the prototype of a weekly newspaper for their use. The Sixth Fleet edition, with ample blue color on the cover, contained news, features, comics, and pictures lifted from the daily paper. It was not a capsule of news written in *Time* and *Newsweek* style; rather, it was a pickup of type and engravings from the daily newspaper.

The twelve-page weekly plus another twelve pages of color comics were transported to Naples by truck — a two-day trip — and then transferred to the navy to be dispatched to the ships at sea. The paper was especially for the men aboard moving ships; shore-based personnel were expected to buy the daily *Stripes*.

The top brass in London liked the prototype, or so said Capt. W. M. Chambliss, senior public information officer of the U.S. Naval Forces in Europe. Chief journalist mate John Wright was assigned to the staff of *Stripes* to be its editor, and Vice Adm. Thomas S. Combs of the Sixth Fleet gave his approval.

It turned out that the sailors liked the weekly and the comics, but the skippers of the ships were not enthusiastic. Instead of ordering several thousand of each issue they settled for several hundred or in some cases several dozen.

"The old man doesn't want a bunch of papers cluttering up his ship. It's OK to have a few in the wardrooms but he won't go for the amount you fellows are talking about," a lieutenant commander told Wright.

That attitude torpedoed the weekly Sixth Fleet edition, and it died a year later. We held on as long as possible because the air force expressed interest in a weekly for its personnel stationed at Tripoli and in Dharan. M/Sgt. Larry Manning was assigned to *Stripes* to be editor of the air force edition, and for a few short months *The Stars and Stripes* included all three services on its roster. But the figures weren't there; the seagoing weekly, which began March 14, 1955, and the fly boy special, born June 6, 1955, both crashed March 26, 1956.

★   ★   ★

The experimental weeklies out of the way, all hands heaved to produce a good daily newspaper. The proposed move to start another edition in Paris was now a part of history. Thoughts were given to make the plant at Griesheim more functional and the living more pleasant for its staff.

Plans were drawn for the removal of the Press Club from the top floor of the main building to a renovated structure near the swimming pool. Plans were also in the works for a new building for dependent housing. It was to be located just off the access road to headquarters — the idea being that if you are going to live and work in Germany you might just as well be comfortable. And to hell with the Russians.

9

Trouble

Once upon a time in a castle known as Kronberg, nestled in the woods at the edge of the Taunus Mountains west of Frankfurt am Main, a captain in the Women's Army Corps of the American occupation forces heard a rumor that there was buried treasure in the basement. She asked an army corporal to check it out and, being a good soldier, he did as he was told.

With the help of a German handyman, the pair searched and searched until they located a box under a stone as well as a large quantity of vintage wine. When the corporal brought the captain to the little room in the basement, she ordered the contents of the box carried to her bedroom on an upper floor of the castle, which was being used that year of 1945 as an officers' club. The corporal and the handyman made the transfer from the lead-lined box up the back stairs to the captain's bedroom.

Dismissing the pair and cautioning them not to speak of the matter, the WAC captain settled down to take inventory. She didn't know it, but what she had spread out on her bed was part of a cache of $1.5 million in jewels belonging to the Countess von Hesse, granddaughter of Queen Victoria and the elder sister of Kaiser Wilhelm.

The captain, the mess officer, and one of a number of Wacs

who operated the officers' club in the eighty-room castle, hurried downstairs to the bar to see if her boyfriend, a full colonel on the USFET G-1 staff, was there. He was, and when he finished his drink, she invited him to her room to show him the hoard — emeralds, diamonds, sapphires, and amethysts. Two heads are better than one, she reasoned, but the colonel thought that in this case three might be even wiser, so the next day he involved an army major, his assistant in the personnel division.

When the three of them had their day in court — it was a year before the final conviction — it was brought out that the major had "fenced" an estimated $50,000 of the loot in Belfast, Northern Ireland. It was also determined that the U.S. mail had been used to transport some of the valuables to the States.

It was not only jewelry that had been taken. There were books, including a Bible once owned and inscribed by Queen Victoria, as well as letters written by her between 1891 and 1893. Other items included bracelets, wristwatches, binoculars, crucifixes, silver cups, and a gold table service.

The captain, who married the colonel shortly after the jewels were discovered (some hinted that this was done so they wouldn't have to testify against each other), managed to get some of the treasure to her relatives in Wisconsin. When agents of the War Department called on the captain's kinfolk, they found gold-plated knives and forks in kitchen drawers mixed up with the everyday stainless steel.

Gold melted out of jewel settings was discovered in a West Virginia backyard, and a box of the loot was found in a locker at the Illinois Central Railroad station in Chicago. A two-star general's name came into the case when it was testified he had taken some of the silver plates and made gifts of them to a Wac officer.

★   ★   ★

Who were the characters in this dime-novel plot? First, there was Wac captain Kathleen B. Nash, thirty-four, of Hudson, Wisconsin. A native of Prescott, Arizona, she joined the Women's Army Auxiliary Corps in July 1942. She was arrested June 3, 1946, in Chicago while on her honeymoon and was given a lie-detector test, which the army said she failed. The charges against her were two counts of larceny, embezzlement, conspiracy, and being AWOL. She was sentenced October 1 to five years at hard labor, dismissal from the service, and total forfeiture of pay.

Her boyfriend and later husband was Col. Jack W. Durant, thirty-six, of Falls Church, Virginia, who was arrested also in Chicago. He had been a lawyer for the Department of the Interior in Washington, D.C., when he was called to active duty in August 1942 as a captain in the Army Air Force. His trial started December 11, 1946, and ended May 1 the following year when an eight-man army court found him guilty of larceny, forgery, and violation of U.S. customs. He was given fifteen years at hard labor, dismissed from the service, and all pay due him was ordered forfeited. He was acquitted of four charges in a trial that ended eleven months after his arrest.

The major was David F. Watson, thirty-six, of Burlingame, California. Arrested June 7 at Frankfurt, where he was assigned to U.S. Forces, European Theater, personnel division, he was charged with larceny, conspiracy, four charges of receiving stolen goods, and one of selling the goods. On November 1, 1946, he received three years at hard labor, dismissal, and forfeiture of pay.

The corporal who, with the German handyman, found the loot was Roy C. Carlton, of Kilgore, Texas. He got off scot-free. He told army investigators he was only following orders and did not at any time see the contents of the packages taken November 6, 1945, from the cache in the basement. He did state that he and the handyman knocked off a bottle or two of Henkell's sekt vintage 1904, which, it turned out, was a good year.

The handyman was Ludwig Weiss, fifty-four, a chauffeur for twenty-one years for the Countess von Hesse. He denied he purposely revealed the family's secret, despite a remark Capt. Nash-Durant made upon her arrest that Weiss mentioned the hiding place of the jewels to Carlton because he hated the sons of the countess.

"There must be some mistake. Both of the princes are very good boys," he said, speaking of Princes Philipp and Wolfgang, both of whom at that time were held in an American internment camp near Darmstadt, where they were confined for their activities with the Nazi Party. Philipp had been governor of Hesse, an appointment made by Adolf Hitler, who was a friend of the Hesse family. He explained his involvement:

> Carlton wanted to look through the cellar. I don't know what he really was looking for, and he took me along with him.

After we found the box, I never did see the jewels. They were all in parcels.

We went through a tunnel and tapped a few stones. Then we came to a little room and on the right side I noticed what looked like new cement but I did not want him to find anything, so I tapped on the left side.

Carlton had a flashlight and he said, "nothing there," pointing to the right side. I tapped, and there was a hollow sound. I lifted it, and we found the box. It was not a very big stone, but it was hard to lift.

Carlton then called Capt. Nash after the lid was pried from the box, and only assorted parcels were disclosed. She came into the room, looked at the box and said, "Bring it all to my room."

And the countess and her family? Did she get her jewels back? Was the castle ever returned to her?

Princess Margareta, the seventy-four-year-old Countess von Hesse, did get her jewels back, but she insisted that there were more of them valued at from $500,000 to $750,000 still missing. Her daughter, Princess Sophia of Greece, and her two sons, Philipp and Wolfgang, were with her at the trial. The sons had been given a pass from the internment camp, so they could assist their mother.

Princess Margareta lived in a cottage near the castle, which was formerly used by the estate manager. In all the time she resided there she never once set foot in the castle, which the family called Schloss Friedrichof, a relic of the once mighty Hohenzollern family.

"They don't want me," she said.

★　　★　　★

In the Kronberg case the key word was greed, but, unlike the Durants and Watson, crown jewels just weren't that readily available to the rest of the occupation forces and their dependents. What was in surplus were large supplies of low-priced coffee, cigarettes, and gasoline. Those who wished to engage in black-marketing had only to make their intentions known.

The Germans were able to buy coffee in their stores for about $4 a pound, of which $3 was tax. As a result, smuggled coffee from nearby Belgium and Holland, plus black markets of coffee sold to American military personnel, were lucrative temptations.

The American part in this scandalous operation revolved around the post exchanges and commissaries. The PXs had been in operation all during the war, but the commissaries proliferated when the dependents started arriving in mid-1946. Coffee had always been rationed in the American stores, but at first the ration was generous — seven pounds per month for each adult. This figured out to fourteen pounds per month for the military or U.S. civilian employee and his wife.

In the early 1950s, married couples were still permitted to buy that amount, but single GIs were cut to two pounds per month. A German government official came up with the figure that if the Americans drank all the coffee they imported, it would amount to twenty-five cups each person per day.

The official said that, although the Americans sometimes used the coffee for gifts to German friends and families, much of it entered the black market. He had a point: while the commissary price was only ninety-five cents per pound, the German retail price was more than four times that.

A German newspaper urged its government to reduce the huge tax on coffee and suggested that the Americans raise the price of their products and, presto, the black market would be eliminated.

This was all before Katherine G. Reed, of Mount Clements, Michigan, was arrested in 1952 and charged with seventeen counts of black-marketing in coffee, cigarettes, gasoline, military scrip, and greenbacks. The German press had a field day, and the American wire services filed thousands of words daily to newspapers back in the States. But the managing editor and the news editors of *The Stars and Stripes* had a mild case of red faces and pulled punches. Why? The reason was that Mrs. Reed's husband was a full colonel in the U.S. Air Force. Not only did he have silver eagles sitting on both shoulders, he was a former commanding officer of the Wiesbaden Military Post. When his wife embarrassed him by getting arrested, he was shifted to another job, that of special assistant to the chief of staff of 12th Air Force.

We received no guidance or complaints from the army about the Reed story; after all, it had nothing to do with that service. To its credit, the air force didn't complain, although it could not have been pleased. Our news accounts were much shorter than the versions sent to the States by the wire services and, other than the one reporting the verdict, appeared on inside pages.

Mrs. Reed, a buxom, forty-four-year-old, dark-haired social leader of Wiesbaden, pleaded not guilty to the charges, which included selling a military gasoline ration book for 140 marks

($33.32); exchanging $1,565 for German currency or military scrip; illegally acquiring 3,900 marks and $2,500 scrip; and illegally dispensing military coupons for 1,800 gallons of gasoline.

A German testified that he bought several cans of coffee at Mrs. Reed's home for 9.5 marks or $2.26 per can. A German restaurant owner testified he had driven a Reed servant and an unidentified man to the Reed home and that afterward the third man "counted about $200 in greenbacks." The restaurateur submitted a photo taken of the transaction, which showed a woman who bore a likeness to Mrs. Reed.

Another German said he bought 200 pounds of coffee from Mrs. Reed for about $2.50 a can. He said he also bought 500 to 600 gallons' worth of American gasoline coupons from her.

"I made plenty of money on the gasoline deal," he testified. He wasn't stretching the truth. Americans paid fifteen cents a gallon, while the Germans' gasoline cost seventy cents a gallon.

An air force finance officer told the court that the Reed family had drawn their full authorized allowance of $200 in greenbacks on several occasions. The defense contended that this money was for legitimate expenses on trips outside Germany.

Toward the end of the trial, the colonel, of Fairfield, Iowa, became irritated when a wire service photographer attempted to take a picture of his wife, and he lunged for the camera.

"Go on, break it — break the camera," his wife pleaded. As the flashbulb flared, Mrs. Reed dashed head down across the courtroom and took her seat. Her lawyer ordered the photographer outside, and said he would call the police.

The Reeds made a formal protest against "molestation" to Judge DeWitte White, who replied that the court was not in session at the time and that such incidents were between them and the photographer.

The picture appeared in stateside newspapers the next day. *Stripes* did not use the photo.

Finally, on July 30, 1952, with her husband and twenty-year-old daughter, Janet, sitting in the courtroom, Mrs. Reed got the bad news. She was found guilty of five of the seventeen charges of dealing in currency, coffee, and gasoline coupons and fined a whopping $3,982. She broke into tears when the judge gave her thirty days to pay the fine or go to jail.

★   ★   ★

The Reed case got the headlines, but there were others —
other dependents too — in the news as the result of illegally selling
coffee, gasoline, and other items. The first wives to get in trouble
were two American women in August 1947, a year and a few weeks
after the first dependent ship landed at Bremerhaven. They were
the spouses of a first lieutenant and a U.S. civilian employee, and
both lived at Russelsheim. The officer's wife was fined $75 after
being found guilty of obtaining silver and crystal tableware in a
trade for three pounds of coffee, one can of chocolate syrup, five
pounds of flour, and one carton of cigarettes. The civilian's wife
was found guilty of having bartered five pounds of coffee and five
pounds of sugar for a crystal bowl, a vinegar cruet, and a vase. She
was also convicted of selling dollars for a total of 4,100 marks
(about $205) and fined $200.

It wasn't just military wives who got involved in the black
market. In Munich, M/Sgt. Thomas H. Carmichael was sentenced
to a year of hard labor and a dishonorable discharge from the army
for assisting in the theft and sale of 350 pounds of coffee.

Cpl. Arthur Mahoney converted a surplus ambulance that he
had acquired into a homemade 750-gallon tank truck. Bribing German clerks in the vehicle registration office to issue him extra EES
(European Exchange Service) gasoline ration coupons, and bribing
gasoline station attendants to accept them, Mahoney did a neat
business on the black market until the army caught him and gave
him a year at hard labor and a bad-conduct discharge.

German frontier customs agents stepped up their campaign
and fired shots when smugglers failed to halt. Hans Schiffer,
twenty, a German, was shot and killed on the border near Aachen.
He was smuggling six pounds of coffee — less than a month's ration
for a married American officer.

★　　★　　★

The examples cited weren't the only ones; they just happened
to get caught. Most of the dependents learned from their husbands,
who had been exposed to the cigarette phenomenon, which began
when the shooting stopped. If he was reluctant to tell her, then her
maid or cook did. She soon discovered that a can of coffee, a carton
of cigarettes, or even a tin of Spam could magically turn into a piece
of jewelry, a Leica camera, or a Meissen china figurine.

When General Clay's wife arrived on the first shipload of dependents in June 1946, it didn't take her long to see that black-mar-

keting was rampant in Berlin. She suggested to her husband that a legal barter market be set up where the Americans could acquire the goods they sought and the Germans might obtain what they and their families needed to survive.

The general authorized the barter mart plan, which the Germans called "tausch ring." It was located at 51 Leichhardstrasse in West Berlin and opened August 9 under the sponsorship of the Office of Military Government, United States (OMGUS), post exchange.

Americans could bring in anything that had not been purchased in the PX or the quartermaster stores, and what they brought was assigned trading points. A team of German appraisers judged the value of the goods provided by their people and it too was assigned points. A jar of coffee was allotted 16 points, a carton of cigarettes 44, a can of beans nine, while a Zeiss-Ikon camera with a 4.5 lens went for 220 barter points.

The store took ten percent of the original price in order to pay for its operation. Two months later, another store opened at 50 Kaiserstrasse in Frankfurt. It too assessed points, slightly higher than in Berlin, and also charged ten percent to pay for overhead.

The other three powers in Berlin didn't bother with such a store. "That's because the Russians don't want it, the French don't need it, and the British are above the idea," one barter official said.

This system continued for two years and worked out well for both the Americans and the Germans. It wasn't too difficult to ask Aunt Minnie in Kansas to send over a carton of coffee or some of her kids' hand-me-downs, and Uncle Ralph wasn't too unhappy with the Rolleiflex camera he got out of the deal.

When it began to get out of hand — someone said the wives of two high-ranking officers in the Frankfurt area had cornered the market on Meissen china — General Clay stepped in and ordered the Berlin and Frankfurt barter markets closed.

This action freed the wives to seek diversion in bridge, babies, and sleeping pills, not necessarily all three or in that order. The blight of any occupation army is boredom, and for dependents it was double in spades. Some of the marriages began to fall apart, as Betty Luros Knorr wrote in the *New York Daily News* on February 26, 1950: "Just how many marriages hit the rocks during those early adjustment days when the occupational male greeted his newly arrived wife by the wrong first name or when his former German girlfriend, now a maid or cook in the house, forgot her new role, has never been ascertained. At least one husband committed suicide at the news that his legal spouse was coming over."

Seven weeks after she arrived in Berlin, an American wife of a civilian employee working for OMGUS served breakfast to her two small children, sent one off to kindergarten, put the other in the playpen, and killed herself with her husband's handgun.

The young American wives had too much time on their hands. They could travel only when their husbands had a pass or furlough time, housework didn't tie them down because most had two or three maids to do the work. Many played bridge; a lot of them drank to excess.

Most of the older American wives got along well and involved themselves in the German communities in which they lived, helping out at hospitals and orphanages and making lasting friendships with their German counterparts. But some young Americans were unable to cope. One of these was Wilma Ybarbo. Another was Yvette Madsen. Still another was Martha Joan Wage.

★　　★　　★

The first American dependent to stand trial for murder was Mrs. Wilma E. "Billie" Ybarbo, twenty-three, of Malden, Massachusetts. She was accused of the shooting death of her husband, Sgt. John Ybarbo, a U.S. constabulary trooper, in September 1948. The sergeant, of Goliad, Texas, was awarded the Silver Star for bravery during World War II.

Wilma received a sentence of twenty years in prison December 28 that same year, but it was reduced to five years by a military court the following March. General Clay, the theater commander, freed her April 15 after she had been detained 107 days, saying "the remorse of her conscience will prove punishment enough." He added that he did not wish to separate her from her six-year-old son, Jimmie.

Wilma's trial, which was held at Marburg, marked the first time an American woman was tried for a capital offense under occupation law. Americans in Germany who were not members of the military were subject to both German laws and Military Government ordinances.

On the witness stand, Wilma said she killed her husband in fear for her life and not because of jealousy. "I thought he would kill me," she said. Her lawyer added, "She did what any decent New England woman would have done."

General Clay, in announcing her release, said, "Mrs. Ybarbo lived in an unnatural environment, drunken parties and a general looseness of life, under which normal behavior could not be expected."

Two days later, Wilma arrived in New Bedford, Massachusetts, and was greeted by her mother, Mrs. Eunice Bailey, and her son.

When Yvette Madsen, an attractive twenty-two-year-old brunette, arrived in Germany to join Andy, her air force husband, she brought along their infant son, Dana, and her Brooklyn accent. Dana was no problem, nor was his sister, Nancy, born a year later, but it was the accent that triggered a fight at a party early October 19, 1949, that ended with the death of her husband, 1st/Lt. Andrew E. Madsen, thirty-two, of Oakland, California.

The wife of a colonel objected to Yvette's Brooklynese chatter at a party in a private home, called her a loud, vulgar person, and then slapped her face.

"Andy, are you going to sit there and let this woman insult me like that?" she said to her husband, who tried feebly to pass the incident off as a joke. With that, Yvette flounced out of the house and drove the family Buick back to their Buschlag home. Buschlag is just across the autobahn from the Rhine-Main Air Base, where the lieutenant was operations officer for the 1629th Air Base Squadron, MATS (Military Air Transport Service).

Madsen, driven home by a friend, arrived at their quarters thirty minutes later. When he entered the hallway into the living room at ten minutes to 3:00 A.M., Yvette shot him through the heart with one bullet from a .45-caliber pistol. He slumped on the floor in front of the sofa.

Yvette Madsen was found guilty March 18, 1950, of murder in the first degree and sentenced to fifteen years in prison. She had been tried by a three-man panel of American judges under Section 211 of the German penal code, which allowed the death penalty for "lustful murder." However, the then new federal government of Germany had just abolished the supreme penalty, so the maximum was life in prison.

Yvette was flown to Andrews Field, Maryland, and then driven to the Federal Prison for Women at Alderson, West Virginia.

Shy little blonde Martha Joan Wage, a nineteen-year-old dependent from Red Wing, Minnesota, shot and killed her air force husband because he brought a German *fraulein* into their quarters at Furstenfeldbruck.

"Look what I brought home," S/Sgt. Dan P. Wage said as he opened the front door on July 26, 1952, and introduced Elizabeth Bartl, twenty-six, a shapely seamstress and unwed mother of two.

While the Bartl woman waited in the front room, Martha Joan followed her twenty-six-year-old husband into their bedroom and demanded, "Where did you go after work?"

"That's none of your business," he replied. Then Mrs. Wage went into the other bedroom and returned with his carbine, pointed it at him and said, "Get that girl out of the house."

"If you're going to shoot, you better make it good," he said, and laughed when she pulled the trigger and the gun didn't go off. He laughed again when the same thing happened a second time. Then he grabbed the carbine away from her, unloaded the clip, and hit her on the side of the head with the butt of the gun.

Reeling back from the blow, she returned to the bedroom, where their two baby daughters were sleeping, found another clip, pushed it into the gun and pulled the trigger, but it failed to go off. She emptied out two shells and pulled once more. The bullet ripped through the sergeant's body and he cried out, "Oh God, no" and slumped on the bed, dead with a .30-caliber bullet through the main artery from the heart.

Mrs. Wage was initially charged with first-degree murder. The charge was later reduced to voluntary manslaughter because under German law a jealous killing is not murder. She was found guilty October 9, 1952, and was sentenced to serve two years and six months in the Women's Federal Penitentiary at Alderson, West Virginia.

★ ★ ★

Stripes printed these stories about dependents in trouble, but not in great detail. The wire services took care of that.

10

Berlin

In the spring of 1948, we learned of trouble in the quadripartite city of Berlin. It shortly developed into a blockbuster story that was to be on Page 1 for much of the next ten months. Little did we realize that it would turn into a blockade by the Russians and that the 2.5 million Berliners would have to be sustained by an Allied airlift which at first was called "Operation Vittles."

My first inkling of trouble came on March 30, when John Livingood, the assistant managing editor, handed me a story from Joseph B. Fleming, bureau chief in Berlin.

"Fleming has a hot story about the Rooskies trying to put the squeeze on us in Berlin. I just talked to him and he said it looks like they mean business. His translators picked up the piece from a Kraut newspaper. I think we ought to go Page One."

I read Joe's story, which quoted Lt. Gen. G. S. Lukianchenko, Soviet military government's chief of staff, as saying that to maintain "the necessary control and discipline" over traffic going through the Russian Zone, new measures would have to be taken.

"I would like to add," the general said, "that the agricultural work as well as the tasks confronting us in reconstruction and developing peacetime economy in the Soviet Zone made an increased utilization of transportation necessary. That has to be thought of in

169

considering the main road, which up to now served as a link between Berlin and the west."

Lukianchenko's statement, which was printed in the Russian-licensed *Vorwaerts*, did not say what measures the Russians would adopt, nor did he explain the connections between an eastern zone transportation shortage and the road to Berlin. The general said Russia would continue to see that provisions for the people of Berlin and the people of the western sections were shipped in, but he said this would be "in a regular manner and with the necessary control."

Our headline was RUSS MAY CUT BERLIN ROUTES. Cut the routes they did. The next day, April 1, the banner and readout on Fleming's story read: RUSS SIFT BERLIN TRAVEL; ORDER TRAINS, CARS SEARCHED.

It was no April Fool's joke. Russia told the Western Allies it was assuming jurisdiction over all passenger and freight traffic between Berlin and West Germany. In separate notes delivered to American, British, and French military governments, the Soviet military administration in effect took upon itself the right to pass on all persons entering or leaving Berlin.

This hardline approach was the aftermath of the Russian walkout of the Allied Control Council eleven days earlier. The council had the task of governing Germany under an agreement reached in London between the Russian, British, and American governments. Gen. Lucius D. Clay's office issued a statement which said, "We have advised the Russians that we are prepared for train commanders to give proper documentation, but we cannot permit entry into our trains as a new procedure."

The crack night express from Frankfurt, *The Berliner,* left on schedule but was stopped at the border just east of Helmstadt. The Russians demanded to be allowed aboard for the purpose of inspecting passports and other identification. When 1st/Lt. Angus Brewer, Berliner commander, refused, the Russians asked him to sign an "agreement" drawn up by the Soviet commandant, a Major Popov, in which all parties acknowledged the U.S. train commander did not allow "everyone on the American train to be checked inside the train by Soviet representatives." Brewer again refused and ordered the engineer to move back to Helmstadt.

The same thing happened to Capt. Raymond B. Bates, commander of the Berlin-bound Bremerhaven train. However, 1st/Lt.

John Asbury allowed the Russian commandant of the Marienborn Soviet checkpoint to board the Berlin-Bremerhaven train and inspect documents. Asbury's train was cleared in fifteen minutes and paused only briefly in Helmstadt before continuing on to Bremerhaven.

The British were quick to respond. Maj. Gen. N. C. D. Brownjoy, deputy military governor, told the Russians, "We do not recognize that Soviet authorities have a unilateral right to determine what persons or goods may enter or leave Berlin."

Previously, the Russians recognized the rights of Berlin's other occupation powers to ship goods freely in and out of Berlin on military trains. Allied travelers needed only army orders with Russian translations on trains. These could be presented by train commanders to Russian inspection, but Russian troops did not board trains.

In Washington, the army said Clay had full authority to act and to "take appropriate action."

The April 1 pronouncement made no mention of air travel to and from Berlin. The only restriction in force then was that Allied planes must travel over a designated air corridor.

To protect the sovereignty of military trains, the British and Americans canceled all traffic to and from Berlin. The French, who had only a few trains, permitted the Russians to inspect one and then canceled the rest. The April 2 headline alluded to the airlift, although it involved only two American airplanes — a C-47 and a C-54. The headline: BERLIN "ISLAND" FED BY AIR.

The two transports landed at Templehof airport in the American sector with 15,000 pounds of commissary food for the 11,000 Americans. The British put two C-47s, which they called Dakotas, in the air to make daily flights into Gatow in their sector.

Meanwhile, all was quiet on the 112-mile autobahn between Helmstadt and Berlin, according to Arthur Noyes, Frankfurt correspondent for *Stripes,* who made the drive without incident. He found the Russians willing to accept ordinary European Command (EUCOM) travel permits issued to correspondents, which had a section printed in Russian, at the two roadblocks on the way to Berlin. The Russians were "polite and efficient and there was no attempt to delay," Noyes said.

Four other correspondents had a different story to tell. Robert Haeger and Wellington Long of the United Press in Frankfurt ar-

rived at the Berlin end of the autobahn somewhat later, after seeing
only seven Russians along the way. At the Nowawes control point,
Haeger and Long reported they were greeted by five Russian captains who were busy interrogating Ed Morrow of the *New York
Times* and Marguerite Higgins of the *New York Herald-Tribune*, en
route to Frankfurt from Berlin. All four were taken to a nearby Russian headquarters for more questioning and then allowed to proceed. Noyes returned to Helmstadt the next day, again without incident.

Mildred Murphy, the other *Stripes* reporter in Berlin and the
daughter of Robert D. Murphy, Clay's political adviser, wrote that
American dependents and women workers for the military government agreed that there was no point in getting nervous about the
Russians' new travel restrictions. Some of the women told Mildred
that they thought the situation "has come to a head," while others
said things were bound to blow over. Despite the outward calm,
however, wives were in the commissaries buying extra butter,
flour, and sugar "just in case." Several married women in the PXs
and commissaries expressed anxiety over their children.

More than fifty percent of air force families put in requests to
return to the States before their sponsors could complete tours of
duty. U.S. Air Force, Europe (USAFE) officials said between 1,500
and 1,600 of the family units answered "yes" when asked if they
wanted to go home at government expense. *Stripes* reporter Russell
Jones said the same source added that the movement would consid-
erably lessen the load on the army and the air force in Europe.
More than thirty-five percent of U.S. personnel were engaged in
purely housekeeping duties, largely due to the presence of the dependents, he told Jones.

The air force plan was to fly the dependents home on the first
available planes, with those from the "isolated areas" such as Berlin and Vienna getting first priority. Other priorities would be
given on the basis of age and number of children, family emergen-
cies, or pregnancies. The International News Service, quoting
Jones's article, added that Clay told its reporter only seventy-two of
the 2,500 American dependents in Berlin had requested permission
to go home.

"I don't want anyone to feel he is being held here. I also told
my staff that nobody will be ordered out. Any American who is

nervous, we will be glad to send home entirely on a voluntary basis," the general said.

The feeling in Berlin was that as long as Marjorie Clay remained at her husband's side, then the wives of other personnel would do the same. Just the opposite view was held in the USAFE headquarters city of Wiesbaden and in the communities near Rhine-Main Air Base, or as one flyboy put it, "Let's get the women and children the hell out. When the balloon goes up we're going to be upstairs and we won't have time to wetnurse the families."

In Washington, the State Department asserted that the U.S. forces intended to remain in Berlin. A day later Secretary of the Army Kenneth C. Royall told a press conference that "Gen. Clay proposed to sit tight in Berlin. In this proposal he has the full support of the department and the government." Royall quoted Clay as telling him that evacuation would be "unthinkable." He said Clay told him the army would maintain itself in Berlin indefinitely.

Also in Washington, Secretary of Defense James V. Forrestal asked Congress to adopt universal military training and draft men from nineteen to twenty-six years of age for military service. Congress was busy too; it appropriated the $6 billion aid proposal designed to check communism across two continents.

Newspapers in New York agreed that the Western Allies communications to Berlin must be kept open despite the Russian squeeze. The *Herald-Tribune* said, "To admit that Western military trains are legitimately subject to inspection is to admit that we are in Berlin only on sufferance from the Kremlin." The *Times* said that the great powers "cannot possibly withdraw from the position they occupy by virtue of their common victory and in accordance with the obligations binding on them all . . . with a loss of face that would jeopardize and weaken their power and influence in Europe and throughout the world."

The *Daily News* put faith in Clay: "It seems to us that the only thing for American people to do is back Gen. Clay to the limit in any course he may see fit to take." The London press said the Western Allies must maintain their position in West Berlin. Capitulation to the Soviet Union, it warned, would be a serious defeat to democracy.

There was a story about sending an armored column, namely tanks, through the checkpoint at Helmstadt and into Berlin, but it was never written and of course didn't get into the paper. Fleming later informed us that Clay told a group of reporters, including himself, in an off-the-record briefing, that he favored such a show of strength, but that he was overruled by Washington.

★   ★   ★

Stripes came in for some kidding in this period of high tension. For some time we had been planning a series of three one-day trips to be called Picnic Tours. The announcement of the proposed feature was on Page 1, the same day the Russians said they were taking over one of our picnic routes. The wire services in Frankfurt hopped on our announcement with glee: the Russians were clamping down on the West and the response of the American forces' newspaper was to go on a picnic. In spite of that, the series started the following Saturday and continued for six weeks.

On that first day, Harvey Sanderson took readers on a trip from Frankfurt into the rolling hills of the Odenwald country via Darmstadt, along the placid Neckar River into Heidelberg, and then back to Frankfurt through Everbach, Michelstadt, and Dieburg. Win Fanning's tour started in Stuttgart and continued through Schwabisch Hall, Lagenburg, and Blaufelden to get to the age-old walled fortress town of Rotenburg on the Tauber River. Julia Edwards's trip out of Munich was to the dream castle of Herrenchiemsee, an island palace built by Ludwig II, the mad king of Bavaria.

All three reporters listed picnic sites, the location of European Exchange Service (EES) stations, as well as churches where visitors could stop and worship. The three tours were spread over two full pages complete with photos and maps. Later, the series was published in booklet form, and I saw to it that the wire services received complimentary copies.

Picnic Tours proved to be a boon for the EES. Its snack bars ran out of food and soft drinks that first day, and we were asked to provide them with advance schedules, so they could be certain of having plenty of supplies on hand. We were pleased to oblige.

★   ★   ★

USAFE increased its fleet of C-47s to seventeen on the second day and flew in twenty-seven tons of food for the American community. General Clay told reporters that the airlift was "good practice" for the air force. Meanwhile, the Russians eased up on their demands, stating that the Western Allies' freight traffic bound for Berlin could proceed normally, but offered no change in their insistence on checking passenger trains entering the Russian Zone en route to the Western sections of Berlin.

The next day 41 planes flew 100 tons of supplies from Frankfurt to Templehof, while 67 flights were flown out of Wiesbaden with 192 passengers and 285,000 pounds of freight. On the fourth day, April 4, the airlift ended. Thirty-eight cargo planes, each carrying two and a half tons, flew into Templehof. The total for that brief emergency period was 399 passengers, 535,802 pounds of cargo, and 90,870 pounds of mail. A pool of 76 battle-tired C-47s was available, and about half of them were kept in operation daily.

Although the planes halted airlift activity, the Russians kept up the pressure. The Americans and the British were asked to vacate their vehicle aid stations on the Berlin-Helmstadt autobahn. The United States agreed to close its Nahmitz outpost, thirty-five miles from Berlin. Great Britain shut down its station as well.

Two days after the flights stopped, a Russian pilot in a Yak fighter crashed into a British European Airways Viking inside the safety zone approaching Gatow, killing himself and fifteen aboard the transport. Witnesses said the fighter pilot buzzed the Viking from behind and, when it rose sharply, the wings of both planes were torn off. Two Americans were among the ten passengers on board the British plane, which carried four crewmen. Typically, the Russians blamed the British, saying that the Viking was hidden behind clouds. The British called the Russians' claim "untrue."

★   ★   ★

Things were fairly quiet the rest of April, all through May, and the first half of June. When the Allies announced on June 18 that currency reform for the Western sections of Berlin was being planned, the Russians promptly denounced it and refused to participate. In a matter of hours, the Russians revealed plans for their own currency reform.

Near midnight, June 23, the teletype in the Berlin Press Center began to chatter. Joe Fleming, in the bar for a nightcap, heard it and hurried over to the machine to read a bulletin from the Soviet-sponsored ADN news agency:

BERLIN, June 23 (ADN) — Transport Division of the Soviet Military Administration is compelled to halt all passenger and freight traffic to and from Berlin tomorrow at 0600 hours because of technical difficulties.

It was too late to call Pfungstadt, where *Stripes* was published. Joe went back to the bar to finish his drink.

On June 25 the Soviets dropped the other shoe. They served notice that Russia would not supply food to the Western section of Berlin. The next day, the American airlift was back in business on a twenty-four-hour basis, taking on the task of hauling supplies to its own staff and dependents as well as the 2.5 million Germans in besieged West Berlin. British RAF planes also resumed flights. Two days later, thirty-five C-54 Skymasters took off from air force bases in Hawaii, Alaska, and the Caribbean to fly to Frankfurt to join Operation Vittles.

The Skymasters, known on civilian airlines as DC-4s, began arriving on the last day of June, the first one touching down at 9:30 A.M. at Rhine-Main. It was loaded and, ten hours and six minutes later, took off for Berlin. Brig. Gen. Joseph E. Smith, the new commander of the airlift, was there to greet the crew. Smith, who had been commanding officer of the Wiesbaden Military Post, served as chief until July 28 when he was replaced by Maj. Gen. William H. Tunner. A veteran of the high-altitude operations over the Hump from India and Burma to China during World War II, Tunner knew how to move freight. He wasn't called "Willie the Whip" for nothing.

Shortly after Tunner's arrival, Operation Vittles was renamed the Air Lift Task Force and the Skymasters flew 339 missions for their first 2,000-ton day. When the British RAF brought in the Yorks, Hastings and Haltons, the name was changed to Combined Air Lift Task Force under Tunner's command.

In order to accommodate the increased air fleet, five airports in Western Germany were expanded and the three runways at Templehof and the two at Gatow in Berlin were improved. There was space for a landing strip in a field next to Tegel in the French sector, which had been used by the German army to train anti-tank divisions, and it was decided to build there. The French had no objection as long as the Americans would build it. Radio Berlin's towers at Tegel were deemed a hazard to landing, and the French commandant, Gen. Jean Ganeval, asked the German officials to remove them. They refused, saying the facility was under Soviet control. The general sent out demolition teams on December 16 and blew up the 400-foot obstructions. The Soviets were furious but did nothing.

Huge rock crushers were needed at Tegel. The machines were delivered to Rhine-Main, cut up into manageable pieces, and loaded on C-54s. Upon arrival in Berlin, they were welded back together and put to work along with 20,000 men and women of Berlin who labored three shifts a day for the going wage plus a hot meal. There was plenty of rubble for the runway's foundation, but tons of asphalt had to be flown in for the landing surface.

With the arrival of Tunner, the airlift became a Military Air Transport Service (MATS) function, although the general answered to Lt. Gen. Curtis S. LeMay, commander of USAFE. Under the table of organization, Tunner was not permitted to communicate directly with the commander of MATS in the States, although he was a MATS officer. The airlift was under USAFE, and all communications had to clear through its headquarters; being able to pick up a telephone to get something done immediately was denied Tunner.

★   ★   ★

In order to be near the Ruhr coal supplies, three squadrons of C-54s were shifted to Fassberg and Celle airfields in the British Zone. GI duffle bags were used to haul the coal. When it became necessary to water the coal down in order to control dust, the water added to the weight. This situation ended when, after about two dozen trips, the canvas bags were in shreds and had to be discarded. Hemp was then used, but was replaced by a five-ply paper container which proved best of all.

★   ★   ★

The air crackled with Big Easys and Little Easys and a lot of Big Willies and Little Willies. "Big Easy 22 Fulda," someone would blast out, and on another headset it was, "Little Willie 38 Fritzler."

The big and the little had to do with the plane's size. "Big" stood for the four-engine C-54, while "little" referred to the two-engine C-47. "Easy" meant eastbound, while "Willie" was westbound. The numeral was the transport's number in the block of planes hauling freight that day, and the town name indicated the position.

The day I flew to Berlin for a first-hand look, I sat in the back end of a C-54 loaded with flour — "Big Easy 54" — all the way to Templehof. I returned the next day in an empty "Big Willie 16."

The first crash occurred July 9, when the airlift was only two weeks old. A C-47 piled into a hill northeast of Wiesbaden, killing three persons. The first C-54 went down in a forest near Rhine-Main October 18 with three fatalities. There were eighteen crashes, causing the deaths of seventy-nine persons, thirty-one of them Americans. Most of the accidents were caused by the weather, particularly the dense fog. November and December were especially wet and foggy, and there was a period of eight days just before Christmas when the airlift faltered but did not shut down, thanks to radar.

Radar made landings possible under almost unbelievable weather conditions. Two systems were used: one to track the plane in the air corridor and as it left the twenty-mile-wide path to enter the approach pattern to the airport, and the other to pick up the transport in the approach pattern and bring it in to the runway. The first system was operated from the tower, the second from the ground. The latter, known as GCA (Ground Control Approach), was a U.S. Air Force favorite but was seldom used by commercial pilots. They preferred another system in which they remained in control, instead of having to take instructions from the ground. The success of GCA in Germany did much to change that view.

To provide experience, pilots en route to Germany were given four-engine flight training at Great Falls Air Lift Training School in Montana, where a duplicate of the air corridor and approach paths were set up with navigation aids exactly like those in Germany. That training paid great dividends.

★　　★　　★

1st/Lt. Gale S. Halvorsen of Garland, Utah, loved kids, and when he looked out and saw all those little faces looking up at him as he approached Templehof, it tugged at his heart and triggered an idea. The next day, while waiting to take off, he fastened a candy bar to a miniature parachute made from one of his clean handkerchiefs. When he reached Berlin and made the glide to the runway, he tossed the parachute out of the ten-inch flare opening behind the pilot's seat. The next day he dropped six more, and Operation Little Vittles was born.

Operation Little Vittles caught on, and more pilots joined in the fun. New handkerchiefs were collected from members of Halvorsen's 17th Troop Carrier Squadron, and supplies of the cloth and candy were dispatched from communities in the States. One large shipment was received just before Christmas from Mobile, Alabama, where Halvorsen had been stationed prior to his assignment in Germany. When Halvorsen was reassigned to the States, he estimated that he and the other pilots had dropped over 60,000 tons of candy for an average of 250 pounds daily. Capt. Laurence L. Casky took over for Halvorsen, and when he rotated he turned over the duty to Capt. Eugene T. Williams.

★ ★ ★

By December, the daily delivery to Berlin exceeded 4,500 tons. In January and February, 1949, it climbed to 5,500 tons. The supplies were requisitioned by the Bizonal Administration in Frankfurt, which coordinated the movement by ships, rail, and truck to the airports in the Western zones, and then the airlift to the three airports in Berlin and the final transfer to German authorities, who saw to it that the Berliners received the food and fuel.

The food came from all over — the United States, Great Britain, butter from Denmark, sugar from Cuba, and coffee from Brazil. West German towns and cities helped too; a special two-pfennig stamp was required in addition to the regular postage stamp, proceeds from the sale going to buy food for Berlin.

★ ★ ★

The Americans started out with two-engine C-47s, which were phased out when the four-engine C-54s arrived. A giant C-74 Globemaster flew nonstop from the States with twenty tons of flour, twice the normal C-54 load. A month later, three twin-engine C-82 Flying Boxcars arrived for duty. The navy participated too. In November the first three of twenty-four U.S. Navy C-54s landed in Germany.

The Yorks, Hastings and Haltons performed well for the RAF, but Sunderland flying boats operating out of the Elbe River near Hamburg got much of the publicity when they landed on the Havel River in Berlin where it widens into a lake in the British sector two miles south of Gatow. The British also had the services of a number of air charters for which they paid forty-five pounds per flying hour, a higher rate than commercial pilots were getting at the time.

★ ★ ★

There was no rest on holidays either. Operation Santa Claus, working out of Fassberg, delivered gifts for 10,000 children in Berlin. One squadron supplied 1,500 gifts on what it called Operation Sleigh Bells. On New Year's Eve, the control board at airlift headquarters showed a total of 100,000 flights. On Easter — dubbed the Easter Parade — the airlift set a new record of a flight every six and a half minutes, carrying 12,940 tons in 1,398 sorties. In Berlin there was a plane landing every three minutes at each of the airports every hour of the twenty-four-hour period.

My family and I lived in a house in a wooded area between Eberstadt and Darmstadt, which was right under the turn path of cargo planes taking off from Rhine-Main. From daylight to dusk, and all through the night, the big transports roared over our home every few minutes.

★　　★　　★

There were rumors galore in Berlin that April of 1949 that the Russians would lift the blockade and when Tass, the Soviet news agency, hinted April 25 that it might happen, *Stripes* started making plans to cover the big event. However, the planes still flew their missions, chalking up a record of 232,263.7 tons or an average of 7,845.5 tons daily for the month.

Then on May 4 the Big Four delegates meeting in Berlin announced the lifting of the blockade. It was the same day that a giant C-97, a Boeing Stratocruiser, landed at Templehof with the first ten-ton load of food. A week later, on May 11, Fleming reported that the autobahn and railroad blockade would be lifted at 12:10 A.M. May 12. It was all over but the flying.

★　　★　　★

The barrier at the Allies checkpoint just outside the U.S. sector in Berlin was raised by Cpl. Hector Cluff of the 3rd Battalion, 16th Infantry Regiment, and a jeep driven by Pfc Horace Scites, also of the 16th, drove through. He was followed by a second jeep containing 1st/Lt. William Frost, and the two led a procession of civilian cars onto the long-forbidden autobahn leading to Helmstadt. A bright full moon shown down while overhead the Skymasters continued back and forth to Berlin and did so until the last day of September, building up stockpiles of food and fuel.

On the first birthday of the airlift, June 27, the fleet hauled 8,944 tons of freight in 992 flights, which was 8,864 tons better than the eighty tons flown the year before in thirty-two of the small C-47s.

Mayor Ernst Reuter said it best at ceremonies marking the anniversary: "The names of the pilots and crewmen who lost their lives for us will never be forgotten in this city. This day concludes a historic year."

Col. John E. Barr, Templehof commander, answered, "As

long as we are needed here, the U.S. Air Force will never abandon you."

As the stockpiles grew, the airlift began to cut back. The British withdrew their civilian fleet August 16 and the RAF pulled out September 23. Capt. Perry Immell flew a load of coal on Flight 276,926 into Berlin on Sunday, September 30, for the Americans' final sortie. The airlift to the no-longer besieged city was over.

The U.S. Air Force Blue Book, Vol. II of 1960, estimated that the U.S. and British governments between them spent about $200 million, but as General Clay pointed out at the time, "There is no expenditure currently being made for training and for national defense that, dollar for dollar, gives a better return."

11

Staff

The Stars and Stripes was GI from its 1942 beginning in London. Officers held the key administrative posts; a handful of them were editorial types but mostly it was an enlisted man operation. British civilians played an active role on that first edition, as did Frenchmen later on the Continent, Belgians in Liege, and Italians on the various Mediterranean papers.

Without Jimmy Frost, the *London Times* composing room foreman, and Bill Jolley, who made up Page 1, as well as a number of others, the paper just wouldn't have come out. Without Alf and Gertie Storey, proprietors of the Lamb and Lark pub and unofficial members of the *Stripes* staff, the whole effort wouldn't have been worth it. Staffers had such a high regard for the Storeys they gave them their mild and bitter trade as well as a postal box in the newsroom. Storey's dog, Deacon, also had a box which just happened to be next to the colonel's. Of course, the mail boxes were unused, but that was the way the staff felt about the Storeys.

Madame Renee Brasier, a spunky little red-haired French woman who was business manager and member of the board of directors of the *Herald-Tribune*, had the building ready for the Yanks when Paris was liberated. She had kept the Germans from using the facilities by telling them that it had been requisitioned by the

Vichy Ministry of Agriculture. When the Americans arrived, she summoned former employees, who had the linotype machines and the press dusted off, oiled, and running in two days. Using her own money, she ordered supplies of metal needed to fuel the linotypes.

Richard Beecher (pronounced Bee-shay), the composing room foreman and an Englishman who had hid out in the Paris suburbs during the German occupation, was glad to see the Americans. Not only might it mean steady employment, but also it was a chance to get an occasional can of evaporated milk to quiet his pains caused by lead poisoning. When I could I filched a can of Borden's from the tables at Chez Mercier, the army mess across the Champs Élysées.

George Barriac's fluent English and business training in school landed him the position of chief of transportation in September 1944. His mission was to set up a program to train 300 Frenchmen to drive U.S. Army jeeps and six-by-sixes — no easy task. After the war he wound up in Pfungstadt, where he worked in the circulation department.

Fernand Martinez, who also spoke English, was the chief mechanic. He set up and operated repair teams at various points in the advanced circulation areas. After the war, Barriac, Martinez, and Mme. Brasier were presented the U.S. Medal of Freedom by Col. Otis McCormick, chief of the Information and Education Division, at a ceremony in Frankfurt.

Maurice de Thier, publisher of *La Meuse*, and Jacques Heyligens, who was on his staff, made our life easier on the Liege edition, as did Joseph Montfort, the copy boy, and other Belgians, including Roget, Armand, and Raymond, whose last names I never knew.

Later along came Julius Peter Katz, whose mother was Czech and his father a German Jew. Because he was an embarrassment to his stepfather, Peter spent much of the war hiding out in Berlin. He was bright and articulate in several languages, and I recall him spending spare moments on the cable clerk's desk studying Greek.

In the early days of the Nice edition (1944) pretty Jacqueline Cauvin, nineteen, was the typist and secretary. Jackie was a great help to the three GIs who put out the paper with two portable typewriters, no teletype machine, and only a tired old radio which sometimes managed to get BBC.

George Serramoglia, the copy boy at Nice, kept the out-baskets clear and the desk supplied with refreshments from the cafe on the ground floor. Pretty secretaries Nina and Cilly decorated the business office and saw to it that the circulation records were up-to-date.

British women played key roles too. Jean Baird was the cartographer at Paris, and her daily situation map of the fighting by the 1st, 3rd, 7th, and 9th armies was a front-page fixture. After the war she spent some time with us at Nice and livened our pages with sketches of GIs relaxing in the sun.

Ella M. Fisher, whom everyone called Molly, started in the subscription department of the London edition in January 1943 and later was chief of personnel at Pfungstadt. She and Willy Benoit were also awarded the Medal of Freedom by Colonel Mc-Cormick.

★   ★   ★

Joan Liddle was English and proud of it. I remember a dinner at the Chateau Meaux in Pfungstadt to celebrate Princess Elizabeth's wedding to Philip at which Joan and the other Britishers donned formal attire and toasted the royal couple and future queen.

After consuming much champagne, they let their hair down and sang a number of songs, including several bawdy verses of "Roll Me Over." One or two of the verses Joan contributed were her own, since writing poetry was her hobby. When she wasn't doing secretarial work in my office, she wrote for *Weekend* magazine and other publications.

Here is one of her poems that I liked best.

THE ENGLISH

The English are a chilly race
They live in chilly houses
They work in chilly offices
(The typists wear warm blouses)
They travel home on chilly trains
And for their evening's cheer
Walk chilly streets to chilly pubs
And sit and drink warm beer.

Joan married Sam Moyers, a civilian employee of Army Ordnance at Heidelberg, and they and his two sons left for the States. They settled in Huntsville, Alabama, where he worked at the Redstone Arsenal.

★   ★   ★

When Monica Thornberry entered a room she did so behind a foot-long silver cigarette holder. A parson's daughter, she arrived in Germany following a brief assignment as secretary to the director of the GI University at Biarritz, France. After a few weeks in the Information and Education Division office at Hochst, she was sent to Berlin to set up an office and billets for *Stripes* reporters Joe Fleming, Art Noyes, and Marie Anne Greenough.

Although Fleming and Noyes preferred their own quarters, the brass wanted the three of them in one place, so they would be more accessible. Monica was up to the task but had a harder time trying to keep track of the jeeps in the motor pool, where young GI drivers were in the habit of joy-riding after hours with their *frauleins*.

Late one night she received a phone call from Noyes to come get him out of jail. A poker game he was in had been raided by military police, and the *Stripes* expense account funds had been confiscated, he told her. A colonel whom she knew sprung Noyes, who then sheepishly admitted that it was his gambling earnings and not the expense money that had been taken. Monica was able to get that back too.

A short time later, she was transferred to Pfungstadt, where she shared an apartment with Joyce Harriott, also a British secretary, who worked for Lt. Col. William M. Summers, editor in chief. Monica was assigned as secretary to the chief of distribution, a position she held until her marriage in November 1950 to slotman Vincent Halloran. Halloran died in 1979 at San Francisco, where he was employed as an editorial writer for the *Examiner*. Monica lives in San Francisco; Joyce Harriott resides in Kent, England.

★   ★   ★

When his native France fell to Adolf Hitler's troops in the fall of 1940, Willy Benoit was sixteen years old. A student at the Lycee of Toulon, he continued his education until he received his baccalaureate and then joined the French Force of the Interior, the Resistance, which spent much of its time harassing the Germans.

Shortly after the Americans landed on the shores of southern France, August 15, 1944, Willy joined up with Company A, 180th Infantry of the 45th Infantry Division. The Thunderbirds came ashore at Ste. Maxime in the center of a VI Corps assault, which had the 3rd Infantry Division landing at St. Tropez on the west and the 36th at St. Raphael on the east.

Able Company needed an interpreter, so William Robert Benoit, who had seven years of English at the Lycee, fit right in. Someone gave him a pair of combat boots, he picked up a spare uniform at supply, and soon he acquired an M-1 and a tin helmet. Willy was in business. Of course, he earned his keep because the GIs couldn't understand the natives, and the French couldn't make out what the Americans were saying as the three divisions advanced up the Rhone Valley to the vicinity of Lyons and then east toward the Belfort Gap between the Vosges and the Jura mountains.

In October, as the division prepared to enter Germany, the word came down from 7th Army headquarters to all units that they must divest themselves of French nationals. This made Willy most unhappy because he wanted to cross the Rhine River with his American fighting companions and chase the Boche back into Germany. Willy instead had to turn in his M-1 and his tin helmet but was permitted to keep his uniform and bedroll.

Soon he was on his way back to southern France, catching whatever rides he could. About this time Cpl. Howard Katzander, a correspondent for *Yank,* met up with Willy, who was standing by the road with his thumb in the air. Howard was driving a liberated German Volkswagen jeep.

When they reached Marseille, they drove to *The Stars and Stripes* office, where they met 1st/Lt. Fred Van Pelt, the officer in charge, who agreed to give Willy work operating the teletype machine, translating, and doing oddjobs around the office.

When the Marseille edition closed March 10, 1945, and reopened the next day in Nice, Willy went along with the rest of the staff. When I joined the Southern France edition in Nice that April, one of the first persons I met was Willy Benoit. When we shut down in October, Willy transferred to Paris and I to Germany. When the Paris edition closed in 1946, Willy was sent to Hochst, where he worked briefly and then joined our staff in Pfungstadt. The following year he wed Monique le Moel and brought her to Germany to live until May 1955, when they emigrated to the United States.

They presently live in San Francisco, where he is a manager with the Pacific Bell Company.

★   ★   ★

Margie Elliott, who worked for the U.S. Navy in London during the war, transferred to the U.S. Army's Information and Education Division in Paris on V-J Day as a BCV (British Civilian Worker). A few days later she was on her way to Germany, where she was assigned as secretary to Lt. Col. William G. Proctor, officer in charge of *The Stars and Stripes* at Hochst.

When Lt. Col. William M. Summers replaced Proctor and moved the editor's office to Pfungstadt, Margie made the shift too as a secretary in administration.

Her marriage to Elmer D. Frank, production manager, ended her employment, but she did fill in from time to time as a vacation replacement. The Franks remained in Germany until 1982, when they returned to the States. They now live in Pittsburg, Kansas.

★   ★   ★

Staff of the London edition of *The Stars and Stripes* spent a lot of off-duty time in pubs. Maj. Earl H. Tiffney, the officer in charge, was no exception. When he wasn't in the Lamb and Lark, he would quench his thirst at Short's Bar in the Strand.

It was there late one afternoon that he met Stan Emery, a Briton working for the OWI (Office of War Information), a U.S. agency, rewriting its handouts for release to the British press. Stan's job was being phased out, he told Tiffney, so the major invited him to try out as a proofreader on the U.S. Army newspaper. He got the job and then a short time later moved with Tiffney to Paris to work with *Stripes*. After eight months in France, he was transferred to Pfungstadt, where he reported to 1st/Lt. Nathan J. Margolin, the assistant officer in charge.

Stan found the proofreading setup primitive, manned usually by whatever two or three GIs weren't doing anything else special that day, each comparing original copy with the galley proof.

"Give me a quiet place in the corner of the composing room," he told Margolin. The next day German carpenters moved in to erect a partition. Stan also asked for a couple of literate soldiers to do the work his way, to read the copy aloud while he checked the galley proof. The paper then started to look cleaner.

Although most of the staff at that time shared the single nickname of Moe, an exception was made in Stan Emery's case. He was called Limey.

When the paper closed in April 1945 and the staff shifted to Altdorf, Stan went along but lasted only three weeks.

"The editor was a Jew and anti-Brit, for which I didn't blame

him after some of the outrages in Palestine, but he didn't have to
piss on me — which he did," Stan remembers.

He packed his duffle bag and caught the courier jeep to Frankfurt, where he stepped into a job on the post newspaper — $75 a
week, PX, commissary, and liquor rations.

"I was in hog heaven," he says. "I stayed there nine years."

Stan returned to England, where he worked ten years on *The
Sun* and then shifted to the *Daily Express*. Now retired, he and his
wife Daphne live in Somerset, England.

★   ★   ★

British-born Anne E. Goddard, a secretary for the officer in
charge of the Altdorf edition, overheard the colonel and the production manager talking about hiring a proofreader. She volunteered.

"What are your qualifications?" she was asked.

"I am English and speak and write English," she said.

That seemed plausible and Annie got the job. It wasn't too
long before she was named chief of the department, bossing young
soldiers who were marking time prior to their return to the States
and discharge from the service.

Shortly after the move from Altdorf to Pfungstadt in December
1946, U.S. civilian proofreaders were hired and some resented
working for a woman — a Britisher at that. But Annie held on for
five years until one day she turned up AWOL.

"I missed my plane," she explained when she reported a day
late for work.

I learned of this when Maurice Kirkwood, the general manager, asked if I could find a position for Goddard. It happened that
I had an opening for a copy clerk's job, and that is how Annie came
to work for editorial. The clerk assisted the telegraph editor, sorting
through the overnight slag and filing stories by subject, so the editors could decide on their use. She kept track of new leads, inserts,
and bulletins, in addition to answering the telephone. Annie also
filled in as my secretary from time to time until 1954, when she emigrated to the Bahamas and later to the United States.

She was always a lot of fun. While her fellow Britons will never
be forgotten — Monica Thornberry, for her foot-long cigarette
holder; Joan Liddle, for poetry; and Joyce Harriott, her demure de-
meanor — Annie is remembered for her clowning at Chateau
Meaux and Press Club parties. Her stock post-midnight act was to

dump a loaded ashtray down the front of her frock. It always got laughs.

She worked hard for the Press Club, was a member and chairperson of its board of directors, and was hostess at several successful dinners and special events.

Born at Newcastle-On-Tyne, as Anne Elizabeth Barclay, she was wed twice. Her married names were Goddard and Southworth. Annie spent her last years in San Diego, California, where she died July 13, 1974, of emphysema.

★   ★   ★

Lor Lizabeth Back — Liz for short — arrived in Pfungstadt in November 1947 to take charge of the photo lab and its files, which consisted of several drawers filled with packets of negatives. True, the packets were dated and the subjects listed with the name of the photographer, but they were dumped helter-skelter in file cabinets. She reorganized the files, set up cross-reference cards, took over much of the scheduling, and maintained the weekly operation reports.

We didn't know she could take pictures until the day in March 1948 when John Livingood, the assistant managing editor, and Dzidra (Ina) Liepa, a lovely Latvian blonde, were married. We needed a photographer to take pictures of the wedding, but there wasn't one on duty; Jerry Waller, photo chief, and the others were all on assignment. Liz volunteered. After that, her lab work suffered some because both John and I kept thinking up special assignments for *Stripes*'s first woman photographer.

Born and educated in Vienna, she was attending the Graphical Institute and working as an apprentice in a photo studio when the Nazis arrived in Austria. She and her sister left for Czechoslovakia in June 1938, where her family owned a brewery and a malt factory. Her mother joined them, but soon the Nazis invaded Czechoslovakia. Liz, her sister, and a cousin fled to England in a small airplane, getting out just four days before the German troops arrived. Less fortunate were her mother, several aunts, uncles and cousins, who died at Auschwitz.

While in a London labor office, she noticed a help-wanted advertisement that the Civil Censorship Division was seeking people who could speak German to work in occupied Germany.

"The pay was terrific. I could never dream of earning that

kind of money in England, but the clincher was that the training was to be in Paris. I jumped at the chance," she recalled.

Liz worked for CCD from 1945 to 1947 and was stationed at Pullach near Munich when the order came to disband the division. As chief of the photo lab, she also took pictures of the staff and re-photographed documents. She was trained to detect secret ink messages, but although one might expect something sinister, the only such messages Liz recalled that her department ever detected were between homosexuals.

Faced with unemployment and a return to London, Liz met a friend who told her to apply at *The Stars and Stripes*, and that is how I met Lor Lizabeth Back. I was impressed with her credentials as well as the fact that she could speak German.

The assignment I remember best was at Konnersreuth, when she and reporter Nan Robertson drove to the little Bavarian town and filed past the bed of Theresa Neumann, who annually during Holy Week displayed the stigmata of Christ. Liz recalled:

> It was a strange and moving experience to see this pale and shrouded figure sitting upright in bed with blood flowing from her hands and head. I was prevented from taking pictures and had to leave the room because of my camera but later returned without it.
>
> This time there was more blood on the bedclothes, she was extremely pale and the room reeked of incense. It was quiet in spite of the many people outside. You could hear the birds singing in the trees. Both Nan and I were moved by the phenomenon; there was no explanation for it. I was perturbed even for days afterwards.

When they returned to Pfungstadt, Nan wrote her story, and Liz's pictures of the Germans and the American soldiers and their wives lined up in front of the house of the Maid of Konnersreuth appeared in the April 18, 1949, issue of *The Stars and Stripes*.

Liz married her boss, Jerry Waller, in 1950, and two children later they moved to Los Angeles, where they presently live. Jerry is retired as photographer with the flood control division of the County of Los Angeles.

Nan Robertson moved from *The Stars and Stripes* to the *New York Times*, where in 1982 she won the Pulitzer Prize for her series on toxic shock syndrome, stories based on her own experiences.

Theresa Neumann, famed for the stigmata, died September 18, 1962. She was sixty-four.

★ ★ ★

Dennis Newstead, a Britisher, did what I did when he signed on with *The Stars and Stripes*. He brought along his bride; she, like Paulette, did not have the proper papers.

Dennis saw an advertisement in London for a printer on an English-language newspaper in Germany. He applied and was accepted by *Stripes*, and he and Doreen took off for Frankfurt.

"There were a couple of touchy moments on the train with the German border inspectors," he recalled. "We got through, however, and arrived in Pfungstadt about midnight. The Chateau Meaux band was playing 'Clair de Lune' to welcome us. Bless 'em!"

Dennis was born in London during World War I. He apprenticed out to a print shop and then joined the Royal Air Force when World War II started.

"I spent four years in the RAF, much of it in France where our ass was ignominiously run out. We boarded a ship at Saint-Nazaire and a day or two later it was sunk by a German U-boat. We bobbed about for a time off the French coast before being picked up by a British tanker and dropped off in England."

Dennis served a couple of two-year stints with *Stripes* as a proofreader and on makeup. During his off-duty hours he practiced the bass fiddle and jammed with the German band at the Chateau Meaux along with Jack Browne, piano, and John Sharnik, violin. He and Rhea Sanders, who later wed news editor Joe Rabinovich, were responsible for talking French guitarist Django Reinhardt into visiting Pfungstadt. They had met Reinhardt in a Frankfurt club where he had been playing. I remember the event well. It was August 9, 1947, and we had the story and a picture of Reinhardt and Browne in *Stripes* the next day. Newstead's fiddle was too big, so it and he were cropped out of the photo.

Dennis and Doreen and their children emigrated to the United States and settled first in Denver and later at Costa Mesa, California, where he operated a printing firm. Now retired, they live on their sailboat, the *Sanderling*, at Port Sonoma, just north of San Francisco.

★ ★ ★

When Belgian-born Yvonne de Ridder came to work for *The*

Stars and Stripes, we had no idea that she was a real honest-to-goodness war heroine. Her pretty face, sunny disposition, and trim figure gave no hint of her inner strength and character. But then, we didn't know what heroines were supposed to look like.

We learned later that with the help of a Catholic priest, Yvonne had hidden a number of British, Canadian, and American pilots in her Antwerp apartment during the war. She had joined the resistance movement in 1941 and had engaged in sabotage and espionage activities until she was denounced and arrested by the Gestapo. She was flogged, tortured, and sentenced to be hanged but was liberated in September by British troops just two weeks before she was scheduled to die on the gallows.

We became aware in 1948 of her activities when Yvonne, a secretary to the adviser of unit publications, was awarded the British King's Medal for Courage in the Cause of Freedom, as well as six Belgian and three French decorations and the Certificate of Merit, issued by the Allied Forces in Europe and signed by General Eisenhower.

The television audience in the United States learned about her exploits in 1955 when she appeared on "This Is Your Life," at which time she was reunited with Father Rene LeClef and three of the pilots she befriended.

Yvonne is wed to Roger Files, a retired U.S. Air Force colonel. They live in Topanga, a suburb of Los Angeles.

★   ★   ★

Upon taking over as managing editor at Altdorf, I found that I was in charge of a number of German civilians who proved to be talented professionals and loyal workers. This came as a mild surprise because GIs had been prohibited from fraternizing and were threatened with a $65 fine if found talking to a German. In the early days at Pfungstadt our chances of getting to know Germans other than linotype and press operators, who spoke little or no English, were nil, since there was a bevy of displaced persons from Eastern Europe there to wait on tables, cook our food, and clean our billets.

So it wasn't until Altdorf in the summer of 1946 that I really got to know the Germans. Without a doubt, our best photographer was Hans Hubmann. His wife, Lisa, was also a fine photographer. Both spoke excellent English.

Johanna Buschner, the research assistant, librarian, and

translator, was indispensable. Before the war she had been editor of the economic newspaper *Europakable*. When we moved from Altdorf to Pfungstadt, we took her with us, arranged for a billet for her, and were saddened a couple of years later when she decided to leave us to work on a German publication.

"What are we going to do without you? What will become of the *Stripes* library?" I asked.

"I have a replacement for you, my sister Greta. She speaks English. She will be here tomorrow to meet you. I plan to work with her for a month and if you are not satisfied with her we will find someone else," she said.

There was no problem. Greta Rache worked out just fine. She was still there when I left the paper several years later.

★   ★   ★

In those early Altdorf days I had a pretty *fraulein* for a secretary. She didn't like to be called a *fraulein* because that implied she was German. She insisted that she was Czech. Her name was Anna-Maria Ernest and she was born in Pilsen, Czechoslovakia. The Allies insisted she was German, since her father, a captain in the Czech army, served with the Germans when his unit was integrated after the Nazis marched into Czechoslovakia.

This was not a small matter for Anna-Maria, since she was going steady with Gordon Skean, an ex-GI from North Carolina, and they had marriage on their minds. Skean came to the paper in Altdorf as assistant to Jack Browne, production manager, and when Browne was promoted to assistant business manager, Skean replaced him as head of production.

As a Czech, Anna-Maria could have gotten married to Gordon and remained in Germany with a house, a commissary card, and all the privileges. But as a German she would have to leave within thirty days. That was the law. They took their vows, *Stripes* lost a production manager, and I lost a secretary.

They traveled to the States, where they lived a short time in North Carolina, and then made their way to the other side of the world, where Gordon joined the Tokyo edition of *The Stars and Stripes*. Later he became its general manager.

Gordon and Anna-Maria's problems were no different from those of thousands of other young lovers in occupied Germany. Gordon had been a serviceman but took his discharge to accept civilian employment before meeting Anna-Maria. If he had remained a serviceman, he would have stayed on the job until his enlistment was up and then thirty days prior to being sent home he could have married. He would have gone home on a troop ship, and later his bride would travel to the States at government expense.

Since Gordon was a civilian working under a contract, he had no choice but to leave thirty days after their marriage. The alternative would have been to live together without being married, but they didn't wish to do that. Anna-Maria felt strongly about Germany and being called a German, and if she couldn't return to her native Czechoslovakia, then North Carolina would just have to do.

The fraternization policy dated to the day that General Ike's troops set foot on German soil. Under that policy it was a $65 fine if you talked to a German. When the shooting stopped, that policy was relaxed to a point where the *frauleins* were even invited to functions held in the American Red Cross clubs.

But marriage? That was something else. Gen. Joseph T. McNarney, who replaced Eisenhower as theater commander when the latter became army chief of staff, imposed the ban on marriages to German girls following a flood of applications. McNarney is said to have felt that Americans with such a close family relationship would have divided allegiance. A member of his staff said U.S. personnel in Germany would not be able to accomplish their mission impartially if they were involved personally with the very Germans they were administrating.

Maj. Gen. James M. Bevans, assistant chief of staff, USFET personnel, put it more bluntly. He said on the air during an Armed Forces Network program that the "ban on American soldiers marrying *frauleins* would be lifted only when Germany adopts democratic principles and is denazified thoroughly." Bevans added: "The policy of non-marriage with Germans is necessary in order to emphasize the relationship between the occupying forces and the defeated Germany. We should not confer the benefits, which come to the wife of a U.S. soldier, upon an enemy of the U.S."

Slowly the army began to change its thinking and, late in 1946, it was decided that military personnel would be permitted to marry Germans immediately prior to their departure from the European Theater. McNarney said at a press conference December 22 in Berlin that the marriage rule was changed because of a legal opinion that it was mandatory under the law. Congress provided for transportation of war brides to the States without distinction between enemy and Allied nations, he pointed out, and the final decision was that soldiers should be allowed to marry before they leave the theater in order to take advantage of it. He explained that he maintained the ban on marriages with Germans by personnel remaining in the theater because he considered it unwise.

The change in the policy was welcome news to lovesick GIs, but many *frauleins* were disturbed when they learned that a thorough investigation of their backgrounds was required before a visa could be issued. Those who could not meet the qualifications would not be permitted to leave. Particular emphasis was placed on the political record of the individual.

★ ★ ★

Some girls will do most anything for love, and in 1947 Doris von Knoblock, a diminutive twenty-year-old *fraulein,* was no exception. A dental technician at the 1st Gen. Dispensary at Darmstadt, she confided to her friend, Sigrid Kraft, also twenty, that she yearned to join her boyfriend in New York.

"Since you don't have much money and no passport, what about going air freight in a box?" Sigrid said.

"I'm crazy in love but I'm not that crazy," Doris replied.

But Sigrid was insistent. She told Doris that she had just shipped a dog to her former boyfriend at a cost of $130 and that the animal got to New York in twenty-three hours. "If he could do it, why couldn't a girl?" she said.

The more Doris thought about it the more she liked the idea, so she wrote to her boyfriend and asked him to send her $150. She didn't tell him about the box but she arranged with a German cabinetmaker to build her a $2x2x2^{1}/_{2}$-foot container complete with air holes and lock that would fasten from the inside. The cabinetmaker didn't question why she wanted such a lock, and she didn't tell him.

On October 2, the day before she planned to leave, she asked Pfc Robert Seidentopf, a fellow worker at the dispensary, if he would come to her house the next day to pick up a box and take it to the airline office at Rhine-Main Air Base. "A personal favor, please, Robert," she pleaded. He agreed because he liked Doris.

Nineteen hours later, Doris heard voices and figured she was in the baggage room, but to be certain she decided to release the latch, open the lid, and peek out. This she did and looked right into the startled eyes of a baggage handler who cried out: "There's a girl in the box! There's a girl in the box!"

The airline supervisor was summoned, and he ordered the now-closed lid to be pried open. There was Doris, curled up inside, wearing only a brassiere, skirt, and socks. She was holding a sweater, but there was no way she could put it on inside the box. Also inside was what was left of her tea in a five-ounce bottle and three slices of bread which were to last her until she reached New York. Tacked inside the box was a small, red heart cut out of a piece of felt.

"Imagine the horror of being in there so long and then being caught," were her first words.

Army investigators took her to the terminal cafeteria for lunch, which she ate eagerly, and then she was driven to their station for questioning. Other investigators picked up Seidentopf at the dispensary; he was shocked to learn that Doris had been in the box. He told them that Doris had spoken to him about shipping a box of tapestry and statuary to the New York address and that is what he thought it was.

At her trial Doris was found guilty of "illegally attempting to leave Germany by plane" and was fined 100 marks.

★   ★   ★

Georg Hofricter was hired by *Stripes* for a three-day job of putting the rotary press at the old Pfungstadt plant into operation. He stayed eleven years, leaving the paper in 1956 to join the *Frankfurter Rundschau*. While with *Stripes* he was superintendent of the press room. His new job with the Frankfurt newspaper was in improvement and planning.

Before the war, Hofricter had been a printing equipment engineer for Albert & Company's printing press assembly plant in Frankenthal. It just so happened that when *Stripes* acquired its new Super Albert 60 rotary press in 1954, it was from Hofricter's former employer. There was even a family tie involved, since Hofricter's son was employed by Albert.

While with *Stripes*, Hofricter built several devices for the plant. When Elmer Frank, production manager, asked for bids on a conveyor system for the rotary press, a German firm offered to install the project for $11,000. Hofricter went to his drawing board, came up with the plans, and got a German firm to do the work for approximately $3,000.

Hofricter left *Stripes* the same week that Elmer turned back the last of the original fifteen linotype machines requisitioned from the Frankfurter Sociatactes Druckerei, owners of the auxiliary plant in Pfungstadt.

★   ★   ★

Over the years *Stripes* had a number of young German men who spoke English and worked as copy boys. They didn't mind going to the third-floor lunch room several times a shift to get coffee for the Americans, but they resented being called boy.

"I'm not a boy," Rolf Feiberger said. "I was three years in U-Boats in the North Atlantic. That was a man's work."

I explained that it was just an expression and that I started in the newspaper business as a copy boy. A lot of us who got out of school in the Depression years had to start at the bottom, I told him.

When I left *Stripes* and returned to the States to work, I found just as many girls doing copy running as boys and they got around the term by calling them copy kids.

★   ★   ★

There was a four-year period in the early 1950s when we became actively involved in the welfare of the German employees. The issue had to do with the paying of a Christmas bonus, a policy practiced by German firms but prohibited by the U.S. Army. We decided to take some action. Here is how I remember it:

"We have to do something to keep our key German employees," Lou Brown, chief of distribution, said.

"I'm losing linotype operators and pressman right and left," Elmer Frank, production manager, replied.

"Why is that?" I asked because, although I had some German employees, I hadn't heard any of them indicate that they might leave.

"The German economy has bounced back and German firms are hiring again. They are taking our best people and paying them more than we are permitted," Frank said.

"I was asked the other day by one of my old-timers if *Stripes* had any plans to pay a Christmas bonus," Brown added.

"I've run into that too," Frank said. "A Christmas bonus is normal in Germany, or at least it was before the war. Some of the firms are reviving the practice and the workers expect it."

"What do you suggest?" I put in.

"We can't meet the pay scale because USAEUR won't permit

it, but maybe we can raise money to pay Christmas bonuses. How about a raffle?" Brown said.

"That's a helluva idea and I think the colonel might go for it. What would the prize be and how much should we charge for the tickets?" I asked.

"How about several prizes — a bicycle, a radio, maybe a phonograph. Sid Gans in the New York office could get the stuff wholesale and ship it over. We could charge a buck a ticket and sell them at our newsstands if the colonel can get the OK from the army," Brown said.

"Postal regulations won't permit announcing the raffle in the newspaper, so we will have to resort to posters," I pointed out.

The colonel liked the idea and sold it to the army, and the German employees' Christmas raffle was born. A committee was formed with Brown as chairman; Frank set about printing the tickets; and Gans shipped a bicycle, a wristwatch, and a food mixer. The 1950 raffle drawing was conducted at the Press Club, and the Germans netted about five deutsche marks each, or a little over a dollar. We were embarrassed by the small amount, but everyone had a lot of fun and it was decided to do it again the following year.

The committee got an early start for the 1951 event and did a little better but not much. A Vespa motor scooter was the top prize. The bonus amounted to DM 20, or about $5 each.

However, for the Third Annual Benefit Christmas Raffle in 1952, we decided to go for broke. We borrowed money from the American Express in Darmstadt for the down payment and ordered a $5,000 Cadillac convertible from Anderson-Martini, the General Motors firm in Copenhagen. When it arrived we hauled it about the Frankfurt-Wiesbaden-Heidelberg area on a trailer. The tickets, sold at *The Stars and Stripes* newsstands, went like hotcakes. We also published a program and sold advertising, with the proceeds going to the raffle.

The raffle was kicked off by a barn dance for *Stripes* personnel and guests in a new addition to the press room. The drawing was supervised by an insurance company agent and the manager of the American Express office in Darmstadt, and the numbers were drawn from a ping-pong ball machine used for bingo games at a service club in Hanau. The winner was Pfc Wilbur Staub, twenty-one, of the 325th Hospital Train, stationed at Landstuhl. The GI from New Oxford, Pennsylvania, had never before owned a car.

A grand total of $51,556 was realized, but the Germans employed by *The Stars and Stripes* only received a total of $18,386, or DM 100 each. This figure was determined in advance and with lesser amounts going to those on the payroll less than a year. They were pleased, but our problem was what to do with the remaining $33,000. This was solved by donating $30,909, or DM 129,817, to the VDK, a German charity federation. Carl Meckes, the Darmstadt representative of the organization, accepted the funds and promised it would be used for orphans under fourteen years of age who were living outside institutions.

We also gave $1,470, or 512,000 francs, to the French Liaison Mission at Orleans, France, who in turn presented it to the Comite National de Defense Contrelat Tuberculosis. This amounted to the percentage of tickets sold in the Com Z area in France. USFA troops in Austria received $679, and $112 went to TRUST forces based in Trieste. Ninety percent of the tickets were sold in Germany, a fact which explained the lesser amounts to the other commands.

Because we netted so much money, the army decided that the Fourth Annual Benefit Christmas Raffle in 1953 would be restricted to only the amount of the bonus requirements. This meant there would be no funds for charitable organizations. The raffle again was a success. We skipped the program with its advertising and ordered a black Cadillac convertible with red leather seats and white sidewall tires. Sid Gans bought it from General Motors in New York and had it shipped to Bremerhaven.

The big event was kicked off with another barn dance held this time in an airplane hangar on the former Luftwaffe air strip across from our offices. The drawing was conducted in the Press Club, with another insurance company agent and the manager of American Express in charge. The winning ticket was held by Pfc Lloyd C. Brett, twenty, a parts man in the motor pool of Detachment A, 17th Signal Battalion at Metz, France.

The German employees received $32,152, or DM 160, per person. We held back $800 in order to finance the start of the 1954 raffle but, alas, it was not to be. The army rejected the idea, and the Germans did not get a Christmas bonus nor did the charitable organizations reap a dividend. We eventually gave the $800 to the VDK, which used the money to aid destitute veterans of the German army.

We later heard that a colonel in Heidelberg felt that the *Stars and Stripes* policy of giving Christmas bonuses to its German employees was unfair to other nonappropriated fund organizations who also depended on German help. We thought it unfair of the colonel and the army, but there was nothing we could do about it.

We thanked our lucky stars that the big winners in the last two raffles were both enlisted men — both privates first class. What if the winner had been a civilian? Or a general?

The army had the last word: no raffle, no Christmas bonus, no money for charity.

12

Critics

"Stories that are pro-Soviet, pro-Communist and anti-American material is printed in *The Stars and Stripes*."
— Rep. George A. Dondero

"*The Stars and Stripes* is a tedious trade journal of the Army."
— Westbrook Pegler

"Whenever I read *The Stars and Stripes,*
Including B-Bag with all its gripes
I never feel I'm quite content
Until I read where the Colonels went."
— Der Verfasser
7807 USAREUR

On February 26, 1948, Rep. George A. Dondero (R-MI) was recognized by the Speaker of the House of Representatives in Washington, D.C. In the twenty minutes allotted him, Dondero charged that "pro-Soviet, pro-Communist and anti-American material" was being printed in *The Stars and Stripes*.

"Whether this is the result of sheer stupidity or the machinations of a Communist clique in the American Military Government, or both, is for our Department of the Army to find out and act upon," he said.

Dondero detailed stories, cartoons by Bill Mauldin, headlines and picture captions to which he objected. Among them was a Page 1 story telling of Czechoslovakia's withdrawal from the Marshall Plan Conference by "unanimous consent of all parties of the National Front government." He said no indication was given that "this National Front is Communist-dominated."

His samples included a story of a CIO attack on the Taft-Hartley Labor Act, a Mauldin cartoon unfavorable to the House Un-American Activities Committee, and "an insulting allusion" to Mrs. Peron, wife of the president of Argentina.

Dondero said *The Stars and Stripes* also printed stories about Soviet charges of U.S. imperialism and of American espionage efforts in Russian-dominated areas without attempting to refute them.

The story went out over the Associated Press wire but major newspapers in the United States, if they used it at all, placed the item on inside pages. However, the charge gained support three days later when Rep. John McDowell (R-PA), a member of the House Committee on Un-American Activities, said that the committee might investigate Dondero's charges.

"If the charges appear to hold water I will put it before the committee for an investigation," McDowell said. He added that most of the *Stars and Stripes* personnel he had known appeared "good, honest hard-working newspapermen — no different from those in the House Press Gallery."

The army was quick to come to the defense of *Stripes*. Maj. Gen. Floyd L. Parks, chief of army public relations, said he was sure that there was no Communist propaganda in *The Stars and Stripes*. The general told a reporter his office had cabled to Frankfurt a resume of complaints made in the House by Dondero.

"We try to give the news as it is given over the wire services in the United States," General Parks said. "The information is no more propaganda than when it is published here."

Gen. Lucius D. Clay, European Command chief and in effect the publisher of *Stripes*, said March 2 that he had never seen any anti-American or pro-Communist matter in the army newspaper.

"I am very proud of *The Stars and Stripes* and I read it every day," he said.

In his talk Dondero said he had studied four copies of *The Stars and Stripes*, and in them he said he found stories that made grist for the Communist mill or would afford valuable intelligence information to the Russians.

"It will be said that most of these stories are press association dispatches for which the staff of *The Stars and Stripes* is not responsible. The question is, however, why were they selected and by whom and why was not a reply of some kind not added," he said. The congressman also noted that

> while officers and privates of the American armed forces constitute the staff of the paper, its masthead calls it the "unofficial publication of the United States occupation forces in Europe." It is not clear to me just what this means. Does it mean that the members of the newspaper staff are free to publish anything they see fit in this paper? Does it mean that the Army assumes no responsibility? Can it be expected that material circulated by this paper in Germany will be considered as unofficial by the German people? To me it would appear as if it were a convenient way for the Army to pass the buck of responsibility for the contents of the paper.

There were a number of other stories that Dondero didn't like, and Phil Bucknell, of our New York bureau, checked back issues of *The New York Times* and the *New York Herald-Tribune* to see how they were used. In most cases the metropolitan editors gave them the same treatment that we did.

Dondero objected to a Mauldin cartoon in the July 11, 1947, issue that showed a drunken American speaking to a youngster as follows: "You kids are the only hope for shick soshiety."

"What grist for the Communist propaganda mill," the congressman said.

He also objected to a Mauldin cartoon published July 13. It depicted the House Committee on Un-American Activities as making the following statement to a young man demanding the investigation of "professional bigots" and the "KKK": "Investigate them? Heck, that's mah posse."

The congressman had reason to read those four mid-July 1947 issues because he made Page 1 in all of them. A story datelined Washington, July 11, was printed at the bottom of Page 1 which stated that Dondero had charged in a House speech that Communist sympathizers in the past had infiltrated into key army posts and that Secretary of War Robert P. Patterson's failure to ferret them out "endangers our national security."

Dondero named ten individuals once with the Department of War who, he said, had Communist backgrounds or leanings. The ten names were printed in *The Stars and Stripes*.

The July 13 issue of *Stripes* carried Clay's denial that there were Communists in Military Government ranks. He said Dondero's charges were unfounded and outdated. The general pointed out that all those accused by Dondero had been screened in the United States before coming to Germany.

One of the accused was Josiah E. Dubois, chief prosecutor in America's war crime trial of twenty-four I. G. Farben cartel executives in Nuremberg. Dubois told the United Press in a story in the same issue that Dondero was the "type (of man) who, so far from deserving a seat in the United States Congress, should not be trusted with responsibility of any kind."

Dubois was formerly an assistant secretary of the treasury under both Henry A. Morgenthau and Fred Vinson and served on special missions for the government in Russia and Japan and at the Potsdam Conference.

George S. Wheeler, U.S. Military Government's manpower allocation chief, and another of the ten accused by Dondero, said in Berlin that Dondero's charges were "ridiculous."

★ ★ ★

Rep. Paul Shafer (R-MI) preferred the Italian editions of *The Stars and Stripes* to the Paris paper. He told United Press in Florence that he considered the Paris edition inferior to the ones in Rome and Naples.

"The Italian editions are 'real newspapers' which carry all kinds of unbiased news, regardless of whether it favors the administration or not, whereas the Paris *Stripes* contains too much propaganda and never publishes unfavorable news."

Rep. Claire Booth Luce (R-CT), a member of the House Military Affairs Committee, visited the European Theater of Operations in the closing months of the war and apparently objected to the use of the word "junket" in a headline in the Paris edition in connection with the committee's fact-finding tour. She didn't complain directly, but the word came down from the "ivory tower" to the copy desk that we were not to use the word "junket" in articles about congressional inspection tours.

★ ★ ★

Westbrook Pegler, the old sportswriter-turned-political columnist, spent four months in Europe early in 1952 and faulted much of what he saw. None of the English-language newspapers on the Continent carried "As Pegler Sees It," but Sidney Gans, chief of our New York bureau, clipped out some of those articles from the *Journal-American* and sent them to me.

Pegler came down hard on HICOG (High Commission of Germany) and especially Shephard Stone, director of the Office of Public Affairs, who was on leave from the Sunday Department of *The New York Times*. John J. McCloy, high commissioner, had broken an ankle skiing and was unavailable for comment.

Of HICOG, this is some of what Pegler had to say: "This machine of this Military Government is now transferred into a colonial bureaucracy. This system of kangaroo courts, making up its own laws as Hitler did, and this new civil administration under a High Commissioner with a colonial cabinet, are not American institutions in the broad sense."

Of Shephard Stone: "He was entitled to eight German civilians to do his bidding as household servants free of cost to him but he only had six."

Of the army: "Something strange is going on here. Lt. Gen. Manton Eddy has a good reputation and there is evidence that his Seventh Army is alert. But in expressing satisfaction over . . . a new supply of trucks to replace a lot of patched and cannibalized rolling stock, he tells me that the first concern of his transport section will be to rush personnel out of the fighting zone back into France. That meant the wives and children of officers and non-commissioned grades who are entitled to the gentle and expensive considerations which the United States shows to family men on active duty."

And of *The Stars and Stripes:*

> Eisenhower and all the generals in this strange command insist that the so-called North Atlantic army is a field army ready to fight. Yet Tuesday's *Stars and Stripes,* a paper which began in fun in 1917 and became a tedious trade journal of the Army, casually reported the arrival of 552 more service wives and children on the liner *Washington*.
>
> This ship has brought over 3,241 dependents, most of them to Germany, since November 20 and the traffic is known as the "diaper run." The *Washington* is augmented by an unsystematic and risky airplane service which gets around Ike's hesitant efforts to bar further additions to the load of camp-followers who will have the

first call on the trucks, trains and planes for an exodus, probably to France, if and when Russia strikes without warning.

The government has chartered the *Washington* for seven trips to "eliminate the backlog of dependents awaiting transportation to the European Command." She has made four already — so the commanding generals tell you they are fixing for a fight and the Truman machine, which is drumming up this army to redeem the crimes of the Roosevelt and Truman administrations, continues to dump American women and children into a potential battle area where most of them may become refugees in winter weather at any minute.

★   ★   ★

Not all of our critics were congressmen or columnists from across the sea. We had a resident carper in Hans Wallenberg, a German-born ex-U.S. Army major who was the civilian editor of the Military Government-sponsored German-language *Neue Zeitung* at Munich.

Wallenberg told twelve visiting American publishers and editors May 28, 1947, that *The Stars and Stripes* "is 90 per cent cheesecake and the rest is not too hot from the standpoint of news coverage."

Wallenberg's assessment was in reply to a question concerning the freedom of news coverage in the German press. Wallenberg explained that if the German papers did not carry the news, the Germans would read it in the *New York Times*, the *New York Herald-Tribune*, or *The Stars and Stripes*.

"One of the worst examples from our point of view is *The Stars and Stripes*," he said. He told reporters after the meeting that he had recommended to the *Neue Zeitung*'s parent, the Information Control Division, that action be taken to curb *The Stars and Stripes*'s freedom of news coverage because of its influence on the German press.

Wallenberg's remarks were refuted the following day by his boss, Col. G. E. Textor in Berlin, and by Col. George S. Eyster, director of EUCOM's Public Information Division and policy director of *The Stars and Stripes*, in Frankfurt.

Textor, chief of the Information Control Division, expressed "deep regret" that a member of his organization had issued a public criticism of *The Stars and Stripes* and said that Wallenberg was speaking as an individual and "without authority." He called the criticism "inexcusable" and said it "certainly does not represent the official view of ICD." He said he thought *The Stars and Stripes* was doing a "good job" and added that he had no intention of seeking to curb the army newspaper's freedom of news coverage because of its effect on the German press. Textor also said Wallenberg's statement was "out of line" and made it clear that operation of *The Stars and Stripes* was not within the domain of ICD.

Eyster pointed out that *The Stars and Stripes* was a publication for the occupation forces in Germany and as such reported news as it happened — "good and bad."

"It is quite obvious from my close association with the editorial personnel of *The Stars and Stripes* that they make every effort to present news in its correct light and to provide adequate balance. The paper appears to do a very able job of news coverage, both foreign and domestic, and does everything in its power to support policies of the U.S. government and the commander in chief in Germany."

Two months later — August 6, 1947 — Wallenberg resigned because of a disagreement with his superiors over policies of the Information Control Division. He declined to state what the "disagreements" were that prompted his resignation.

Wallenberg had emigrated to the United States from Germany in the 1930s and had returned to his homeland as an American army officer. His father was a former newspaper publisher in Berlin. At the time of his resignation he was a civilian and had guided the *Neue Zeitung* since March 1946.

Neue Zeitung's Munich edition had a circulation of 550,000, while its counterpart in Berlin printed 140,000 daily.

★   ★   ★

There were others in the civilian branch of the U.S. government who criticized *The Stars and Stripes,* though they were not as vocal. Their complaints, like Wallenberg's, stressed the point that some articles published in the army newspaper harmed German-American relations, this despite the fact that the English-language publication was not available to Germans.

There was never a direct order from the State Department or Military Government to suppress a story. Instead the diplomatic person-to-person approach was often used in urging that *The Stars and Stripes* be sympathetic in maintaining good U.S.-German relations.

Stripes reporters Omer Anderson and James M. Quigley in Bonn relayed advisories from public affairs and political officers as to how they would like to see a story presented that dealt with the Germans. Most suggestions were sound, and all were considered.

The most memorable advisory had to do with an American army Wac's mammary glands and her relations with a German doctor. In this instance, a political officer in Bonn approached his army counterpart in Heidelberg requesting that the colonel exercise his good offices to maintain a minimum amount of publicity on the story in *The Stars and Stripes*. The colonel forwarded the request without comment. The result was that we assigned a reporter to the story and published several accounts of the trial, but we did keep it off Page 1.

Reporter Jon Hagar covered the trial of the Wac, a sergeant in her thirties who brought the suit in a High Commission of Germany (HICOG) court seeking 250,000 marks ($62,500) against a Heidelberg University Clinic's plastic surgeon. She told the court she went to the doctor to inquire about an operation to remove "excess fat" from her breasts. After viewing before and after photographs of other patients, she submitted to the operation. She returned to duty three days later but had to quit work when she became ill.

Another German doctor, in private practice, told her she had developed a gangrenous condition and advised her to see American doctors at the nearby 130th Station Hospital. She did, and they transferred her to the 97th General Hospital in Frankfurt, and from there she was evacuated by air to the Brooks Army Hospital at Ft. Sam Houston, Texas.

At the trial in April 1953 she testified that the doctor's alleged "carelessness and gross negligence" left her "sick, sore, lame and disabled" and forced her to "lose both breasts and to submit to further painful surgery to close open wounds."

The plastic surgeon testified that she left his clinic against his recommendation. The two-month-long trial ended with the surgeon being cleared. The judge said the Wac's attorney failed to prove any "lack of special skill, care and treatment by the doctor."

★ ★ ★

Stripes's coverage of the war in Korea drove some in the State Department up the wall.

"Why do you have to use such words as 'blood baths,' 'slaughter' and 'murder' in your news accounts from Korea?" one asked me at a HICOG policy meeting I attended. "It has such a bad effect on the Germans."

I pointed out that the news articles were from the wire services, had been cleared by the censors, and reflected the official view of Gen. Matthew B. Ridgway, who had replaced Gen. Douglas MacArthur. Ridgway's offensive was called "Operation Meat Grinder," which reflected the mood in the Pacific at that time.

Discussion came to an end when someone suggested that a letter be sent to the Pentagon with a request that something be done to tone down the general.

★　　★　　★

Criticism of *The Stars and Stripes* came with the territory. We expected it and probably deserved some of it. There was nothing we could do about a Dondero who swung from the floor of the House of Representatives with his wild charges. Pegler's comment about *Stripes* being "a tedious trade journal of the Army" was without malice and perhaps partly true. Wallenberg's statement that *The Stars and Stripes* was "90 per cent cheesecake and the rest not too hot" was off-the-cuff, and the reporter knew it when he wrote the story.

What did hurt was the criticism from some officers of the U.S. Air Force, not in the immediate family but a cousin of sorts. Most families spat from time to time, but this turned out to be a real brouhaha.

Spread over a large area of Europe, parts of North Africa and Asia, and with too few public information officers to send in news releases, the air force suffered from a lack of publicity. As a result, some of the brass in blue suits reacted unfavorably to much of what the newspaper did. Unhappy with the distribution of the paper, books, and magazines, the air force set up its own system only to return it to *Stripes* when its own people could not improve on the service or make a profit.

Displeased with its share of the *Stripes* financial pie, the air force asked for and was given a seat on the newspaper's board of directors, then assigned a major as assistant editor in chief and a number of years later brought in a full colonel to be editor in chief.

The handling of accidents, the real bad news, was what caused most of the problems *Stripes* had with the air force. The issue came to a head March 11, 1952, when an F-84 Thunderjet crashed practically on top of our heads. It landed on a barn one-half mile from our plant, killing the pilot and a German woodcutter. A story we could hardly overlook, it was the second biggest story on Page 1 the next morning.

Reporter Bernard H. Liebes was on the scene minutes after the accident and, as soon as he collected what on-the-spot information he could, he telephoned USAFE (United States Air Force Europe) at Wiesbaden. He was told the plane was one of three on a flight from Fuerstenfeldbruck Air Base near Munich. His story stated that the F-84 plunged to the ground 50 yards from a two-story house only 100 yards from Rhein Strasse, the main street linking Darmstadt to the autobahn and the headquarters of *Stripes*.

Harold McConnell, night news editor, was in his house 150 yards away when he heard a terrific roar followed by balls of flame that shot skyward. Debris, some of it flaming, was strewn all over the ground near where he, his wife, and two sons lived.

Capt. William R. Moran and 1st/Lt. Truitt W. Harris of the 1st Division Air Section, whose airstrip was adjacent to *Stripes*, said the plane came hurtling out of an overcast sky. They immediately took off in their L-5 and sighted the body of the pilot and his un-opened parachute on the ground behind the autobahn snack bar.

Reporter Jon Hagar talked to an air force lieutenant in charge of removing the pilot's body from the woods. The lieutenant told Hagar that four or five Germans working nearby had seen the pilot bail out and that they recovered the cockpit canopy. The pilot's seat and unopened chute had been found 125 paces away.

John Livingood, assistant managing editor and day news editor, gave the story second play treatment to the Associated Press report of the New Hampshire primary race between Sen. Robert A. Taft and Gen. Dwight D. Eisenhower. The crash story rated a larger headline, however.

Col. C. K. Rich, deputy commander of the U.S. 12th Air Force, was furious the next day when he picked up *Stripes* and read the story. Upon arrival at his office, he dictated a letter to Maj. Gen. Daniel Noce, chief of staff of the European Command, stating that the newspaper "gave [the story] a slant which we consider to be detrimental to military objectives," and asked that the subject be discussed at the next policy meeting. His letter continued:

> The paper devoted approximately 2,500 words, much of which was not even factual, plus 35 column inches of pictures to this accident. In addition to this sensational treatment, *The Stars and*

Stripes failed to contact this headquarters concerning this incident. Neither did they request clearance on any of their stories. They left the impression that the plane was engaged in low-level maneuvers over a metropolitan area, whereas the planes were maneuvering at 26,000 feet when one went into a compressibility dive from which the pilot was unable to recover. Publicity of this negative type by one of our semi-official publications is not considered to be in the best interests of the Department of Defense.

The story written by Liebes did not state that the plane was engaged in low-level maneuvers over a metropolitan area. USAFE in Wiesbaden had been contacted, but not the 12th Air Force, to which the plane belonged. Since the name of the pilot was not used, and no attempts by Liebes and Hagar were made to obtain it, we failed to see the harm. We had long observed the practice of not releasing names of casualties for a period of forty-eight hours to give the military time to notify the families.

"The crash got full and quick coverage since it almost hit our plant. You don't need clearance on eye-witness stories. What's to clear?" Livingood said.

Three weeks later, Lt. Col. Henry J. Richter, the editor in chief, Maurice R. Kirkwood, general manager, and I attended the policy meeting in Gen. Thomas T. Handy's office. Col. Rich didn't attend, but he sent a Colonel O'Leary and Capt. James Brady, 12th Air Force public information officer.

The complaint was brought up by O'Leary near the end of the session, but Handy closed off discussion by stating that "*The Stars and Stripes* had gained its reputation by the way it presented the news and not by the way the military wanted it presented. Many things we must leave to their judgment if they are going to run a newspaper. They must not be under wraps."

I was pleased to hear the general's remarks, which were a restatement of the original Eisenhower view of the mission of *Stripes*. It also was in keeping with Clay's "goldfish bowl policy" on publicity.

O'Leary and Brady stopped off at Griesheim on their return from Heidelberg, and we had a long chat. I knew Brady from the days when we were both cub reporters at *The Sacramento Union* before the war, so I felt I could speak frankly. Both officers asked us to help the air force maintain morale by always mentioning that the planes were "on a training mission" and added that "another aspect was that the Air Force must be careful about the reaction in

France, Belgium and other NATO countries who are presently receiving jets from America."

They pointed out that the USAFE headquarters in Wiesbaden had control over only a supply depot at Chateauroux, France, while the 12th Air Force was in charge of all other installations. We agreed that in the future *Stripes* reporters and editors would call Brady's office.

The following year 12th Air Force completed a move of its headquarters to Landstuhl, where a twelve-story aircraft-control tower looked down on a vast undertaking scratched out of the forests. Other 12th Air Force bases, which served as advance sites for jets of NATO's defense fleet, were located at Bitburg, Hahn, Spangahlem, and Sembach, all located in the French Zone and, like Landstuhl, well west of the Rhine River.

Relations between *Stripes* and the 12th Air Force improved; but then, there were no major accidents in the next few years before I returned to the States. To completely please the flyboys would have been to omit all mention of air crashes or to restrict coverage to a couple of paragraphs.

I wasn't around when the air force colonel took over as editor in chief. I have often wondered how he would have reacted if one of the fighters came roaring out of the sky to land near his office.

13

People

Professional newspapermen in uniform gave *The Stars and Stripes* its stamp of authenticity and flavor right from the beginning. The war kept the staff more or less intact from the paper's birth in ·April 1942 until a few days after the end of hostilities in May 1945. Redeployment caused the number and quality to fall by the wayside, and the few editions that survived hung on with short-time help from the replacement depots.

When the army became convinced that *Stripes* could not survive with a military staff, it agreed to give civilian jobs to those GIs who wished to remain in Europe and bring over professional newspapermen from the States. It took time, but *Stripes* regained its professional look and tone and went on to bigger and better editions to be read by more and more people.

To maintain morale and give a meaning to marriage and family life, dependents were permitted to enter occupied Germany and join their husbands and fathers. Lives that had been interrupted by Pearl Harbor were slowly returning to normal and resumed fully when the ships carrying dependents started arriving in the warm spring of 1946.

Pretty American women in their stylish clothes appeared on the sidewalks of the cobblestone streets of the German cities and villages and drew puzzled stares from dowdy German housewives. Well-stacked *frauleins* were awed by the well-scrubbed American girls who enrolled in high school classes in Berlin, Frankfurt, and Stuttgart.

The wives mixed well with their fellow American women from other states and with the foreign-born wives of soldiers and civilians. They fitted in nicely with the British and other Allied women who worked as secretaries and in other clerical jobs with the army, air force, and Military Government.

The *Stripes* colonels' ladies — Eulalie, Sadie, Jan, Inez, and Frances — assumed leadership roles in church and charity functions with German agencies. Orphanages and youth clubs, as well as schools, benefited from the generosity of these women and members of their committees who gave time and money to help the less fortunate.

Bridge, bingo, and social events at the *Stripes* Press Club filled spare moments, as did golf, tennis, and swimming. Picnics were planned, and softball games took over Sunday afternoons. Bowling vied with University of Maryland classes on weeknights.

The need to start or restart families became important, and before long the maternity wards in Frankfurt, Wiesbaden, Heidelberg, and Munich were turning out little *Stripes* issues. After that it was PTA and Cub, Brownie, Boy and Girl Scouts, as well as German youth activities such as the soap box derby, where the overall Germany winner donned *Stars and Stripes* colors and participated in the finals at Akron, Ohio.

★   ★   ★

Nancy Elaine Lampron wasn't the first child born to a *Stripes* family — that honor went to Roberta Browne — but Nancy was the first born in the back seat of a stalled jeep.

Her mother, Jacqueline, a French war bride, told her husband, Emil, about 10:00 P.M. that she was feeling pains and he called the *Stripes* dispensary. Cpl. Joseph Smiley drew a new Willys Jeep station wagon out of the motor pool, collected Capt. Glenn Weaver, a physician-surgeon assigned to the Bensheim-Pfungstadt area, and they drove to Lampron's billets in Pfungstadt.

Lampron, a printer from Spencer, Massachusetts, made Jackie comfortable in the back seat with a couple of pillows and a blanket, and they set off for the 130th Station Hospital in Heidelberg.

"It's a good thing we have this new civilian jeep," Smiley said as they headed south on the autobahn. "I'd hate to have to depend on those piles of junk in the motor pool."

Smiley spoke too soon. About five miles out of Pfungstadt, the jeep's engine cut out and he coasted to the side of the autobahn. He decided it was the fuel line, but he had no time to try to repair it; Jackie was in labor and gave birth right there to a six-and-a-half-pound girl.

The hospital records her birth at 2330 hours September 22, 1947.

★   ★   ★

The only *Stripes* employee to be fired because he goosed his commanding officer was Joseph Alvin Kugelmas. Well, perhaps "goose" isn't the right word. Joe actually kneed the army officer at a party in a private billet at Pfungstadt.

Lt. Col. William M. Summers, editor in chief, was on the receiving end of the indignity as he entered the room filled with guests. Joe slipped up behind him and lifted his knee so that it touched the colonel's posterior. The colonel whirled and said: "That's it, Kugelmas. You're fired!"

Since I was standing nearby and witnessed what had happened, I grabbed Joe by the arm and pulled him into the kitchen.

"Why the hell did you have to do that?" I asked. "We just got everything smoothed over, and now you go and goose the colonel."

"I didn't mean any harm," Joe pleaded. "I really like the guy. I'll go and apologize."

"You will not," I said. "You go home and we'll talk about it on Monday. You can see the colonel then. This is not the time or place to discuss business."

Joe and his wife, Elizabeth, left the party. When I had a chance to talk with Summers a few minutes later he was furious.

"Can you believe that guy? After my going out on a limb for him?" the colonel said.

Summers had indeed gone out on a limb for Kugelmas, who joined the staff as a copyreader in May 1949. A member of the editorial staff of the New York newspaper *PM*, he applied for a job with *Stripes* and, after being cleared by federal agencies, was flown to Germany. His family followed a few months later.

One day in February, Joe stepped into my office and said he

wanted to talk. He had a confession to make because he had obtained the job with *Stripes* under false pretenses.

"I didn't tell you that I am an ex-convict, and I think you should know that I served a year in prison for larceny," he said.

I just sat there dumbfounded and then finally told him that we should go see the colonel. I phoned the colonel's secretary, telling her that I had an urgent personnel problem to discuss, and a few minutes later Joe and I walked in and sat down.

Joe told Summers what he told me. The colonel wondered aloud as to why the Federal Bureau of Investigation, and other agencies that check all potential employees, hadn't turned up the prison record. But then his decision took both Joe and me by surprise.

"I don't see a problem, Joe. From what I have been able to observe you are doing good work on the copy desk, and you write well. The fact that you are man enough to reveal your past counts for something. I'll mention it to Heidelberg, but I think everything will be all right."

"What a helluva guy," Joe said as we returned to the newsroom. The next night, the Saturday before Valentine's Day, a Valentine party was planned at the billet of Howard and Shirley Katzander. The theme was the Valentine's Day Massacre, in memory of the Chicago gangland killings.

The Kugelmases were there when my wife, Paulette, and I arrived. A short time later Summers and his wife, Sadie, walked through the door into the living room where the goosing incident took place. Two weeks later Kugelmas was en route to the States with his wife and two children.

★   ★   ★

Francis "Red" Grandy was one of the few people I ever hired who had never previously worked on a daily newspaper. It wasn't his photographs; it was his smile, boyish charm, and the intervention of a friend that influenced me, and I am glad I made the exception.

Red went on to win many prestigious awards for his work, as well as having his photos reprinted in leading newspapers, magazines, and the *Encyclopedia Britannica*. Three years later, after almost not getting the job, I appointed him chief of the photo department.

Grandy walked into my office early in January 1951, and although I liked what I saw of his few samples, I turned him down because all the experience he had was classroom and campus work at the University of Southern California.

Betty Kaye, a friend living in Wiesbaden, phoned the next day to put in a word in his behalf. She asked if I would see him again and look at more of his work.

"What I saw in his scrapbook is good," I told her. "But you know he has never worked on a daily newspaper. He doesn't know about deadlines, has no experience when it comes to news. Taking pictures of girls, flowers and sunsets is something else."

"I understand, but I think you should make an exception in his case. He is good and his work is outstanding. Please talk to him again," she pleaded.

I finally agreed because Betty, an air force dependent, was also a booking agent for stage shows and often brought her productions to our club to preview before sending them out on the military post circuit. I certainly didn't want to offend her, and she was a friend. Grandy returned the next day and I called in Jerry Waller, the chief photographer and department head, and a couple of the news editors to see his work. He walked out an hour later with the job. I have never regretted changing my mind.

Three months later, April 11, Grandy took the now famous photo of General Eisenhower that won him first prize in the *Editor and Publisher*'s 1951 contest, an award from Kent State, inclusion in the *Encyclopedia Britannica,* and inclusion in the volume of the best news pictures of a quarter-century published by *Life* magazine. It was a photo of Ike's reaction to the news that President Harry S. Truman had fired Gen. Douglas MacArthur.

The incident occurred at Coblenz and we used the photo on Page 1. The three major wire services immediately requested copies, which later were published on the front page of *The New York Times,* in *Time* magazine, *Newsweek,* and hundreds of other publications.

Two weeks later Grandy was in Vienna and took a picture of Robert A. Vogeler greeting his wife, Lucille, following his release from a Communist prison at Budapest, where he spent seventeen months of a fifteen-year sentence following his conviction of an espionage charge. That touching and timely photograph was published April 30 on Page 1 and was also requested by the wire services. It too was reprinted in major publications, including the *Saturday Evening Post.*

In both cases Grandy proved that he knew how to take news photos. In both instances he demonstrated that he could work in tandem with reporters — in Coblenz with Art Noyes and in Vienna with Ernie Reed.

At Coblenz, Ike had just finished reviewing French troops and stood chatting with two French generals, their interpreters, and a number of press representatives. He had just removed one glove and during a lapse in the conversation Richard O'Malley, an Associated Press reporter, spoke up: "Excuse me, General Eisenhower, have you heard the news about MacArthur?"

Ike looked at O'Malley and said, "No, what happened?" Then O'Malley told him that President Truman had relieved MacArthur of his Far East command and that he had been replaced by Gen. Matthew B. Ridgway. Eisenhower looked to one side, Grandy clicked his Speed Graphic and the general said, "Well, I'll be darned." Eisenhower then asked O'Malley how he learned of the firing, and the AP reporter said it was on the 10:00 A.M. radio news broadcast.

After Grandy finished his assignment he returned to Griesheim and processed his film, made contact prints, and took them downstairs to the news editor. It was almost 8:00 P.M. and the news editor was rushing to get out of the office to catch a train to start his vacation. He told Red that the Page 1 dummy was already made up and tossed the contacts into the in-basket. Downhearted, Grandy left the newsroom.

When John Livingood, the assistant managing editor, came in the next morning after his days off to take over the news editor's job, he found the contacts. A few minutes later he brought them into my office.

"Grandy's got some good stuff here on Ike's visit to the French command at Coblenz. Here is a great shot of the general's face reacting to the news that Truman fired MacArthur."

I looked at the contact and agreed that we should use it on Page 1. Livingood pointed out that since it was a candid shot the brass in Heidelberg would probably object because Eisenhower was caught off-guard.

"We won't show it to them. We're already a day late as it is," I said.

John was right. One colonel in Heidelberg did protest, but Ike liked the photo and later autographed a copy for the photographer, which said, "For Red Grandy: who in this picture surprised an old soldier. D.D.E."

The photo appeared two days after it was taken and caused a sensation. We published it two columns at the bottom of the five-column page. The Associated Press, United Press, and International News Photos sent their drivers down the autobahn from Frankfurt to pick up free copies of the print. It was our policy to give photographs to the agencies without charge as long as they gave *Stripes* credit.

The New York Times published it on its April 16 front page with credit to both *The Stars and Stripes* and the Associated Press. The *New York Daily News* and *Life* magazine also used the picture with credit to *Stripes*, but *Time* magazine and *Newsweek*, in their April 23 issues, did not. *Newsweek* followed up May 7 by giving proper credit.

Roy W. Boyd, Jr., of *Time* magazine in New York, explained: "While we never had *The Stars and Stripes* in the picture credit, it was mentioned in the original draft of the story, but unfortunately was edited out. I am very sorry this happened. It was a fine picture and should have been properly credited. Extra precautions will be taken to see that it doesn't happen again."

Even the Russians got into the act, according to Leonard Lyon's column in the *New York Post: "Pravda* used Ike's photo under the caption: 'This is how Gen. Eisenhower looked when he learned of the outcome of the French elections.' "

When Reed called from Vienna to say that Vogeler, a thirty-nine-year-old vice-president for Eastern Europe of the International Telephone and Telegraph Company, was expected to be released soon, I dispatched Grandy to Vienna. He was there a few days early, but that gave him time to become acquainted with Vienna, and through Ernie he met Lucille, Vogeler's wife, and her sister, Pia.

When it was announced that Vogeler was to be released the morning of April 28 the press gathered outside his home at 15 Max Emmanuel Strasse to wait.

"It was a long wait punctuated by a thunderstorm, and the entire press corps, about thirty of us, got pretty wet and jaded after three hours," Grandy remembers.

Due to his and Ernie's relationship with Lucille, a beautiful Belgian-born blonde, Red struck up a friendship with one of the guards provided for her protection by the U.S. State Department. Through him Red learned the license number of the State Department's black Chevrolet sedan that was scheduled to bring Vogeler to his house.

"While the rest of the press were gathered under a tree across the street I noticed this black sedan approaching the corner house where the Vogelers lived, so I drifted across the street and got organized. My first shot was one of him getting out of the car and the second was when Lucille came running out with their two young sons and embraced Vogeler," Grandy said.

Since there were no wirephoto capabilities in Vienna, Red's problem was to get the film back to Griesheim. Reed put him on the Mozart night train to Munich, and the next morning he borrowed a Chevrolet from the Munich News Bureau and drove to Griesheim in three hours and forty minutes, a record since several of the war-damaged bridges still had not been replaced.

The picture, taken on Saturday, didn't get into *The Stars and Stripes* until Monday, April 30 — a day late, but it still beat the stateside press and was picked up by the three wire services, again for free, and was published in U.S. newspapers, including a half page in the *Saturday Evening Post*.

A year later, on March 12, 1952, the day following the New Hampshire primary election, General Eisenhower stepped off an airplane at Rhine-Main Air Base near Frankfurt. Grandy and I were there, hopeful of meeting him and congratulating him on his victory over Sen. Robert A. Taft. That was the same election in which Sen. Estes Kefauver defeated President Truman and forced the latter out of the race.

We had approached Gen. Thomas T. Handy, who headed the reception party, and I told him I wanted Grandy to meet General Ike. "Go to it, son," Handy said.

When Eisenhower reached the bottom of the stairs and before he drew abreast of the color guard, I stepped forward and introduced myself and then Grandy. Ike's face broke into that famous grin and he reached out and shook Red's hand while still photographers clicked and newsreel cameras whirred.

That picture of the three of us was printed in thousands of newspapers the next day and in magazines and shown in movie theaters the following week.

★   ★   ★

We had other good cameramen: Bud Kane, Dick Koenig, Herb Palmer, Larry Riordan, and Joe Brignola during the war; Bob Merritt, Chris Butler, George Penn, Tony Vaccaro, Jerry Waller, Ted Rohde, and Ed Killpack in the postwar years.

Waller, a photographer for the American Red Cross while the fighting was going on, was chief of the photo department and planned the move from Pfungstadt to the new studio and darkroom at Griesheim. Now retired, he lives in Los Angeles with his wife, Lor Lizabeth, also a former *Stripes* photographer.

One of Waller's photographers was Sam Vestal, a young soldier who was there in 1953–54. When his enlistment expired, he returned to California and resumed work on the *Register-Pajaronian* at Watsonville. Shortly afterwards, he took a picture that exposed misconduct of the district attorney of Salinas County and touched off an investigation of corruption. The picture and the story won a Pulitzer Prize for his newspaper.

Another *Stripes* photographer during the Waller-Grandy era was Henry Toluzzi, a former Grenadier corporal in the Swiss army. He had been working for the U.S. Army Special Services. When his contract expired in late 1949, he came to Pfungstadt, where Waller and I interviewed him.

Being a Swiss national, he was paid on the Continental Wage Scale, which had been set by the Allied governments, and meant that he would receive less money than the American photographers. This didn't please him, but Jerry and I pointed out that he didn't have to pay income taxes to Uncle Sam as we did.

One of Henry's most memorable photos taken while with *Stripes* was of General Eisenhower seated in a jeep in the little town of Dornheim during the 1951 autumn military exercises. He was smiling that famous Ike smile and talking to three young German boys.

Thirty years later the Toluzzi picture of Ike and the three boys was reprinted in a German television magazine and the German daily *Bild Zeitung*. With its publication in 1983, the three boys — now grown men — came forward.

"We immediately recognized Gen. Eisenhower when the jeep stopped. We were always seeing him in the German newsreels. So we knew who he was. He asked how we were and an American took the photographs," Roland Imhof, forty-one, said. V Corps public information officers rounded up Imhof, Guenter Koop, thirty-nine, and Guenter Kohlross, forty-two, and gave them copies of the photo Toluzzi had snapped September 30, 1951.

"The photo was taken right outside of the elementary school. We were on our way home. I was eleven years old," Imhof added. Now a technician in a hotel, he is the father of two children. Koop, a production manager for a large electrical firm, has a French wife and a daughter. Kohlross owns a factory which makes machinery that manufactures sausage skins. He is married and has two daughters.

And Toluzzi? He left *Stripes* in June 1952 to do free-lance photojournalism and later hooked up with NBC News for worldwide assignments. Birth certificates of his and his wife Sonia's children are a tip-off to some of those stories: Peter Michael born in Hong Kong, 1956, and Anne Helene born in Kenya in 1961. Toluzzi now lives in retirement on his yacht *Takiri* in Australian waters.

★　　★　　★

Although the editorial staff of *The Stars and Stripes* was predominantly civilian, we had a number of enlisted personnel working on the newspaper. While a few held down jobs on the copy desk, most were assigned to sports, photo, and clerical work.

A lot of them knew sports from either playing or writing about the games for high school or college newspapers. Photographers in uniform, especially those who trained in film classes at Ft. Monmouth, New Jersey, more than held their own and even taught *Stripes* civilians the latest techniques.

The editor of B-Bag was an enlisted man, and among those who handled the letters to the editor in a professional manner were Lee Patterson, Lonnie Towe, David Iteen, Bill Shrum, and John H. Conner.

When a GI demonstrated that he was proficient and wanted a civilian job, he was offered a contract. Cecil Neth of Huntington Beach, California, Douglas K. Jennings of Topeka, Kansas, and Nicholas Raymond of New York were among those selected, and all did well. Neth moved on to be an editor of *Overseas Weekly* and after that a newspaper in the States. Jennings worked in the Salzburg news bureau and later held down a public relations job in Los Angeles. Raymond started in the New York bureau and then became an assistant editor of the military news section of *Stripes*.

Soldiers John Raita and Hugh F. Harty joined the staff as proofreaders, and when their enlistment was up they accepted civilian employment and remained for a number of years.

Victor Wheeler and Max Hill Weir, both regular army non-commissioned officers and printers by trade, served more than one hitch with *Stripes*.

Wheeler made the transition from hot to cold type on his several assignments and is now living in retirement in Southern California.

On his second tour there was no vacancy in production, so Weir worked in editorial as picture editor and was responsible for booklets entitled *Castle Tours* and *Trizonal Towns*. Also, with the help of proofreader David Danziger, he produced a three-dimensional cover for the feature section, complete with colored glasses.

I'll never forget Larry Kaufman. He was with *Stripes* eight months in 1953, writing sports and features in the tradition of *Stripes* veteran Jimmy Cannon. A soldier in the tradition of George S. Patton he was not; he had to be reminded to keep his uniform clean and to have his hair trimmed. Not to worry, Kaufman would say, he was not going to make the military his career. He left in December from Bremerhaven on board a ship bound for New York assigned to guard prisoners. Larry didn't mind; he had served his time.

After a short period in New York, he accepted a job as sports editor of the *Wilmington* [Delaware] *News* and changed his name to Larry Merchant. I often see him on Home Box Office television reporting boxing and football.

Pvt. Lou Rukeyser came along early in 1955 and took over the B-Bag editor's chair. He had graduated from Princeton before entering the army and while in college worked as campus correspondent for the *Baltimore Sun*. When he left *Stripes* in January 1956, he was a specialist third class, and after taking his discharge from the army he returned to the *Baltimore Sun*. He made an easy transition from army to civilian life, from print to the electronic media, and now has his own television program. We see Louis Rukeyser's "Wall Street Week" every Friday evening on public television.

14

War

It was called a war — a newspaper war — and it was all of that in the early 1950s: a circulation war involving five newspapers published in Europe. Instead of bullets, the sky was filled with brickbats, lawsuits, lucky bucks, World Series tickets, transfers for some army officers, and the firing of a top *Stripes* civilian executive.

Editor and Publisher, the newspaper trade journal, was the first to identify as a war this contest for the serviceman's nickel in an article published August 7, 1954. Quoting United Press correspondents as its source, the story listed the "contenders" as "*The Stars and Stripes;* the *American Daily,* a five-day-a-week tabloid; the *Overseas Weekly,* a flashy publication that was once banned by the U.S. Army for being 'too sexy'; the European edition of the *New York Herald-Tribune;* and the *Daily American* in Rome."

The trade journal added that the *New York Times,* with a Continental edition published in Amsterdam from mats flown daily out of New York, was apparently aloof from the scramble. *Editor and Publisher* said the target for the contenders was the estimated 400,000 Americans in Europe, North Africa, Greece, and Turkey.

The German press reported August 25 that the *Herald-Tribune* accused the *American Daily* of "unfair competition" with its lucky bucks campaign and suggested that it might be an illegal lottery.

Lucky bucks involved a list of serial numbers of one-dollar scrip bills (a total of $250 a week) published in the paper. If the lucky GI had a bill in his pocket that matched one of the numbers, then he had a lucky buck and was the winner of the jackpot. The story also said the publisher of the *Daily American* in Rome protested the *American Daily*'s similar name.

The Associated Press followed with a story datelined Frankfurt, November 14, which told of a new letter press that *Stripes* put into operation in August and its new twenty-four-page daily edition with more comics, more sports, and more features.

The expanded daily was something we had wanted for a long time, and it took the Paris *Herald-Tribune* brass to get us off dead center. Charles Spann, the *Herald-Tribune* circulation manager, asked me to stop by and see him the next time I was in Paris. A week or so later I dropped in on him and he immediately called in Eric Hawkins, managing editor, and Art Buchwald, the *Herald-Tribune* columnist. Spann wanted to know all about the battle with the *American Daily* and what our next moves were. I told him the best I could.

"To beat Ryder at his own game, *Stripes* should come out with a bigger paper with more news, more sports and more comics," Spann said.

I took his suggestion back to Germany and presented it to the editor in chief and the general manager. We decided to abolish the twelve-page *Feature Section* and use four feature pages in the daily plus more news, comics, and sports. With the new press it was a natural, and Information and Education Division in Heidelberg approved the concept. Spann was delighted and informed us that the *Herald-Tribune* planned to add comics, which was something new for the Paris-based paper. The battle lines were drawn and we were ready.

Yes, we had a war on our hands and the war-born *Stripes* has the scars to prove it. I think we were all a bit scarred by the happenings, which, as I recall, began at a cocktail party in my home in south Darmstadt in the summer of 1948.

A young man who introduced himself as Dick Donnelley accompanied one of the invited guests from Frankfurt. I was told that he was the stepson of Melvin Ryder, the president of the Army Times Publishing Company in Washington, D.C., and publisher of the *Army Times, Navy Times,* and *Air Force Times,* all weeklies and all packed with advertising.

Toward the end of the party Donnelley got in a heated discussion with Lt. Col. William M. Summers, editor in chief, and me over the use in *Stripes* of free advertising for the post exchange and the commissaries. It was true that we printed public service ads featuring the food special of the week or some item that the PX or commissary happened to be pushing. We felt that it was part payment for the use of newsstand space in the post exchange, and we told him so. We also informed him that *Stripes* did not receive revenue from the ads. Donnelley left the party threatening to protest to higher-ups in the Pentagon. That's the last I ever saw of Dick Donnelley, but I sure heard plenty of him as the years went by.

Ryder had been an enlisted man on the staff of the World War I *Stripes* in Paris. He worked in circulation as a field agent. After his return to the States and civilian life, he published a newsletter for the military and eventually expanded it to the weekly *Army Times.* Later he added the *Navy Times* and after World War II the *Air Force Times.* Unlike his stepson, he was friendly to *Stripes* and me.

The three weeklies were printed in the States and shipped to Europe, where they were displayed and sold on the *Stripes* newsstands. Packed with advertising and articles about the services, they sold well. Then, in 1953, we began to pick up rumors that the Ryder interests had their eye on Europe and planned to start a daily newspaper. On July 15 the Army Times Publishing Company launched the *Air Force Daily,* a six-column tabloid printed by the *London Times.* Ryder and Donnelley were listed as publishers and executive editors, Dale White as editor, and Fred Shaw managing editor. Their lead story was about the Korean War.

The *Air Force Daily* didn't set any circulation records, but it was on the newsstands in the United Kingdom nearly a full day before *The Stars and Stripes* arrived from Germany. The newsstands in the UK were operated for a time by the Ryder interests, but after a few months and many complaints about the service, the Air Force Exchange (AFEX) took them over. AFEX was the air force version of the army's European Exchange Service (EES).

There was also criticism from the publisher of the *Rome Daily American* of Ryder's use of the words air force in the name of the paper, but the Washington publisher solved this by changing it to the *American Daily.* At the same time he moved the operation to

Germany, where most of the troops were stationed, set up shop in Giesen (twenty miles north of Frankfurt), and published the first Continental edition on July 2.

The owner of the *Rome Daily American,* Ray Vir Den, a New York advertising executive, didn't like the new name either. He said it was too much like the name of his paper and threatened court action.

We objected to the *American Daily*'s use of Milton Caniff's comic strip "Steve Canyon." We didn't protest when the paper was printed in England, but when it moved to Germany, I wrote to the syndicate pointing out that our territorial rights had been violated. The syndicate agreed and canceled the *American Daily*'s contract.

Two days after the final Canyon strip in the *American Daily,* we rolled out our big gun: a chartered two-engine airplane to fly the papers to England. If the *American Daily* was deserting its readers in the United Kingdom, then *Stripes* would fill that void. So reasoned Anthony "Tony" Biancone, chief of distribution for *Stripes.* The daily airlift to London with a stopover in Paris proved a big success, missing only a few missions due to fog. Readers in western France and England were receiving a twenty-four-page newspaper plus a sixteen-page color comic section on Sundays, a full day ahead of the competition.

Biancone and I had the full support and backing of Lt. Col. Arthur L. Jorgenson, the editor in chief, and Maj. Warren H. Scheffner, the general manager. Both worked hard to change the newspaper's role from passive to active and to obtain approval for some of the things we wished to do from Armed Forces Information and Education Division as well as *The Stars and Stripes* Fund Council.

The climate changed when Scheffner was transferred to Heidelberg to another job within AFIED on September 8 and Jorgenson was relieved October 9. Scheffner, of Kansas City, Missouri, was with *Stripes* two years and one month and Jorgenson, of Spokane, Washington, only eighteen months.

There was no way of our knowing the reasons for their early departures, but we blamed Col. Edward R. Ott, the new chief of U.S. Army, Europe, Armed Forces Information and Education Division. Ott, a former high school teacher and later assistant dean at Louisiana State University, had taken over the post June 26, 1954, from Col. Maurice G. Stubbs. Two months after sitting down at his desk he shook up the *Stripes* command.

Scheffner's post was not filled immediately, but Lt. Col. Lother B. Sibert, also a former schoolteacher, was assigned to replace Jorgenson. We knew Sibert, a stern and humorless person, because he had been making a study of the *Stripes* operation for several weeks before assuming the editor-in-chief post. He told me later he had been checking to see if we had any homosexuals on the staff, but if he found any he didn't say.

After working a few weeks without a general manager, Sibert promoted George Close, the communications director, who originally came from Aledo, Illinois, to acting general manager. Close had served thirteen years in the army and was a captain when he left the service. With no experience on a daily newspaper and with only eighteen months at *Stripes*, Close took over just in time to get himself and the colonel bloodied in a dispute with the *Rome Daily American*.

Biancone had agreed to sell the Rome newspaper on the *Stripes* newsstands, but because someone protested Tony's decision, Sibert fired him. Biancone, a platoon sergeant who landed on Utah Beach in June 1944 with the 5th Amphibious Brigade and an eight-year veteran of *Stripes* who came from Riverside, New Jersey, was doing what he was paid to do. We suspected that the *American Daily* had something to do with it, but of course we couldn't prove it.

Biancone said he was told by Sibert and Close that the reason for his firing was that he "embarrassed" *Stripes* by agreeing to distribute the *Rome Daily American*.

"The Army had been caught in the middle of a fight between two civilian newspapers and when a mistake hurt one, a scapegoat had to be found. I'm it," he told reporters.

Sydney Label of Philadelphia, a circulation supervisor, took over Biancone's job as chief of distribution.

Three days later USAEUR headquarters blamed Biancone for "flagrant disobedience of orders," which he called "an outrageous lie."

In Rome, Vir Den said he had asked *The Stars and Stripes* to distribute his newspaper on the same basis as the *New York Times, New York Herald-Tribune*'s international edition, the *Army Times, Navy Times, Air Force Times,* and the *American Daily.*

Vir Den was quoted in a news story that "a letter from Biancone had agreed and the *Rome Daily American* had informed the distribution organization of its plans to begin delivery on November 2."

"But a last-minute cable from Sibert told us to disregard the letter of his distribution chief and added that a letter from his office would follow," Vir Den said.

The publisher said he waited ten days and when he didn't hear from Sibert he cabled him demanding an explanation but still had heard nothing from the colonel.

Vir Den praised the *Stripes* distribution service, saying it "is one of the finest in Europe, one which no individual publisher could afford but if it is open to one it should be open to all new papers. Since when can a few army colonels in Heidelberg and Frankfurt sit in judgment on what or whose newspaper can be distributed by the U.S. Army? It is nothing more than a dictatorial action that strikes at freedom of the press."

In Washington, Ryder said "there is absolutely no connection between the Pentagon and our publications. We are a private organization."

Private or not, the Ryder papers had a number of retired officers on the staff, including John M. Virden, whose column appeared several times a week.

Ott and Sibert took it on the chin when Assistant Defense Secretary Fred A. Seaton ordered Gen. William Hoge, U.S. Army commander in Europe, to put the *Rome Daily American* back on *Stripes* stands in Germany for a thirty-day trial. Sales were only average, and after a time Ray Vir Den stopped shipping the paper to Germany.

The *American Daily* lasted only a few more months and then closed for good on February 28, 1955, approximately a year and seven months after its debut in England. I hired Dale White, its editor, and Fred Shaw, the managing editor, to work on the copy desk, but both left for the States after a few months. If there were winners in the newspaper "war," then they must have been the *Herald-Tribune* and *The Stars and Stripes*.

The loser was Tony Biancone. After his firing by Sibert, Biancone flew to the States to visit his family and returned a week later to marry his fiancée, Elizabeth Medart. He then went to work for Marion von Rospach's *Overseas Weekly*. It came out of the "war" without a scratch and must be considered a winner, since it was still being distributed on *Stripes* newsstands despite a 1953 hassle with the army. Sibert was also involved in that fracas.

★   ★   ★

The *Overseas Weekly* was the brainchild of Air Force Maj. James A. Ziccarelli, of Carmichael, Pennsylvania, and he launched the twenty-eight-page publication May 14, 1950, to give the troops in Europe "a touch of home — away from home." The twelve-page news section featured columns by Billy Rose, Leonard Lyons, Earl Wilson, and Grantland Rice, and the sixteen-page color comics included "Bringing Up Father," "Prince Valiant," and "Flash Gordon."

After determining that *The Stars and Stripes* could set the type and print the weekly as well as distribute it on the newsstands, Ziccarelli obtained a license from USAEUR to go into business. He also needed something to do because he was soon to be discharged from the service.

Not too long after the debut of the *Overseas Weekly*, the Korean War started, and Ziccarelli's hopes of becoming a civilian were dashed when the air force refused to release him. The army and navy were also calling up reserves and recruiting. Faced with more time in uniform, Ziccarelli put the *Overseas Weekly* up for sale.

Cecil and Marion von Rospach bought the fledgling weekly for a little down and a promise to pay off the balance. That was good enough for Ziccarelli; he had received no other offer. The Rospachs (they didn't use the "von," although it was on both of their passports) were Californians; he from Placentia, near Los Angeles, and she from San Francisco. They had been traveling in Europe following their graduation from Stanford.

I first met them that same year when they drove into the parking lot at Pfungstadt. They had just come from Madrid and were looking for work. I didn't need copyreaders then but I was looking for a woman to handle the women's page. The result was that I put both of them on the payroll for a three-month period.

Before his contract expired, Cecil found a job as news chief for the USAFE public information office in Wiesbaden and later switched to the State Department as information officer with the U.S. Information Agency in Frankfurt. We offered Marion an extension on her contract, but she opted to follow her husband, where she found a job with the air force in Wiesbaden editing the *Air Lift Times,* a publication featuring articles about the Berlin airlift.

It was while working in Wiesbaden that Marion learned of Ziccarelli's attempts to sell his paper. She talked it over with Cecil, and he was all for buying it, but because of his government job his role was that of silent partner. No problem: Marion, who had been an editor on the *Stanford Daily*, was more than capable.

She hired a managing editor and several advertising salesmen and slowly and steadily built up the circulation, mostly by using sexual-oriented features. The principal package included King Features color comics and columns, but she also depended on press agents in New York and Hollywood for photos of scantily clad young women to spice up the product. The circulation climbed, and so did the advertising lineage.

In 1953 she published a series of articles written by Christine Jorgensen, the ex-GI George Jorgensen who underwent a sex change in Denmark. It was a graphic tale and the paper's sales soared. Another series followed, this one by Pat Ward, the teenage girlfriend of twenty-two-year-old Minot "Mickey" Jelke III, heir to an oleomargarine fortune, who was convicted of pandering and living off the earnings of prostitutes.

Because of the sexual slant, GI readers were soon calling the paper the *Oversexed Weekly*, and this and the Jorgensen-Ward series didn't amuse the army. On May 5, 1953, USAEUR yanked Marion von Rospach's license to print and distribute through *The Stars and Stripes*. She was given until June 30 to make other arrangements. Marion yelled foul.

She caught a plane to Washington, D.C., with a suitcase filled with back copies of the *Overseas Weekly* to show to the two California senators, William R. Knowland and Thomas Kuchel. While there she filed suit in federal court against Defense Secretary Charles E. Wilson, seeking to delay the army's action.

Publication of the Jorgensen-Ward articles was the army's excuse for the ban, but what really irritated the colonels and generals was the newspaper's practice of reporting court-martials, especially those in which GIs were involved in sex crimes. Lurid details of what this or that *fraulein* was or was not wearing at the scene of the crime titillated the weekly's readers, and circulation jumped to 40,000 a week.

The army's letter to her telling her of the ban stated in part: "It has been evident that the *Overseas Weekly* no longer serves the purpose for which it was licensed, i.e., to advance the education and enhance the morale of the U.S. Army personnel." The letter also complained "that the paper carried stories of sex and prostitution which affect military and dependent personnel in the command."

We learned of the ban the day after Marion received the word from USAEUR because she immediately informed production and distribution officials at *Stripes*. But when we tried to confirm the story with the public information office in Heidelberg, we were told that "negotiations were still going on" and that we would have to wait for an official release from their office.

Newsweek didn't wait, however. Its May 8 issue reported that "spunky Marion von Rospach, 27, had taken on the U.S. Army and is in Washington seeking a court order to block the army's action." The U.S. District Court judges refused her appeal, stating that there had been no showing of "irreparable damage." She vowed to take it to a higher court.

"I can't believe that the Army wants to kill an independent, free American paper. We are being run out of business. This is an encroachment on the concept of freedom of the press," she was quoted as saying.

Upon her return to Germany, she appealed the ban May 11 in a letter addressed to USAEUR and asked for an extension from June 30 to July 28 so as to complete her printing contract with *The Stars and Stripes*. Her request was approved.

Marion shifted the typesetting and printing to the *Frankfurter Rundschau* and adhered to the USAEUR deadline, but the army backed down on the distribution ban because, as *Time* magazine stated, "she fast-talked a few congressmen into getting the ban lifted."

As a gesture of good will, she toned down the editorial content a bit but not much, and as a sop to the dependents she later started *Overseas Family*, addressed to the servicemen's wives, and *Overseas Traveler*, a tourist guide.

15

Taps

Carrol Sprague signed out of the photo lab at 9:00 A.M. January 29, 1948, to join in a search of the French Alps for a downed C-47 carrying twelve persons, including three American dependents and their five children. The search plane he was in crashed and Sprague and eight others died. I felt the loss of the twenty-seven-year-old corporal keenly because I had assigned him to the flight.

Sprague was the fourth GI newspaperman on *The Stars and Stripes* to lose his life in the line of duty. By coincidence, his death was within seventy-five miles of the spot where another *Stripes* man died of a machine-gun burst across the chest. He was Al Kohn, a reporter who was killed near Grenoble shortly after the invasion of southern France.

Others who died while getting the news were Greg Duncan, killed by artillery fire at Anzio, and Paul Connors, shot down during an air force bombing mission.

The drama that took Sprague's life began at 11:37 A.M. two days earlier when a Rhine-Main-based Air Force C-47 took off from Istres, France, to fly to Udine, Italy, with three American dependent wives and five children plus four crew members. The women and children had arrived January 23 at Bremerhaven on board the army transport *Gen. R.E. Callan* and were en route to join U.S. servicemen in Trieste.

A specially equipped B-17 with Sprague and the others aboard took off to join the search. Another plane had spotted the downed Gooney Bird on White Horse Mountain about fourteen miles northeast of Digne, France. Three hours later the B-17 crashed and exploded in the same area. There was one survivor, S/Sgt. Angelo A. LaSalle of Des Moines, Iowa. The death toll of the two crashes was set at twenty-one persons.

The pilot of still another search plane said the B-17 circled the wreck and then started to gain altitude to pass over the ridge. A wing struck and broke off and the big bomber exploded and crashed 100 feet from the crest of the ridge.

Sprague, whose home was in Farmington, Maine, was survived by his mother, Mrs. Flossie Webster. He was on his second hitch in the army and had joined *The Stars and Stripes* in July 1946 from the 645th Air Force Service Squadron.

A friend of mine was also on the same flight. He was 1st/Lt. Maurice "Mike" Casner, Jr., thirty-four, assigned to the USAFE public information office. Casner, a member of the Associated Press staff in New York City for six years before receiving his army commission in 1944, was survived by his wife and two children.

Six days before his death, Casner joined in escorting a group of touring Russian newspapermen through the Pfungstadt plant of *Stripes* and had their pictures taken by Sprague. The Russians issued a statement expressing their deep regret and sympathy at the death of the twenty-one Americans in the two crashes.

Memorial services were conducted February 5 for Sprague by Chaplain Laurence Hertzog of the EUCOM Quartermaster School at Darmstadt. Attending were the civilians, dependents, officers, and enlisted men of *The Stars and Stripes*. A few weeks later Lt. Col. William M. Summers, the editor in chief, ordered the enlisted billets at Pfungstadt to be named Sprague Barracks in the dead photographer's honor.

We all grieved in our own way for Carrol Sprague. Reporters Albert Burchard and Norbert Ehrenfreund were on other planes over the Digne area and could have been on the B-17. Photo chief Chris Butler had been on another assignment that day or he might have been on the ill-fated flight himself.

I'll never forget that it was Carrol Sprague who answered the telephone in the photo lab the day I called to make the assignment.

★　　★　　★

Henry Wilbur Trescott, forty-six, a copy editor for *The Stars and Stripes,* died of heart problems February 24, 1951, at the 97th General Hospital in Frankfurt. Although a veteran, he was not eligible to be buried in a military cemetery overseas, and since he had no close relatives in the States, I bought a plot for him in Frankfurt.

Henry made out a will and named me executor on the day before he died. He left everything he owned to Kathe Hitpass of Pfungstadt, whom he listed as his fiancée.

On investigation I found that there was no such thing as a lifetime plot in this cemetery; it was either space for twenty years or forty years. I opted for the latter, which will expire in 1991 unless someone renews it. If not, what remains of Henry Trescott will be moved and the plot will be resold.

My duties also required the disposal of his clothing and personal effects, a Hillman Minx and several hundred dollars in back pay. His only relative was a cousin, Paul Trescott, an editor of the *Evening Bulletin* in Philadelphia, who informed us that Henry had severed all his ties at home, and he felt it best if the burial would be in Germany.

Henry was a copy editor for the *Knickerbocker News* in Albany, New York, in 1946 when he learned that *Stripes* was hiring. Because he was a bachelor and housing for singles was not a problem, we were able to fly him to Germany and get him started on February 7, 1947. A graduate of Princeton in 1927, he also took graduate studies at Harvard and Columbia and taught school for eight years. He was an assistant history professor at Russell Sage College in Troy, New York, and prior to that taught history in Eastern private schools.

Henry was a quiet person and for a long time he seldom was seen at Press Club functions. After he met Kathe, who was young and attractive, he started going out to theaters and restaurants. When he became ill and complained of chest pains, it was Kathe who insisted he see the medics. He died as he lived and worked — quietly.

★   ★   ★

When Arthur Noyes became so ill with tuberculosis that he couldn't work, his German doctor put him in a *krankenhaus* at Nieder-Ramstadt, where he died April 6, 1954. If he had remained with *The Stars and Stripes,* which he had joined in 1945 and left in 1952 to work for the New York *Daily News,* he probably would have been treated in the 97th General Hospital in Frankfurt and no doubt been evacuated by air to the States for specialized care.

Larry Rue, *Chicago Tribune* correspondent, and I visited Art the day before and found him terribly wasted. It was sad to see our thirty-seven-year-old friend so gaunt, his weight for his six-foot frame down to eighty pounds.

There, too, that day and with him when he died was his wife, Geraldine. Their two children, Arthur, Jr., and daughter Geraldine, as well as Dennis, a son by a former marriage, survived.

Baptist services were conducted in the hospital chapel by Chaplain (Maj.) J. C. Solomon of the 322nd Signal Battalion V Corps, Darmstadt. The casket was transported from the chapel to the cemetery in a horse-drawn, black-draped Leickenwagen. The horses wore black ear pieces known as *trauerumhang*. Chaplain Solomon read the 23rd Psalm as the casket was lowered in the grave atop the hill overlooking the 750-year-old town of Nieder-Ramstadt.

Art contracted the lung disease in July 1948 while assigned to the Munich news bureau and wound up in the 97th General Hospital there. A month later, when he had used up his sick leave, he was flown by the army to the Murphy General Hospital in Waltham, Massachusetts. A short time later he was transferred to the Veterans Hospital at Rutland, Massachusetts. Slowly he regained his strength and put on weight and was able to get a clean bill from the Veterans Administration. He headed back to Germany in August of 1950 — after an absence of two years.

Arthur A. Noyes, a native of LaFayette, Indiana, worked as a radio announcer for station WGN in Chicago and as a reporter for the *Chicago Tribune*. He joined the army in 1942 and came overseas with the 65th Infantry Division in 1945. Shortly after his arrival in Germany he transferred to the Altdorf staff of *Stripes* and worked in various bureaus, including Vienna, Trieste, Berlin, Munich, and Frankfurt. He was one of several reporters who covered the International Military Tribunal at Nuremberg in 1946 for *The Stars and Stripes*.

Art left our employ in January 1952 to work for the *Daily News* and the *Saturday Evening Post*. He got out of a sickbed against his doctor's orders and his wife's wishes to cover the Big Four foreign ministers' conference in the bitter cold of Berlin in February 1954, where he had a relapse and was taken to the hospital in Nieder-Ramstadt. He left there in a black-draped Leickenwagen.

★ ★ ★

At the time of her death December 10, 1954, in a sports car accident in France, Kate B. Lewis was the only woman executive on the staff of *The Stars and Stripes*. She was the assistant distribution manager, and because her boss had recently been fired, her work had doubled. In addition to her own schedule, she was breaking in his replacement. This wouldn't have been too difficult, but she was due for home leave and a flight out of Paris.

Instead of leaving Darmstadt before noon as she had planned, she didn't get away until nearly midnight and then took off in her Porsche coupe for Paris, where she planned to visit friends and leave her car prior to flying home to spend Christmas with her mother, Mrs. Katharine T. Lewis of Bethesda, Maryland.

Sometime in the early morning hours the Porsche crashed into a concrete road marker near Esternay on the route between Nancy and Paris, and Kate died of a fractured skull.

Kate came to Europe in 1950 as administrative assistant to the director of the University of Maryland overseas campus. She transferred to *The Stars and Stripes* in April 1952, where she started as a sales supervisor trainee. She became sales supervisor in September and was named assistant distribution manager in April 1954.

The funeral was held in Bethesda.

16

Brass

Despite our relative low rank, the managing editors of *The Stars and Stripes* got along well with the top brass; it was the colonels and majors who gave us problems. With the exception of 1st/Lt. Robert L. Moora, all the MEs I knew were enlisted men.

Shortly after V-E Day, Brig. Gen. Paul W. Thompson, chief of the Information and Education Division, invited the managing editors of the London, Paris, Nice, Pfungstadt, and Altdorf editions to a reception in the George V Hotel in Paris. After the scotch was poured and the hors d'oeuvres passed, we met the general and his staff. There was no business transacted. The social gathering marked my first drink with a man with stars on his shoulders who called me by my first name.

I was told later that Thompson was shocked to see that the people getting out the newspaper had less rank than his driver. He was right. Art Force, in charge at Altdorf, was a private first class; I had a corporal's two stripes; and the ranking noncom there was Pfungstadt's Paul Elliott, a buck sergeant. Shortly thereafter, the general managed to get the freeze on promotions lifted and I advanced two grades in three months.

★   ★   ★

The Stars and Stripes owed much to Gen. George Catlett Marshall, the army chief of staff, who put it into business. His message setting policy for the newspaper was on Page 1, April 18, 1942, of the first World War II edition, printed in London for American troops stationed in Northern Ireland.

Marshall pointed out that on Gen. John J. Pershing's authority in the previous war, he had assurance that "no official control was exercised over the matter which went into *The Stars and Stripes*" and that it "always was entirely for and by the soldier."

"This policy," Marshall said, "is to govern the conduct of the new publication. A soldier's newspaper, in these grave times, is more than a morale venture. It is a symbol of the things we are fighting to preserve and spread in this threatened world. It represents the free thoughts and free expression of a free people."

That said it all and should have been the final word, but some officers in England and later on the Continent saw it differently. To restate and underline Marshall's order, Gen. Dwight D. Eisenhower took time out from fighting in late 1944 to meet with a captain and a sergeant to tell them that *The Stars and Stripes* must remain free as long as it lived but that the editors must use discretion on anything that might be detrimental to the best interests of the army. He cautioned them on printing material that might undermine confidence of the command. He also cleared once and for all the use of his nickname; he told them it was permissible to use "Ike" in headlines.

Even with Eisenhower's backing, there remained different interpretations of policy and incidents of interference with the operation of the newspaper. A combat general refused to permit *Stripes* to be circulated in his command because of a slight to his outfit in a story that had been cleared by the censor. Ike set the general straight, and *Stripes* was back in the dugouts the next day.

★ ★ ★

Capt. Harry C. Butcher, the general's naval aide, told in his book *My Three Years With Eisenhower* of a letter written April 11, 1945, by Ike to Lt. Gen. Ben Lear, his deputy. The letter said in part: "A great deal of pressure has been brought on me in the past to abolish such things as Mauldin's cartoons, the 'B' Bag, etc. You will make sure that the responsible officer knows he is not to interfere in matters of this kind. If he believes that any specific violation of good sense or good judgment has occurred, he may bring it to my personal attention."

Butcher added that he had received a letter from Lt. Col. Arthur Goodfriend, editor in chief of *The Stars and Stripes*, following Ike's order to Lear. It said: "Thanks to you, the *S&S* is at long last 'liberated.' "

★   ★   ★

Eisenhower's nickname prompted questions after the general entered politics and was nominated for president of the United States. While campaigning in Little Rock, Arkansas, one newspaperman asked if he would "still be Ike" or would it be "Mr. Eisenhower" if he were elected president.

The general grinned, grabbed the reporter's hand, and replied: "Son, if I get to be president, you can call me anything you like."

Following his victory over Adlai Stevenson, I wrote to the president-elect and sent him copies of our election edition with the headline: IKE WINS. Along with my congratulations I also asked: "And this is a personal request which harks back to Versailles when you answered a similar question 'Do we still call you Ike?' "

His reply: "The answer is the same as it was in Versailles and, for the record, it always will be!"

★   ★   ★

After Eisenhower returned to the States to replace Marshall as chief of staff, Gen. Joseph T. McNarney became the American commander. A pilot in World War I and commander of ground forces in Italy in the closing days of World War II, McNarney didn't quite know what to make of his newspaper. We did receive a letter thanking us for our handling of the scrip conversion, but that was his only show of gratitude or interest that I was aware of.

McNarney's replacement, Gen. Lucius DuBignon Clay, was quite the opposite. He knew how to get along with the media, believed that the public had the right to know what was going on with its tax dollar, and he instituted what he called his "gold fish bowl" policy. It endeared him to the press and certainly to us at Pfungstadt. He defended *Stripes* on more than one occasion when it came under attack by a visiting congressman, and he called off the predators in his command who tried to interfere with our operation.

I gave his name to my second son, born in 1953 at the 97th General Hospital in Frankfurt, and Roger Clay Zumwalt still has the sterling silver coin bank from Tiffany's that the general sent to him.

Lt. Gen. Clarence Ralph Huebner, who rose from enlisted man to be Clay's deputy in Germany, was a strong supporter of *Stripes* and was always accessible. I recall being in Col. Otis Mc-Cormick's office when the general telephoned to ask a question about a story in that morning's paper. When McCormick, chief of the Information and Education Division and head and shoulders the best officer to fill that post, said he had the managing editor in his office, Huebner asked that both of us come to see him immediately.

He greeted us warmly and, after telling us to be seated in his I.G. Farben building office, began by saying that we were on the right track in the handling of the news. However, there were a couple of points he wished to make about stories concerning movement of American troops and the location of border-crossing points.

"We want no advance stories on the movement of our own people," he said. "There is no use telling the other fellow what we are up to. He will find out soon enough. It is permissible to report the arrival of the units at their destination but only then."

It was the crossings along the East Germany and Czechoslovakia borders that caused concern, he said. "If a story gets in the paper about a shooting or some incident at a specific point then that crossing is plugged. You can help these people by just not mentioning the incident."

One of the problems, the general pointed out, was that some Communists were also fleeing across the border and posing as refugees. A few weeks later we were advised to cease using the word "deserter" in stories concerning persons crossing the borders and instead call them "escapees" or "defectors."

Huebner didn't mention it since it had occurred earlier, but *Stripes* had been cautioned not to print stories about the departure of a number of German rocket experts and scientists from Bremerhaven to the United States. That story was never published in *The Stars and Stripes*, although our Bremerhaven reporter was aware of it. We did not know at the time that Wernher von Braun, the father of the U.S. Army's effort at White Sands, was one of the America-bound contingent. It turned out that the group was just one step ahead of the Russians.

"Keep up the good work, the army is behind you all the way, and I am here to help all I can," Huebner said as McCormick and I left. I recalled what the general had told a Frankfurt Press Club gathering only a few nights previously: "The army will take care of you, feed you and see to your housing, and when you drop dead we'll send your remains home in a box."

Those subjects — troop movements, border crossings, and German rocket experts — were the only restrictions placed on *The Stars and Stripes* during my ten years-plus tenure. We didn't consider it censorship, although in the broad sense it was; to us it was following orders from the publisher, who happened to wear stars on his shoulders. Those were the big issues. The little issues were usually petty or caused by misunderstanding and solved by a telephone call.

★   ★   ★

There were other generals who supported us and kept us from straying off the policy path. I remember Thomas T. Handy, all four stars of him, telling me privately to "never get in a pissing contest with a skunk" when I suggested that *Stripes* rebut charges by a German editor that Americans were selling coal from the Ruhr on the black market and that the U.S. Army was more or less condoning the practice.

Brig. Gen. Frank L. Howley, the dapper U.S. commander in Berlin; Gen. Anthony C. McAuliffe, he of "nuts" fame and later top officer in Heidelberg; and raspy-voiced Maj. Gen. Ernest Harmon, commander of the Constabulary, who danced with my bride and called her "a cute little filly," were all good friends of *Stripes*.

The "daddy" of *The Stars and Stripes* was John E. Dahlquist, who presided at its birth and then left town for Salerno and Cassino. He brought his 36th Infantry Division ashore at St. Raphael in southern France, fought the battles for the Vosges, Colmar, and Belfort before grinding to a halt in Austria.

A colonel, Dahlquist was G-1 of the European Theater of Operations (ETO) when the order came in 1942 to supply a cadre for the Northern Ireland troops' weekly newspaper.

"We had just been assigned a censor, Maj. Ensley Llewellyn who was also G-3 of the 34th Infantry Division. I put him in charge of *The Stars and Stripes* and gave him all the help I could," Dahlquist said. It was necessary to assemble a staff and locate printers, newsprint, and equipment.

"I also called in Kingsbury Smith of International News Service and Edward W. Beattie, Jr., of United Press and asked for their help. Smith talked King Features Syndicate into providing free comic strips, and both were helpful in getting permission to publish a number of columns, including that of Walter Winchell."

Joe McBride recalled: "Yes, I remember Dahlquist. We didn't call him 'Daddy,' though. He was 'Bivouac John' and, boy, was I glad to get out of that outfit."

Dahlquist finished up the war as a major general. McBride spent forty-one years on the staff of *The Stars and Stripes* before he retired.

★   ★   ★

While the editor in chief of *Stripes* dealt with the parent Information and Education Division, we in editorial worked closely with public information officers.

Col. George S. Eyster was an outstanding officer and a good friend. Others who worked well with *Stripes* and its staff were Colonels Bjorne Furuholmen, Robert Shinn, and Barney Oldfield; Lt. Col. Hattilu White-Addison; and Maj. Reade Tilley. Without the public information officers and their people in the field, we would have been unable to fill the pages of the newspaper. Many of the PIOs had worked on newspapers back home and were aware of our needs and space problems.

★   ★   ★

Every newsman's favorite colonel the warm summer of 1954 was a serious fellow by the name of Dilley. If one could hide behind his office door, this is what might have been heard:

"Anything for the daily bulletin, colonel?" his secretary asked.

"Yes, here is something I've written. See that it gets general distribution," Col. John R. Dilley, commander of the Frankfurt detachment, said as he handed the paper to his Wac aide.

She took the note and this is what she read: "Official attire of dependents: No bare back, halter-type sun suits to be worn without a jacket or wrap; no bare-midriff costumes; no strapless, low-cut dresses except in clubs at appropriate social functions; no shorts on teen-agers; no jeans on mature women."

As she typed the colonel's words on the stencil before sending it to the mimeograph room, she thought to herself, "There will be a hot time in old Frankfurt town when the women read this."

She was right. There was a hot time that August 1954 afternoon in Frankfurt/Main when the dependents learned of the edict.

The post newspaper headlined the story, "No Jeans on Frankfurt Fatties."

The furor didn't bother Dilley, a forty-three-year-old West Pointer, combat veteran, and native of Kansas City, Missouri.

"I noticed that some women fell below standards as far as dress is concerned. Someone had to tell them. It might as well be me. I wrote the order myself. Yes, sir. I didn't even consult my wife," he said.

His wife, mother of a fourteen-year-old son and a nine-year-old daughter, said: "I would never wear such scanty dresses myself. There is such a thing as decency."

The next day hardly a teenager wore shorts and no middle-aged women were seen in blue jeans. Most complied with Dilley's order. The *Overseas Weekly* and the wire services had a field day with Dilley, whom one reporter called Colonel Dior. The *Daily Express* in London published a story and a three-column picture of two Frankfurt shoppers, one in tight jeans and the other in a bare-back dress, on Page 1 of its August 6 edition. The more conservative *Stars and Stripes* printed the story on an inside page.

The U.S. Army stepped into the dispute between Dilley and assorted female employees, wives, and daughters by backing the colonel to the hilt. Without mentioning Dilley or his edict, the USAEUR declaration said: "It is desired and expected that dependents and civilian employes clothe themselves appropriately at all times. It is further emphasized that standards considered appropriate in the United States are not necessarily appropriate in foreign countries."

Colonel Dilley added fuel to the fire when he told an Associated Press reporter that he also frowned on the practice of some women wearing curlers in their hair while shopping in the PX or commissary.

"They look awful," he said.

The story the next day called women who wore such devices "ironheads."

After the initial jolt, the women began to surrender one by one.

Famed Paris couturier Pierre Balmain joined with Dilley in his view of the bare midriff. "Women should not wear a bare midriff costume in public because it is a place where weight shows the most," Balmain told the International News Service.

In Berlin, the *Taegliche Rundschau*, official Soviet High Commission newspaper, said that instead of worrying about low-cut dresses, bare backs, and blue jeans, Dilley could improve American-German relations by banning "gangster films," the "raping" of German women, and by getting his troops out of Germany.

Dilley received a lot of mail; the first week 150 letters poured into his office from the United States, England, France, Italy, and Germany. What pleased him most was that American women began dressing like American women should while living in a foreign land.

★　★　★

Sometimes the children of the brass made news. One was pretty Cynthia Burress, a twenty-three-year-old dependent, who was tooling down the autobahn one spring day in 1947 in her late model Chrysler convertible. Up ahead she saw two Constabulary troopers waving a red flag.

"Where's the fire, ma'am?" a beefy, red-faced corporal asked. "We clocked you at 84 miles an hour over a measured mile in 43 seconds."

"You mean you have a speed limit here in Germany?" she said sweetly. "My family and I just arrived last week from the States."

"Sorry, ma'am. I have to ticket you. Be in the Military Government court room in Darmstadt at 9:00 A.M. next Wednesday."

When her ticket turned up at Constabulary traffic division the following afternoon, the captain did a double-take when he saw the name Burress.

"Geez! If that's who I think it is we're in big trouble. At least that fat-assed corporal is going to catch hell, and that's for sure," he said.

"Why's that, Cap?" the first sergeant said.

"For Christ's sake, read the ticket. Burress. That's the same name as the old man who's taking over this frigging outfit come the first of the month. She's twenty-three years old. She must be his kid."

"Maybe we'll luck out and it will be another Burress. Neither *The Stars and Stripes* nor the post newspapers print traffic violations anyhow, so what's to worry?"

"Let's hope so."

It was true that *Stripes* didn't print news about traffic violations unless there was a fatality, but the Military Government court calendars were checked on a routine basis. In this case the reporter found that Cynthia Burress, twenty-three, daughter of Maj. Gen. and Mrs. William A. Burress, had been fined $50 and had her driver's license suspended for sixty days. The general's family had recently arrived at Bremerhaven.

Cynthia paid the fine, the captain caught hell from the major in Public Relations, and the major heard from his colonel when the item appeared in the April 23 issue of *The Stars and Stripes.*

"How can you people be so gawddam stupid?" the major told the captain. The captain chewed out the corporal, and the two-striper went out that night and got drunk. "I'll never make sergeant in this chicken-shit outfit," he mumbled.

The general was not amused, but, when asked by reporters for a comment about his daughter's arrest, he said he was pleased that the Constabulary troopers were alert and doing their job. Cynthia was back driving her convertible in time for the Fourth of July picnic on the banks of the Neckar River.

★   ★   ★

The 7th Army's all-GI production of "Mr. Roberts," the Broadway stage play, opened March 31, 1951, at a gala premiere in the Sylvan Theater at Vaihingen near Stuttgart. Movie star Tyrone Power, who played the title role in the same play for six months in London, was in the audience as the guest of Lt. Gen. Manton E. Eddy, commanding general of the 7th Army, and Mrs. Eddy.

After the play, Power said the performance and staging were "absolutely miraculous."

Stripes reporter Otto Friedrich, who much later became a senior editor for *Time* magazine, said the standing-room-only audience of 400 gave the play an enthusiastic reception.

Tryouts of the play by the twenty-nine-man company had been held earlier at Landsberg Air Base, Furstenfeldbruck Air Base, and Patch Kaserne at Augsburg, all to standing ovations. The airmen especially enjoyed the story of the little supply ship AK-606 plying the backwaters of the Pacific, "delivering more Kleenex and toilet paper to the fighting troops than any ship afloat." All responded to the salty language.

Eddy praised the production and cast in the printed program, stating, "I am confident this play will provide many enjoyable hours for audiences of the Armed Forces in Germany."

But Eddy didn't take into account the effect of the play and its four-letter-word-spouting crew on audiences that had more stars than his on their shoulders. A week after the play's opening, the wife of Gen. Thomas T. Handy, commanding general of

USAEUR and Eddy's boss, arose during the second act and walked out. The play continued but the lady's departure put a damper on the performance. We didn't know anything about it because the event had not been publicized and no reporters had been invited. We learned three weeks later that it was Mrs. Handy who did the walking when we read about it in Walter Winchell's column.

What we did learn was that the upcoming performances at Darmstadt and Rhine-Main Air Base had been canceled "due to technical difficulties." The last press release and the last word on the "Mr. Roberts" affair from the army was dated April 9 and stated that future showing of the play had been "temporarily suspended."

The next day the United Press quoted an unofficial source as saying that the 7th Army decided the seafaring language was "too rough" for soldiers' ears.

Joshua Logan, who wrote the stage version from the popular book, told the UP in New Orleans that whoever closed the play "is creating a far greater evil than any found in the play. If the Army sees fit to close 'Mr. Roberts' it is denying the troops what I consider a true morally uplifting wholesome entertainment. I cannot believe it is too strong for Army ears. The dialogue is mild in comparison to the true speech of servicemen."

Logan said he had agreed to let the army produce "Mr. Roberts" free of royalties because he believed it would help morale. He also said he had agreed to eliminate reference to the deity but would not let another word be deleted.

In New York, the *Times* had this to say on its editorial page under the headline "Soldiers Are People Too":

> One of the difficulties of being a soldier is that some misguided souls, although perhaps well-meaning, forget that he is a human being with a human being's capacity for using his brain. Thus he is sometimes deprived of these simple pleasures which are afforded to the person who does not wear a uniform. In Germany, for example, the American Army of Occupation's production of the play "Mr. Roberts" had been closed because someone thought the language too strong.
>
> Joshua Logan, co-author of the play, said millions of men and women have seen "Mr. Roberts" without objecting to any of the language in it. Its dialogue is mild compared with the true speech of servicemen. "Mr. Roberts" is a funny and at

times moving portrayal of servicemen in war. It has been a success wherever it has played.

Surely if we have to put men in uniform to protect and preserve our freedoms, as we must, we ought to allow them to enjoy some of those freedoms. We think the play should be reopened. If the troops are going to be corrupted by seeing "Mr. Roberts," then they corrupt more easily than any other people we have heard about.

"Mr. Roberts" did not reopen. Seventh Army and USAEUR had nothing further to say on the subject.

★   ★   ★

For the most part we got along fine at the newspaper with the brass in other organizations; it was a few in our own family, the Information and Education Division, that gave us problems. Dealing with some of them was an education in itself.

With the exception of McCormick, West Point class of 1924, we were stuck with either regular army colonels on their last assignment before retirement or reservists who had been schoolteachers in civilian life. Most of the latter, especially those from the South, resented the highly paid ex-enlisted men who occupied key positions on the newspaper. Their resentment showed.

Lt. Col. William M. Summers, editor in chief from 1947 to 1950, endeared himself by assigning a new *Stripes* Chevrolet sedan to the I&E office in Heidelberg. At least one colonel complained to the chief of staff because he had to draw his transportation from the motor pool.

Lt. Col. Henry J. Richter, editor in chief from 1950 to 1953, continued this practice, and relations with headquarters remained good until several changes in command later started things going downhill. For reasons known only to the I&E brass in Heidelberg, *Stripes* lost both of its top officers — Maj. Warren H. Scheffner, general manager, and, a month later, Lt. Col. Arthur L. Jorgenson, the editor in chief who had replaced Richter. Jorgenson had been in command eighteen months.

Lt. Col. Lother B. Sibert, an infantry officer and a Cedar Bluff, Alabama, schoolteacher in civilian life, took over from Jorgenson. George Close, an ex-Signal Corps captain-turned-civilian and the newspaper's communication chief, replaced Scheffner as general manager.

One of Sibert's first administrative acts was to assume control of the outgoing correspondence. Letters written by department heads had to be signed by him; the body of the letter was not altered nor questioned, but his signature appeared at the bottom of the page. The only clue as to the originator were the initials, along with those of the typist. When I closed a letter to a business contact I knew well, I often asked to be remembered to his wife. That went out over the colonel's signature. I often wondered what my friends thought when they received a letter from me. Not only did the colonel sign, but also copies of the letter went into the central file as well as a reader file so that other *Stripes* department heads could read what was said, and I, of course, could read their mail. The result was that we wrote less and used the telephone more.

Sibert also abolished the weekly operations report in favor of a daily report so that the first hour I spent in the office was devoted to that chore. Reporters and district circulation managers had to submit like reports. This wasn't always easy, since most depended on army and air force teletype machines.

"Tell them to use the telephone," Sibert said.

We did get some relief for a few weeks in 1954, when Sibert got himself involved in a battle with Ray Vir Den, the publisher of the *Rome Daily American*. The fighting was intense and as a result we lost Anthony "Tony" Biancone, *Stripes*'s chief of distribution. Sibert was out of his element doing battle with a civilian publisher, but for a time it kept him occupied and out of our hair. He fired Biancone, and that action triggered the resignations of key personnel in a number of departments and greatly affected the morale of those remaining on the job.

Sydney Label of Philadelphia, an ex-navy pharmacist mate during the war and a former European Exchange Service employee, replaced Biancone.

John W. Livingood, assistant managing editor who had been with *Stripes* since the summer of 1946, gave his notice and took off in May 1955 with his wife, Ina, for Pennsylvania's apple country. They moved into a new house on the outskirts of Robesonia. John had been a teenaged soldier in World War I and worked for the Office of War Information (OWI) during World War II.

The Livingoods left the same month that the Allies had agreed to end the occupation of Germany. The Americans would remain, but not as occupiers. It seemed a good time to make the move.

Losing Livingood was a severe blow to me because I learned a lot about newspapering from him in the nine years we were together. I had recently celebrated my fortieth birthday and, because publishers of newspapers back home weren't too keen on hiring anyone over that age, I had started making inquiries about jobs.

James Quint of San Mateo, California, and a San Francisco newspaperman, replaced Livingood as assistant managing editor. He had been with the American Red Cross in Italy during the war and had worked for *Stripes* for four years.

Sibert showed no favorites: he was just as hard on his military staff as he had been with Biancone. Two months after he took over as editor in chief, Sibert welcomed Maj. Ralph Gaither of Morris, Oklahoma, a World War II and Korean War veteran, and gave him the title of assistant editor in chief. He was there two months and then sent on his way.

Lt. Col. Andrew Hayes, an infantry officer from Louisville, Kentucky, replaced Gaither but sixty days later he too was gone. Something was wrong, and the brass in Heidelberg reacted by putting Sibert on orders. He was replaced by Lt. Col. Byron R. King, an armored officer, and the tension eased. It calmed down so much that I gave pause in my thinking about leaving.

There was also talk of a retirement plan for the civilian staff, something we had been told was not possible for overseas employees of nonappropriated fund organizations. Under consideration was a plan in which the employee would put in a percentage of his pay each month and that figure would be doubled by the organization. It was to be retroactive, and this sounded good to me since I had nine years of civilian service at *Stripes*. If this plan was approved in Heidelberg we couldn't afford to leave, I told my wife.

The bubble burst when King left the editor in chief's post after only eight days. We never heard why but assumed that he didn't care for the I&E way of doing business. He was replaced by Lt. Col. Donald A. Bartoni, an infantry veteran with the 95th Infantry Division and a native of California.

A week or two later the other shoe dropped. We were informed that the retirement plan had been disapproved in Heidelberg, and that if it had gone through, it would not have been retroactive. It was right then that I made up my mind to leave. Although I liked Bartoni — he was far more reasonable and understanding than Sibert and he did offer me another two-year contract — I felt it best to leave. The decision not to have a retirement plan was the clincher. I talked it over with Paulette and she concurred, so I typed out my resignation. It was a hard decision for her, since she would be leaving her family in France and traveling half a world away, taking our two boys, Richard and Roger, with us.

I didn't say so in my letter but I was tired — tired physically and mentally. I was tired of the tug of war between Heidelberg and Griesheim, tired of the constant bickering over things not connected with getting the news to the readers. I had been with *The Stars and Stripes* eleven years, nine as a civilian, and I had worked for a platoon of officers — seven field-grade officers (Jorgenson, Scheffner, Sibert, Gaither, Hays, King, and now Bartoni) in the past thirteen months. I needed a rest. In fact, that is what I told a reporter from the *Overseas Weekly* when he telephoned the next day. "I'm tired and I want to go home," I said.

I recommended Quint to succeed me as managing editor and Bartoni gave him the job. "I'll stop off at the Fairmont Hotel bar when I get to San Francisco and drink to your success as managing editor," I told him as we parted. It was in that bar where I had interviewed him for a job in the fall of 1951.

Heidelberg wasn't through making management moves. This time it was Maj. James A. Ziccarelli, an air force officer, who joined the staff as assistant editor in chief. His and Quint's names went into the staff box the day after mine was deleted.

Ziccarelli, who had twenty-eight bombing missions over Europe with the 95th Combat Wing, was to be the first of a number of U.S. air force officers to be assigned to *Stripes*. The air force had long wanted a say in the management of the army newspaper, and Ziccarelli was the point man.

A resident of Carmichael, Pennsylvania, he had been a newspaperman in civilian life and had started the *Green Countian,* a weekly. He also launched the *Overseas Weekly* in Germany in 1950 but had to sell it after he was denied permission to leave the service when the Korean War started.

Bartoni gave me a fine letter of appreciation, but the one I treasure was from Gen. Anthony C. McAuliffe, USAEUR commander and the hero of the Battle of the Bulge. Here is what he said:

> I want to express my thanks and appreciation to you for your eleven years of constructive and helpful service during which the paper has grown from a modest beginning to its present size and importance. It must be a matter of deep satisfaction to you to know that you have made large and substantial contributions to that growth and can take credit for a job well done.
>
> Although we will miss you here in Europe, I extend my best wishes for a pleasant journey home and continued success in your new work.
>
> Sincerely,
>
> A. C. McAULIFFE
> General US Army
> Commander in Chief

Those were special words from the man who was famous for his letters, the man who wrote "nuts" to the Germans at Bastogne.

★   ★   ★

Paulette, Richard Albin, Roger Clay, and I sailed from Cannes on the Italian liner *Andrea Doria* on September 21, 1955, for New York. The ship sank to the bottom of the Atlantic the following year, but by then we were in San Diego, California, where I was working on the copy desk of *The San Diego Union* and living with my family in a beautiful home on Point Loma overlooking the Pacific Ocean.

Epilogue

Circulation of *The Stars and Stripes* continued to climb, and the financial picture improved as the years went by. Two years after I left my job as managing editor, a retirement plan went into effect. It called for an employee contribution of four percent of basic earnings and an eight percent contribution by *Stripes*. The plan, underwritten by Continental Assurance Company, was termed a group elective annuity contract and began June 30, 1957. Although it wasn't retroactive, it certainly was a step forward.

Lt. Col. Donald Bartoni, the editor in chief, and James Quint, the managing editor and my replacement, got along just fine. Also, relations with Heidelberg improved, especially after Col. Edward Ott, chief of the Information and Education Division, left for the States and retirement from the army. He was replaced by Col. Morton P. Brooks, former 4th Army deputy G-3 at Ft. Sam Houston.

In July 1957, Bartoni's assignment was up and he was replaced temporarily by Lt. Col. Thomas J. Cunningham, Jr., who in turn gave way two months later to Col. John D. Nottingham. A former *Houston Post* photographer, Nottingham was the first U.S. Air Force officer and the first full colonel to take over the editor in chief's post. The army had always assigned lieutenant colonels to the position. Cunningham stayed on as assistant EIC.

For reasons known only to himself and his wife, Anne, Quint gave notice in March 1958 that after two years and six months he wanted out as managing editor and returned to San Francisco to work on the *Chronicle*. Nathan J. Margolin, a longtime *Stripes* employee dating back to early Pfungstadt days, took over as managing editor. A former company-grade officer, Margolin didn't get along with Nottingham and, eighteen months after his appointment, he resigned.

253

"Mr. Margolin had violated a standing policy and resigned in protest," the colonel told reporters.

"Col. Nottingham gave me a written reprimand for having made an assignment which he did not later approve," Margolin replied.

Bernard "Barney" Kirchhoff, a Chicago newspaperman and assistant managing editor, held down the ME post until Nottingham got around to naming Arnold Burnett in March 1960 as managing editor. Burnett came to *Stripes* in June 1958 after three years with the Pacific edition in Tokyo. He had previously worked on the *Miami Herald, Oklahoma City Oklahoman, Baltimore Sun,* and was a former managing editor of the *Peoria* [Illinois] *Journal and Sun.*

Nottingham's three-year term as editor in chief came to an end in August 1960, and Col. Ridgway Smith, Jr., USA, took over. He stayed four and one-half years, the longest period of any of the EICs. His successor was Lt. Col. William W. Coleman, USAF, who was on the job only two years.

Lt. Col. James W. Campbell, USA, replaced Coleman and almost immediately became engulfed in labor union, personnel, and censorship problems. For starters, Campbell banned George Deojay, a former employee and union shop steward for the American Federation of Government Employees (AFGE), from the *Stripes* installation. Deojay was escorted out of the Press Club and off the premises by military police. His eviction came only three days after the end of a series of union grievance hearings against the paper. The grievance was filed by the local AFGE chapter in Deojay's behalf when he was relieved as the result of the RIF (reduction in force) program. He had worked in the circulation and sales section of *Stripes.* Deojay had the last word, however. Three years later he was reinstated with all back pay and allowances by an arbitrator.

Burnett had his problems with Campbell and finally resigned November 15, 1967, after receiving a "chewing out" from the colonel because of a letter Mrs. Burnett wrote to Defense Secretary Robert S. McNamara complaining of the reduction in fringe benefits for civilian employees of the military. Viola Burnett concluded her letter by saying: "I realize quite well that my innocent husband will probably be fired on some pretext or other because I have written this letter."

How Campbell learned of the letter to McNamara is not known, but he did and he chastised Burnett for his "inability to control his own wife." Campbell told Burnett: "A man has certain responsibilities to keep his wife under wraps."

Burnett was quoted as saying that Campbell told him that his failure to prevent his wife from writing the letter to McNamara was an indication of his "lack of leadership" ability. Burnett's reply to Campbell was published in *Overseas Weekly*'s family section. It said: "Since you came to *Stripes* you have made it clear to us and to every one else that you are the boss, that you alone are running *Stripes*, that you make the decisions. You are the spokesman, you are the man to contact."

Shortly after his brush with Campbell, the Burnetts left on a previously planned home leave and Kirchhoff, the assistant managing editor, again took over. While vacationing in Florida, Burnett accepted an offer of a desk job with the *St. Petersburg Times*. He mailed his letter of resignation to Campbell and sent Viola back to Germany to pack up their belongings, pick up their pets, and check out of the military post. She paused long enough to write a second letter to McNamara and then flew off to Florida to rejoin her husband.

Campbell appointed Mert Proctor, Jr., a former reporter and copy editor for the *San Antonio Light*, as managing editor on February 29, 1968, to replace Burnett. Proctor had been with *Stripes* nine years.

On February 2, 1967, Campbell relayed a message from USAEUR to kill an Associated Press story that Ambassador George McGee's son, Michael, nineteen, had been arrested in California on a charge of driving a car while under the influence of LSD. The story was of interest because the elder McGee was the U.S. ambassador to West Germany and the German newspapers used the story, as did the international editions of the *New York Herald-Tribune*, *Washington Post* and *The New York Times*.

The article was killed when Col. George E. Maranda, USAEUR's public information chief, called from Heidelberg to order its deletion. It turned out that Albert Hemsing, the embassy's public affairs counselor at Bonn, had called Maranda and asked that the story not be used in *Stripes* at least until the case went to court. Maranda objected on the grounds that it was news, and when he told Maj. Gen. Francis Pachier, USAEUR chief of staff, about Bonn's request, the general ordered him to comply. When Maranda objected a second time, the general gave him a direct order, which he followed, but by then two editions had already been printed. The story was kept out of the next two editions, one of which was read in Bonn. Maranda was sacked after serving only seven months of a three-year tour and was sent back to Washington to work in the Pentagon.

On the eve of his departure from Germany, the staff of *The Stars and Stripes* awarded Maranda a certificate making him an honorary lifetime editor. The citation read: "In recognition of his having daringly espoused and cherished the cause of a free press by remaining contumacious in the face of critics."

This incident of news management and fifty-two others were submitted by unnamed and disgruntled *Stripes* employees to the Freedom of Information subcommittee chaired by Rep. John E. Moss (D-CA) and introduced into the March 16, 1967, *Congressional Record* by Rep. Donald Rumsfeld (R-IL).

One of the other incidents mentioned was the criticism of *Stripes* by a USAEUR colonel because the newspaper published a wire service story about President Lyndon B. Johnson's speeding while drinking beer on a Texas road. It was "disrespectful to the commander in chief," the colonel said.

An attempt was made that same year by the Department of Defense to merge the New York news bureau of *Stripes* with a news bureau in Arlington, Virginia. The idea was to centralize the flow of news to military publications, especially the Tokyo edition of *The Stars and Stripes*. The Pentagon insisted the proposal was aimed at efficiency and economy, not news management, but it was successfully blocked by Moss and his subcommittee and died a quiet death.

Despite all of this, the newspaper prospered and increased in size on March 11, 1969, when it upped its pages from twenty-four to twenty-eight. Magazines and book sales were also up.

Campbell was replaced by Lt. Col. F. S. Michael, Jr., USAF, and following his next assignment in Saigon as chief of public affairs he was named to take over as editor in chief of *The Stars and Stripes* in Tokyo. Before he reached there he was quoted in a news story as calling the Tokyo paper the *Hanoi Herald*. He never made it to Japan, his travel orders were rescinded, and he was reassigned.

In 1972 managing editor Proctor set up a team of investigative reporters, and their efforts won the newspaper the Overseas Press Club prize for the best business story of the year, which exposed a land sale rip-off being worked among American servicemen in Europe.

Three years later, September 30, 1975, *The Stars and Stripes* entered the electronic age, the phasing out of metal type casting in favor of computer-set copy. Typesetting and paste-up shifted from the production department to the editorial newsroom, where it was written, compiled, and edited.

The international publishers organization, FIEJ, maintains a technical research center in Darmstadt and takes most of its visitors to Griesheim to show them what a modern newspaper editorial and printing plant looks like.

Recent editors in chief include: Col. David B. O'Hara, USAF; Capt. Edward G. McGrath, USN; Col. James H. Taylor, USAF; Col. Billy E. Spangler, USA; Col. Ruby Rose Stauber, USA, the first woman editor in chief; Col. Robert P. Everett, USAF; Col. Richard L. Horvath, USA; Capt. Dale K. Patterson, USN; and Col. Jeffrey M. Cook, USA.

Censorship problems again surfaced in 1983 when America's highest-ranking officer in Europe ordered *Stripes* not to print any stories concerning the enforced early retirement of his West German deputy for allegedly becoming a security risk.

Gen. Bernard Rogers, NATO's supreme commander, Allied Forces Europe, gave his order in the wake of confirmation that West Germany Defense Minister Manfred Woerner had forced early retirement of four-star Gen. Guenter Kiessling on grounds he had become a security risk. Woerner claimed he had to treat the fifty-eight-year-old Kiessling as a security risk after learning that the general frequented homosexual bars in Cologne. Kiessling denied the charges unconditionally and brought a criminal suit against his unnamed accusers and sued before an administrative court to reverse his early retirement.

Asked by newsmen why *Stripes* had printed no stories about the Kiessling case, a spokesman for Gen. Richard Lawson, USAF, deputy commander in chief of the U.S. European Command, confirmed the gag order, explaining that news reports of the affair had been "highly speculative and sensationalistic" and that officers there "decided that had these news reports appeared in *The Stars and Stripes*, they might be detrimental to the good order and discipline of a readership that includes many U.S. military personnel who work and train closely with their German allies."

This angered Proctor and his news editors, and finally the gag was loosened slightly after about a week to allow the newspaper to print a UPI dispatch reporting the European command prohibition order.

Kiessling was reinstated and exonerated by Chancellor Helmut Kohl.

Meantime *Stripes* picked up a strong ally in Sen. William Proxmire (D-WI), who said on the floor of the Senate February 15, 1984, that General Lawson had barred *Stripes* from using the story "on the forced retirement of a West German general in the wake of unproven allegations of homosexuality."

The senator said the general had sent him a telegram stating that "speculative reports will not be permitted to appear and that reading speculative and sensational news reports such as this could possibly result in undisciplined behavior in the form of innocent but ill-chosen and uninformed remarks or actions."

The senator added: "Imagine that. The general decided that the military personnel are so weak of character that they must be protected from news stories so they don't say something wrong. What nonsense!"

But the brass didn't give up easily. Navy Capt. Jay Coupe, a EUCOM spokesman, defended Lawson's censorship order and justified it on the grounds that Kiessling was reinstated. Obviously, EUCOM and Lawson learned nothing about the role of the press in a free society. Far from apologizing for the error, Lawson and company remained defiant.

Former members of the *Stripes* family would not have known about the Woerner-Kiessling-Lawson-Proxmire story if Wellington Long's report hadn't appeared in the trade journal *Editor and Publisher*. News about newspapers gets little play in the American press, and the paper that I read each morning didn't bother to carry it. At least, I didn't see the story.

Thanks to Bernard Kirchhoff, former assistant managing editor of *Stripes* and now an executive with the international edition of the *New York Herald-Tribune* in Paris, I was able to follow the story from clippings he sent from his newspaper. He also suggested that, as a former managing editor of *Stripes*, I might wish to write to Proxmire. I did so, and a week later I received a note from him dated March 27, 1984:

Dear Kenneth:

You can bet that I will keep the pressure on until we find
some way to relax these censorship efforts by higher command. It is absolutely intolerable in a free society.

Sincerely,

William Proxmire, U.S.S.

It didn't end there. Three years later, on May 4, 1987, Senator
Proxmire introduced a bill in Congress calling for an investigation
into charges of military censorship of the European and Pacific editions of *The Stars and Stripes.*

"We simply cannot in good conscience send troops abroad to
lead the struggle for freedom and censor *The Stars and Stripes* at the
same time. Our people overseas deserve better than second-class
treatment," Proxmire said.

The senator's bill required that the secretary of defense ap-
point five civilian journalists to serve on the commission, which
would report its findings to the secretary and the Congress.

"This issue has dragged on for too long. Nothing has been accomplished. It is important that this long-running dispute end soon
so that *The Stars and Stripes* can get on with its vital mission," he
said, concluding:

> The problem has gone beyond complaints. A top-level civil-
> ian editor at the Pacific edition recently gave notice that he was
> resigning because of censorship. In Europe, a Navy captain who
> left as editor in chief and retired from the military last August,
> said in an article published (January 1987) in the distinguished
> *Columbia Journalism Review:* "The degree of command influence
> became intolerable to me. It was getting progressively worse. It
> got to the point where I was getting calls on weekends from un-
> derlings speaking for generals and admirals. I just got sick of it."
> It's possible that the military command has too much con-
> trol over *The Stars and Stripes.*

Shortly afterwards, he announced that he would not seek re-
election when his present term expired.

Persons interested in freedom of the press will miss the senator
from Wisconsin. He will be especially missed by staff members and
alumni of *The Stars and Stripes.*

★★★★★★★★★★★★★★★★★★★★★★★★★★★★
Duty Roster 1942-1955
★★★★★★★★★★★★★★★★★★★★★★★★★★★★

These names, taken from files of *The Stars and Stripes*, Army orders, letters and books, are from the Europe, North Africa, Italy and Hawaii editions. If you served with Stripes between 1942 and 1955, and your name is not on this unofficial list, please contact the author in care of Eakin Press, P.O. Box 23069, Austin, TX 78735 in the event there is another printing.

— The Author

A

Abbey, Byron W.; Aberle, George J.; Aboyoun, Albert; Abraham, Mary I.; Adams, Frank; Adams, Joanne; Adler, Milton R.; Addison, Peter N.; Agar, Frank E., Jr.; Agee, Boyd H.; Ahakuelo, Abraham J.; Ahlberg, William A.; Ahlin, William; Aiello, Frank; Albach, William; Alberg, Clarence; Albrecht, William; Alexander, James S.; Allwin, Francis J.; Alter, John E.; Althen, Harlow; Alty, Hal; Allen, Walter; Amador, Charles J.; Ames, George S.; Ames, Walter R.; Amsel, David; Amsel, Milton; Andella, Eugene; Anderson, Alexander; Anderson, David; Anderson, Omar; Andrews, Irene; Anfuso, Salvatore J.; Angle, Charles R.; Ankner, Ingebrod; Annis, Robert J.; Antonucci, Peter; Argyrakis, Stratis; Armor, Cheva; Arnold, Lawrence; Asarese, Tovie; Asdel, Wallace R.; Ashmon, Ann T.; Askins, Loren E.; Avedon, Charles and Averitt, Clifford W.

B

Bach, John S.; Bachmann, Horst; Back, Lor Lizabeth; Badamo, Michael; Badiner, Jacob S.; Baenitz, Karl Heinz; Bagley, Joseph D.; Bagnoche, Alfred; Bailey, Joseph, Jr.; Bailey, Joseph O.; Bailin, David; Baird, Jean; Baird, John W.; Baird, Maurice; Baitz, Stanley; Baj, David; Baker, Frank R.; Baker, Fred M.; Baker, Myron; Balajti, Ernest J.; Ball, Whitney G.; Balota, William R.; Banasik, Gordon; Bandemer, Norman S.; Bane, Gene; Banham, Albert; Barb, Gail L.; Bardi, Gino; Barley, Jack L.; Barrett, Vance T.; Barriac, George; Barsi, Vincent G.; Barth, Irving; Barton, William; Bartoni, Donald A.; Bassett, James O.; Batko, Emil; Bauer, Judy; Bauer, William B.; Bauham, Albert; Baum, Jasper; Bauman, John E.; Bauman, William; Baumwell, Louis; Bausch, Edith; Bayer, Willi; Beach, Bruce; Beach, Peter K.; Beam, John E.; Beatty, James H.; Beck, Augustus; Beck, McVicker; Becker, James; Beers, Fred C.; Begon, Jack; Belafsky, Tobias; Bell, L. E.; Bell, Wendell; Bell, William; Bellis, Milton D.; Bellis, R. L.; Bender, William; Benjamin, Arthur L.; Berman, W. I.; Bennett, Kenneth S.; Bennis, Joseph C.; Benoit, William; Benson, Edward O.; Benton, Melanie; Berenbach, Nita; Bernard,

260

Thomas; Bernstein, Lester; Bernstein, Walter; Bersig, Glenn; Bertram, Neil; Betwee, Arthur H.; Biancone, Anthony D.; Bibikow, Helen V.; Biederman, Alfred; Bigger, Charles J.; Biggs, John A.; Billing, Herbert; Billing, Martin S.; Billings, Clarence E.; Billings, Stephen E.; Billingsley, Oliver; Binckley, Cristy; Bing, Ralph; Birnbaum, Herbert; Bishop, Willie G.; Black, Creed; Black, James H.; Blackburn, Louis A.; Blackman, Morris; Blackwell, George; Blair, Willie J.; Blalock, Lew R.; Blanford, James T.; Blankfort, Lowell A.; Blay, John S.; Blechner, Toni; Blinn, Thomas C.; Blood, Jack; Bloom, Murray T.; Blosser, Burt; Blum, Ludwig; Bluman, Herbert; Blumenfeld, Samuel; Bodiford, Burette A.; Bolstead, Ellsworth; Bogert, Frederick W.; Boles, William; Boldender, F. J., Jr.; Bond, Raymond L., Jr.; Bond, Richard W.; Boni, William F.; Bonnell, Clarence J., Jr.; Booth, Robert M.; Bordine, Gordon W.; Bornscheim, Eduard; Borowiak, Thomas; Boswell, Dean; Bothroyd, Dorothy J.; Bougadis, Peter; Bourgin, Simon; Boyle, James; Boyd, John W.; Braden, Joseph; Bradley, Robert A.; Bradshaw, Red; Brainsfarther, Bruce; Braley, Russell N.; Brame, Wyly; Bramlett, Mary; Brandell, Arthur; Branetigram, Hal; Brantley, Mellanie; Breger, Dave; Brehm, Conrad; Brekke, Gerald W.; Bres, Jerome F.; Bressler, Elden; Bridgman, Albert C.; Briggs, Harold; Brignola, Joseph B.; Brillstein, Sidney; Brinkley, William; Briordy, William J.; Britton, Leonard C.; Brix, Richard O.; Brody, Marian Jean; Brown, Elden; Brown, H. M.; Brown, Jack; Brown, James W., Jr.; Brown, Johnny M.; Brown, Louis H.; Brown, Milton; Brown, Peter C.; Brown, Robert A.; Brown, Roger C., Jr.; Browne, Charles C.; Browne, Clyde J.; Browning, Henry L.; Brophy, William; Broome, Dean C.; Bruce, Raymond A.; Bruggmann, Winnie; Brune, Oscar A.; Bruner, Richard; Bryant, William C.; Bryngelson, Donald E.; Buatti, Nat; Bucknell, Phillip; Buchwach, Aaron; Budnick, Adam; Bunn, Quentin S.; Burbach, Emmy; Burch, Charles H.; Burchard, Albert S.; Burchard, James; Burger, Franz; Burke, Bryce W.; Burkhardt, Robert; Burks, Cecil E.; Burleson, Lewis B.; Burn, Blackie; Burnham, Daniel; Burton, Elmer; Burton, Bernard; Burton, James R.; Burnham, Daniel M.; Burzinski, Joseph S.; Busch, James; Buschner, Johanna; Bushong, Earl M.; Bushell, Harry; Bussoneaud, D. J.; Buster, Frank V.; Butler, Chris; Butler, John; Butler, John C.; Butler, Marilyn; Butler, Norman; Butts, Wilbur N. and Byrnes, Howard.

C

Cable, Homer; Caborn, Jimmy; Cahil, William G.; Cahn, Richard F.; Calbert, Maurice; Caldwell, Jack; Caldwell, William J.; Caligor, Leopold; Callagan, John; Callaghan, Harry L.; Callaghen, Robert F.; Callahan, Jerry; Callicotta, Morris; Camp, Carolyn; Campbell, Charles J.; Campbell, James F.; Campbell, John H.; Campbell, Robert E.; Cannon, Jimmy; Cannon, Robert P.; Capers, Edward H.; Caratini, Henry W.; Carey, John R.; Carpenter, Keith; Carpenter, Kenneth G.; Carsons, Morris; Carter, David; Carter, Hodding; Carter, John; Carter, Ron; Carter, William H.; Cartwright, William C.; Casey, Thomas F.; Cashon, Herman H.; Cassini, Igor; Castel, Jack; Cato, Jack; Caudill, Oscar; Caugney, Jack N.; Cayton, Ralph C.; Cazeneuve, Arturo; Ceblasio, Francisco; Chabot, Burton; Chambers, P. F., Sr.; Chamberlain, John R.; Chamberlayne, Edward P.; Chambliss, Charles; Chandler, Wayne S.; Chaplin, George; Chapman, Melvin S.; Chapmond, Selma; Charlton, Richard F.; Checkoway, Joseph A.; Cheek, Ross; Chillingsworth, Kingston; Christenson, Charles; Christenson, Robert J.; Christianson, Beulah; Christianson, Charles T.; Christman, Siegfried; Christy, John;

Chojecki, Richard; Chunis, Clem T.; Cibuzar, Paul A.; Ciccotelli, Geno; Ciklin, Julian; Clancy, John; Clancy, Catherine P.; Clark, Edward; Clark, Russell; Clarke, Robert J.; Claughton, Maggi; Clay, Hiland H.; Cleary, M. A.; Clift, John; Close, George; Clouse, John N.; Coberly, Edward B.; Coe, Richard L.; Coffee, Edward S.; Cogswell, Floyd R.; Cohen, Abe; Cohen, Eldon Scott; Cohen, Richard L.; Colborn, Robert L.; Colby, Gerald C.; Cole, George E.; Coley, Howard L.; Colegrove, Vivian R.; Coleman, John H.; Coleman, Martha; Coleman, Warren R.; Coll, Thomas; Collins, David J., Jr.; Collins, Robert; Collins, Richard M.; Collona, Jerome V.; Colosimo, Anthony C.; Compsom, Henry G.; Concannon, Robert S.; Conlon, Joseph T., Jr.; Connelly, Hope S.; Connolly, Francis; Conner, John H.; Conners, Paul; Conrad, William J.; Conway, Hugh; Cook, James M.; Cooke, Herbert H.; Coomer, Vance E.; Cooper, Robina; Cordaro, Anthony; Cornell, George W.; Cortese, Louis M.; Cosimano, Anthony J.; Costello, Arthur R.; Costick, Theodore; Cotton, Joseph S.; Couch, Ferris S.; Courtney, Eugene; Cowden, John P.; Coyte, Ben L.; Cozby, John L.; Cuffe, John F.; Culler, Austin C.; Cullivan, Joseph T.; Curteman, William; Curvan, Gordon C.; Crabb, Riley; Craft, Roy; Cramer, Harley L.; Crandall, Robert S.; Cranston, Alan; Crawford, Robert A.; Creek, Hansell C.; Crew, Donald N.; Crist, Catherine F.; Croft, Albert; Cross, Howard; Crumbaugh, A. W.; Cruz, Salvador; Cunic, Robert F. and Cunningham, Joseph G.

D

Daiber, Karletta; Dahlen, John C.; Dallaire, Victor; Daniels, Clifton; Dann, Alvin A.; Dann, Reginald; Dantzic, Gerald; Danziger, David; Darnell, James D.; Darte, Margery; Darte, Parkman; David, Lester; David, Miles; Davidson, Alan; Davidson, Arthur Ray; Davis, Alvin; Davis, Blaine E.; Davis, Clifford B.; Davis, Donald; Davis, Frank R.; Davis, Gordon W.; Davis, Harry; Davis, J. L., Sr.; Davis, John O.; Davis, Morrow; Davis, Ralph T.; Davis, Ronald G.; Davis, Sherman; Davis, Stanley; Davis, William W.; Day, Ronald G.; Day, Roscoe; Deakin, Alfred; Dean, Ben; Deaton, Jess; Deaton, Robert; DeChaine, Myron L.; DeGard, Jack A.; Deiss, Ursula; DeJong, Klas P.; Delaney, James K.; Delahoussaye, Curtis M.; DeMaza, William; DeMio, Angelo J.; DeMedica, Peter P.; DeMotte, Edward L.; Denney, Roger; Denton, Royal S.; Dennis, Herbert; Derevjanik, Joseph; Derrick, Loal L.; Deshotels, Matthew; Devaney, John F.; Devendorf, Leo E.; Devine-Jones, E. C. L.; DeWillgen, Henry C.; Diamond, Alan H.; Dickison, J. P.; Dickson, Richard J. M. III; Dicks, Elton W.; Diehl, Joseph D., Jr.; Diggle, Arthur; Dilliard, Irving; Dillner, Robert; Dineen, Daniel W.; DiPuma, Benjamin A.; Dittler, William J.; Divietro, John; Dixon, James, Dobiasch, Karl; Doescher, Hedy; Doherty, Cornelius A., Jr.; Dolan, Thomas; Dombrowski, Jordan L.; Domeck, William; Donohue, Peter T.; Donley, Paul; Donnary, Edward G.; Donnelly, Richard C.; Donoghue, John D.; Donovan, Jack; Donovan, John C.; Donovan, Robert J.; Dorazio, Arthur J.; Dornheim, Arthur; Dorsey, George; Doty, Clayton C.; Dougherty, John P.; Downie, Charles E.; Dowling, Lyle; Downing, Norman J.; Dowell, Edwin E.; Dragon, John; Dragovich, H. M., Jr.; Drake, Edward N.; Dranoff, Albert; Dreyfuss, Allan; Duchatelet, Henri P.; Duff, James P.; Duff, Mary; Duke, John L.; Duliniski, Steven C.; Dumper, Robert S.; Dunbar, William; Duncan, Gregor K.; Dunlap, Harold T. K.; Dunlap, Roy J.; Dunlevy, Thomas M.; Dunphy, Robert; Duren, William C; Duscher, Edward and Dwyer, John J., Jr.

E

Eadgyas, Janos; Eagan, Louis C.; Eales, Raymond H.; Eathorne, James B.; Eaton, Jack; Earl, Harvey D.; Ebert, George C.; Ebert, Robert B.; Echt, Eric; Eck, Loy; Eckert, Robert; Edgington, Doyle A.; Edgren, Kenneth H.; Edmiston, Donald M.; Edmonds, Charles; Edward, Robert; Edwards, John; Edwards, Julia S.; Eeg, Einar; Eggart, John P.; Ehrenfreund, Norbert; Eisch, William; Elauf, Willy E.; Eldridge, Frederick L.; Elkin, Sam; Elliott, Janet; Elliott, John; Elliott, Marjorie; Elliott, Paul; Elliott, Richard B.; Elliott, Vernon; Elmslie, Donald A.; Ellis, Armin J.; Ellis, Edward; Elizondo, Manuel F.; Emery, Frank W.; Emery, Stanley; Emerson, Richard W.; Emmer, Leonard L.; Emmons, William; Enger, Theodore G.; Engle, Erich; Ensworth, Robert; Enyeart, Henry S.; Epstein, Henry S.; Erickson, Clarence L.; Erickson, Darwin A.; Ericson, Earl; Estes, Walter; Estoff, William D.; Essenbreis, Philip A.; Eustis, Bert; Evans, Albert B.; Evans, Dave K.; Evanston, Jerry; Everett, Merritt; Ewald, William H.; Evert, Earl C. and Eynon, David L.

F

Fadden, Thomas E.; Fagerholm, Gustav H.; Falk, Roderick A.; Fall, Leonard B.; Faller, Kenneth; Fannin, O.; Fanning, Winthrop C.; Farquhar, David; Farrell, Thomas J.; Farson, Daniel N.; Faulkner, Forrest; Faulkner, George E.; Faska, Paul F.; Fay, William C.; Feinstein, Martin; Fenney, George J.; Fenney, Harry J.; Fernandez, Robert I.; Ferrara, Fred V.; Fiedler, John W.; Field, John V.; Fick, Rudolf; Fields, Jack; Fields, Paul S.; Fifield, Flora; Fink, William N.; Fischetti, John R.; Fischer, Kurt; Fisch, William L.; Fishbach, Henry; Fishbein, Gerson W.; Fisher, E. Mollie; Fisher, Joseph L.; Fisher, Richard E.; Fleisher, Robert; Fleischman, William J.; Fleming, Joseph B., Jr.; Fleshman, Ruth McClung; Flower, Stanley A.; Floyd, Reginald C.; Floyd, William; Flynn, Leon; Fogel, Richard H.; Foinstein, Gilbert; Foisie, Jack; Folson, Mark P.; Fontaine, Paul; Force, Arthur R.; Forman, Robert P.; Foss, Jack E.; Forrest, Jean B.; Forster, Thomas; Forsberg, Franklin; Forsythe, Clarence C.; Foster, Jack; Fox, Gilbert; Fox, Seymour; Francolini, Andrew J.; Frank, Elmer D.; Frank, Joseph; Frankel, Harold M.; Franklin, Robert C.; Freed, Virgil R.; Freeman, Dexter L.; Freeman, Harry; Freeman, William M.; Freidline, Ralph J.; Friedman, Belle,; Friedman, Julius; Friedman, Harold; Friend, Phynas O.; Fricker, Edmund J.; Friedrich, Otto; Fritz, Richard; Fritz, Jakob; Frye, William; Fuller, M. C. and Furst, Peter.

G

Gaertner, Arthur G.; Gaines, John L.; Gaither, Ralph; Gallagher, William F.; Gallitscher, Thomas; Gallo, Anthony; Gallop, Luis A.; Gannon, James; Gans, Sidney; Gault, Louis J.; Gauvin, Joseph L.; Gauvin, Alfred J.; Garnett, William G.; Garrick, Ray; Garrick, Marvin L.; Gaspar, Alexander S.; Gass, Kathleen; Gebbie, Conley; Gelfand, Ivan; Genest, Claude; George, Thomas R.; Geraci, Philip C.; Gervers, James; Giacobbe, Peter; Gianino, Frank P.; Giblin, Leonard P.; Gibson, William; Giebert, Robert P., Jr.; Gies, Dorothy; Gigante, William; Giger, Joseph T.; Gilham, Willard M.; Gilmore, Michael; Gilpan, DeWitt C.; Gilstrap, Max K.; Ginsberg, Miles D.; Gissone, Joseph L.; Gitchal, Thomas W.; Gitlin, Richard; Gladwell, Gooch; Glass, Donald R.; Glaze, Wilbur; Glover, Foy E.; Glover, Lorraine; Glover, Peggy; Goddard, Anne E.; Goddard, Robert C.; Godfrey, George H.; Goetz, Horace; Goforth, Robert E.; Gold, Richard L.; Goldblatt,

Norman F.; Golden, Dwight E.; Goldenberg, Henry; Golding, David; Goldman, David; Goldman, Irvin; Goldsmith, Arnold; Goldsmith, Peter; Goldmuntz, Lawrence A.; Goldstein, Bernard; Goldstein, Edward; Goldstein, Jack; Goldstein, Harry; Goldstein, Meyer D.; Golellner, Hans; Goode, James A.; Goodfriend, Arthur; Gordon, Craig; Gordon, Daniel; Gordon, Dave I.; Gordon, David, Sr.; Gordon, Donald; Gordon, Sue; Gorman, John; Gorman, Samuel; Gozdecki, Roman R.; Grad, Jules B.; Graff, Gene; Graham, Nancy; Graiey, Bernard F.; Grainey, James P.; Grand, James; Grandy, Francis "Red"; Grant, Larry; Grant, Peter; Gray, George H., Jr.; Gray, Thomas T.; Gray, Thomas J.; Green, Paul S.; Green, Roger; Greenberg, Philip; Greene, Albert; Greene, Clyde D.; Greenhalgh, Walter; Greenough, Marie-Anne; Gregor, Lieselotte; Gregory, John C.; Gregson, James J.; Greim, Friedrich; Griffing, Lawrence D.; Groark, Thomas; Grobe, Lawrence D.; Grobe, Laurin V.; Grodzicki, Casmeir F.; Groebel, Lise; Gross, Don; Gross, Francis; Grossman, Max; Grueneberg, Richard U.; Gruner, George; Grout, John L.; Grover, David; Groves, David; Gudebrod, Morton P.; Gunno, Claude D.; Guotil, Thomas W.; Gusky, Joseph C.; Gutman, Denton; Gutshall, William S. and Ghio, Walter.

H

Habein, Richard F.; Haberzeth, Anton; Hackel, Martin; Hadfy, Leslie; Hadlock, Royal D.; Hagar, Jonathan N.; Hagler, Jimmie A.; Hahn, Charlotte; Hahn, Harry; Hain, Herbert W.; Haines, James; Hakim, George; Hall, Donald R.; Hall, Earl; Hall, Frank; Halligan, Richard; Halloran, Vincent J.; Halpin, Edward R.; Halverson, Oroville; Hamilton, Andrew J.; Hancock, John P.; Handelman, Theodore; Hanks, Earl D., Jr.; Hannifen, Daniel C.; Hanrahan, John J.; Hansson, Peter T.; Haransky, Al; Harcher, Harry A.; Hareld, Richard C.; Hard, Adrien C., Sr.; Harmon, William M., Jr.; Harrell, Alex; Harrigan, James J.; Harrington, John M.; Harriott, Joyce C.; Harris, Gene B.; Harris, Irving; Harris, Leighton G.; Harris, Martin; Harris, Richard; Harrison, John S.; Hart, H. Peter; Harte, Walter F.; Hartley, Harry P.; Hartman, Wallace C.; Hartnet, Gene B.; Hartsell, Loretta; Hartzell, Mahlon P.; Harty, Hugh F.; Harvey, Joseph M.; Harwood, Ralph L.; Hastings, John J.; Hause, Eugene R.; Hauser, John A.; Hauswirth, Barbara; Hayes, Andrew W.; Haynes, Elliott; Hays, John R.; Haywirth, Barbara; Hayworth, Cyril; Hawkes, Hugh M.; Heald, Jack B.; Heath, James F.; Heather, Weston; Hecard, Calvin J.; Hedeman, Gloria H.; Hedges, Glen E.; Hedges, William B.; Heinrich, Frank J.; Heintz, William F.; Heist, Annalie; Helfrich, Robert J.; Helfont, Nathan; Helm, Harry R.; Henderson, Billy O.; Henderson, Steward M.; Henrickson, Robert F.; Henkin, Daniel Z.; Henn, William E., Sr.; Henry, Edward J.; Henry, Jack; Herman, David; Herman, Jacob; Herman, Vic; Hernandez, Stephen A.; Herron, Francese; Hesse, George F.; Hessler, Charles W.; Hetler, Walter F.; Hey, Daniel; Hickey, Gerald; Higgins, Joan B.; Higuchi, George K.; Hilfiger, Mark; Hill, Edward; Hill, Howard; Hill, John I.; Hill, Robert F.; Hines, William A.; Hirsch, Louis; Hirsch, Richard L.; Hitchcock, Wallace C.; Hoback, Arthur B.; Hobart, John; Hobbs, John F.; Hocking, Dean N.; Hocking, Leonard A., Jr.; Hodenfield, G. K.; Hodes, Antonius H.; Hoffman, Eddy; Hoffman, Vincent E.; Hofrichter, Georg; Hogan, Charles A.; Hogan, Edmund F.; Hogan, William; Hoge, Herman J.; Hoge, Thomas; Holden, Lawrence R.; Hollway, Elmer D.; Holdman, Kenneth R.; Holdway, Elmer D.; Holiday, Roy; Hollabaugh, Wayne S.; Holler, Ernest W.; Holl, Franz; Hollie, Theo K.; Hollyman, Thomas B.; Holloway,

Jonny; Honig, Milton; Hoover, Floyd; Hopper, Cyril F.; Hopper, Thomas; Horkan, Kay; Horowitz, Paul; Horowitz, Lloyd; Horton, Howard H.; Hosey, James H.; Hosier, Harold E.; Houchen, Charles R.; Houghton, Jerry; House, Clyde; Howard, Oliver G.; Howard, Ray O.; Howard, William E.; Howden, Beverly; Howland, Kenneth A.; Hritz, Edwin; Hubbard, Carlton R.; Huberman, Julian J.; Huberts, Breginus; Hubbell, Frederick H.; Hubman, Hans; Hubman, Lisl; Huck, John; Hudson, Richard; Huether, Walter; Hufford, Thomas V.; Huggins, Edgar J.; Hull, George M.; Humes, Carleton; Hummel, Martin; Hunn, LeRoy; Hunter, Francis F.; Hunter, Merle; Hunter, Charles E.; Hunt, Ray S.; Hurte, Walter; Huston, Kenneth G.; Hutcheson, William D.; Hutchinson, Alexandria; Huthmacher, Leland R.; Hutton, Oram Clark "Bud" and Hyde, Frederick D., Sr.

I

Iannacio, Anthony; Iglehart, Robert; Igon, James T.; Ingersoll, Robert D.; Ingles, Frank W.; Insley, James F.; Ireland, David J.; Irvin, David L.; Irwin, Edward A.; Irwin, Joel L.; Irwin, Robert Ray; Isadore, Moses N.; Isonio, Emilio V.; Iteen, David D.; Itterly, Harrison M. and Ives, Joseph.

J

Jackson, Francis M.; Jackson, Joseph A., Jr.; Jackson, Nathan; Jacob, Walter J., Sr.; Jacobs, Francis T.; Jacoby, Norman; Jacovino, Vincent M.; James, Earl R.; Jameson, Ron; Jandoli, Russell J.; Jarvis, Joseph M.; Jelinski, John J.; Jenkins, Fred C.; Jenkins, William A.; Jennings, Douglas K.; Jensen, Bernard; Jensen, Orma G.; Jesperson, Chester W.; Jessup, Virgil E.; Jococks, Frank; Johnson, Byron; Johnson, Eugene C.; Johnson, Harry E.; Johnson, Paul; Johnston, Phoebe; Johnston, Thomas E.; Johnstone, Eugene C.; Jonas, Henry M.; Jones, Alton C.; Jones, Andrew N.; Jones, Arthur C.; Jones, Barbara; Jones, Charles E.; Jones, Charles W.; Jones, Dorothy E.; Jones, Gaylord; Jones, Paul H.; Jones, Richard; Jones, Russell; Jones, Wade; Jordan, Lew; Jordan, Wayne; Jordy, William; Jorgenson, Arthur L.; Joyce, Thomas; Judge, John F.; Julian, Robert L. and Junfin, Joseph.

K

Kalb, Gerald J.; Kahn, Sanford; Kalish, Harold A.; Kammerman, Eugene L.; Kane, Maurice R.; Kapchuk, Harry; Kaplan, Ernest H.; Kaufman, Lawrence H.; Karlstrand, Einar W.; Katz, Erving; Katz, Julius P.; Katz, Pauli; Katzander, Howard L.; Katzander, Shirley S.; Kearney, John O.; Keating, Thomas G.; Keith, Ollie B.; Kelder, Robert; Keller, Philip B.; Kelliher, Harry; Kellog, Donald H.; Kelly, Daniel J., Jr.; Kelly, John F.; Kemerly, John B., Jr.; Kendall, Dean E.; Kennan, Ralph; Kennedy, David; Kennedy, Martin; Kennedy, William H.; Kent, F. R., Jr.; Kenz, John; Keola, Henry, Jr.; Kern, Raymond D.; Kerrigan, Peter; Kestler, Hal C.; Kidby, Clarence; Kieffer, Jeanette A.; Kiehl, Marya C.; Kile, Claire V.; Kile, Corwin M.; Kiley, Charles; Killingsworth, Edward; Killpack, Edward S.; Kilzer, Bernard A.; Kimber, LeRoy G.; Kinder, Edith; King, Byron K.; King, James L.; Kinsby, Richard G.; Kinsby, Robert; Kinsey, Richard G.; Kirchhoff, Bernard; Kirk, Weir Richard; Kirk, William C.; Kirkwood, Anne S.; Kirkwood, Maurice R.; Kittler, Emil; Kleege, Robert K.; Kleeman, Martin; Klein, William; Klemfuss, Robert B.; Kline, Al; Kline, Phil; Kline, Seymour S.; Kline, Sidney; Kline, William; Klippel, Wilhelm; Knapp, Leroy C.; Knederowicz, Anthony; Knight, Afton W.; Knopf, Paul; Knorr, Renata; Knorr, Richard; Kochel,

Richard E.; Koenig, Richard; Kohler, Alfred V.; Kohn, Alfred N.; Kohn, Jesse F.; Kolber, Laurence; Kollath, Eugene O.; Kolodinski, Alexander; Konkel, Joseph; Konzelman, Carl; Korb, William W.; Korbchen, Walter; Korman, Jerry; Kornmann, Karl; Korver, John A.; Koster, Richard C.; Kott, Anthony J.; Koyen, Kenneth A.; Kraatz, Hans B., Jr.; Kraft, Henry; Kraft, Wilheim; Kramer, Arthur; Kramer, Barry; Kramer, Ellis; Kramer, Frank; Kramer, Norman; Kresslein, John H.; Kristak, Edward J.; Kroll, Milton J.; Kroner, Svend; Krotozyner, James M.; Krug, George H.; Kruh, Louis; Kruth, Louis; Krysa, Karol E.; Kuchciak, Teddy D.; Kuehn, Eugene L.; Kuest, Frank H.; Kuenzel, Joseph; Kugelmas, Joseph Alvin; Kuhn, Mary; Kuhns, John C.; Kullgren, Peter; Kunkel, Andrew W.; Kupsick, Robert H.; Kuzmicz, Marianne and Kwiatkowski, Leon.

L

Label, Sydney; Ladshaw, Archibald A.; Lagle, Walter; La Harte, Edward J.; Laing, Alex C.; Laird, Milton G.; Lake, James L., Jr.; Lakos, Steven R. J.; Lallemand, Raymond A.; Lamb, Latimer W.; Lamb, Loyal C.; Lampron, Emil A.; Landau, Joseph; Landsdoune, Paul; Lane, William F.; Lang, Paul C.; Langham, Willard G.; Lantz, Charles M.; Lapov, Norman; Larkin, Warren E.; La Rochelle, George J.; Larsen, Betty; Larsen, Carl W.; Larson, Sidney W.; Laschever, Barnett D.; Lasky, A. Victor; Latta, Robert M.; Lattanzio, Peter E.; Lauterwasser, Theodore; Lawrence, Raymond V.; Lawrence, Edward; Laxer, Edith; Lazarony, Phil; Learned, George; Lebelhuber, Franz; Lacacheux, Robert; LeClaire, Haydn; Lee, Francis J., Jr.; Lee, Ray; Lee, Robert H.; Lee, Sidney; Lee, William B.; Leff, Bernard S.; Lefler, Jack; Lehman, Milton; Leialoha, Elmer A.; Lieberman, Leonard; Leiser, Ernest S.; Leisee, Kaida; Lenehan, Peter; Lesher, Robert H.; Lesperance, Francis D.; Lester, William P.; Leszko-Sokolowski, Wladyslaw; Leuterio, Roger; Levenhagen, Don; Levin, David; Levin, Eugene; Levin, Jonathan V.; Levin, Maurice W.; Levine, Leonard H.; Levine, Leo; Levinson, Irving; Levinshohn, Harold; Lewicki, Alexander; Lewis, Clyde H.; Lewis, Gordon W.; Lewis, John B.; Lewis, Kate B.; Lewis, Marion F.; Lewis, Moe; Lewis, Richard; Ley, Hermann; Lichtenberger, Al; Lichenstein, Julius; Liddle, Joan; Liebes, Bernard H.; Lieberman, Leonard; Lillenberg, Ray E.; Lindgren, Robert E.; Lindsey, Raymond; Lindsey, Helen; Lindsey, Thomas E.; Link, Joseph F., Jr.; Lipsky, Horst; Lisagor, Peter; Little, Billy G.; Livingood, John W.; Llewellyn, Ensley M.; Lobenthal, Joseph S.; Lockberg, Eric G.; Lodzinski, Gregory G.; Loeb, August L.; Loeb, Jacques, Jr.; Loebl, Elliott D.; Loimann, Erich; Lombard, Robert; Long, Harold D.; Long, Robert; Looker, Reginald E.; Lord, Sterling; Lorenson, Ernest H.; Lorenz, Jules; Loughlin, William; Lowman, Harry C.; Lucas, Clarence B.; Lucas, Joseph W.; Luce, Joseph H.; Luft, Walter E.; Lukas, Fred M.; Lumpkin, Frances J.; Lund, Leonard M.; Luros, Betty; Lusk, Theodore R.; Lyman, James D.; Lyons, Hilary H. and Lyons, Tommy.

M

MacArthur, John N.; Macauley, Thurston; MacGregor, Robert B.; MacGregor, Robert M.; Mackay, George; Mackey, Joseph; Maginnis, Charles S., Jr.; Magner, Raymond P.; Mahoney, William G.; Major, Ralph H., Jr.; Makey, Joseph; Malick, Eugene L.; Malinowski, Frank J.; Mall, William W.; Malm, Richard K.; Malone, Henry T.; Maloney, F. Robert; Maloney, John; Malshers, Edwin I.; Malum, Steve; Mancini, John L.; Mandell, Irving J.; Mann, Isador; Mann, Klaus; Manning, Harold G.; Manning, Larry G.; Manos, John T.; Marazzo, Joseph; March-banks, Bromet D.; Marchewka, Edward A.; Marcocciom, Adolfo; Marder, Irving; Mardis, John; Margolin, Nathan J.; Marks, Robert M.; Marley, Brent F.; Mar-rian, Helen; Martone, Roland A.; Marsh, Bert E.; Marshall, Ernest N.; Marshall, Jean B.; Marshall, Joseph S., Jr.; Marshall, Robert A.; Marshall, Robert H.; Marshburn, Alvin H.; Marta, Robert E.; Martin, Edward; Martin, Eldon C.; Martin, Mark T., Jr.; Martin, Marie "Rusty"; Martin, Ralph G.; Martin, Rich-ard E.; Martin, Richard H.; Martinez, Fernand; Martinez, Jose; Maroon, Si; Marotta, Anthony C.; Marron, John; Marta, Robert J.; Martley, Michael; Marx, Morton; Marzen, Leonard F.; Maskin, George J.; Mason, Don W.; Mason, John S.; Massimino, Roman M.; Mata, Rudolph M.; Mather, Brian; Mathes, Ray-mond; Matteo, Henry S.; Mauldin, Bill; Mauer, Gilbert; Maxfield, A. F.; Maxim, Wallace; Mayo, Augustus; May, Fred W.; May, William F.; Mayer, June B.; Mazo, Earl; Mazur, Robert F.; Meader, Henry C.; Mealing, Frank; Medart, Edith; Medart, Elizabeth; Medine, William; Medlin, Boyce C.; Meier, Kurt; Meister, Robert; Melcher, Jack; Meleng, John R.; Mellen, Paul C.; Meltzoff, Stanley; Melzi, Ross; Meomartino, James J.; Mendelson, Oscar; Menendez, George; Merillat, Charles C.; Merryfield, Leonard; Merritt, James R.; Merritt, Robert; Mertinke, Fred G.; Messerschmidt, Horst; Metzger, Paul J.; Metzger, Robert; Meyer, Arthur E.; Meyer, Edward C.; Meyer, Elizabeth; Meyer, Robert, Jr.; Meyer, Rhinehart C.; McAteer, Hugh; McArthur, Arthur J.; McBride, Joseph F.; McBride, Ralph A.; McCabe, Joseph P.; McCabe, Robert K.; McCall, Thomas; McCarter, Arthur J.; McCarthy, Daniel J.; McCarthy, John; Mc-Clelland, Marshall K.; McClintic, Robert G.; McClure, Brooks; McConnell, Charles V.; McConnell, W. Harold; McCormick, William B.; McCoy, Trulen C.; McCoy, Vasco; McCulla, James W.; McCullough, Glenn M.; McCur, Joseph A.; McDade, Donald; McDonald, John R.; McDonald, Marylou; McDonald, Matt C.; McDonald, Robert F.; McDonald, Warren F.; McDonald, William J.; Mc-Elwain, Benjamin; McElwain, William; McElwee, Robert M.; McEvoy, J. Ed-ward; McFarland, Edwin O.; McGill, James D.; McGlade, Edward; McGowan, Gordon H.; McGowan, Michael; McGowan, James H.; McGraw, Preston; Mc-Gregor, Robert M.; McGuigan, Bernard; McGuinis, John L.; McGuire, John; McGuire, Harold L.; McHarry, Charles K.; McHugh, Leroy; McIntyre, Robert; McKenna, Philip C.; McKinney, William B.; McLaughlin, Dean E.; Mc-Laughlin, Dorothy G.; McLauchin, Harry J.; McLean, James V.; McLeod, John E.; McLoughlin, Alvin; McNamara, William; McManus, Terrance; McMullan, Frank; McNitzky, William H., Jr.; McNulty, Jack; McQuaid, B. O.; McQuaid, Elias H.; McRae, Thomas; McSwanson, Clement S.; Michel, Gisela; Mignerey, Lester; Mikez, Stephen J.; Milam, James L.; Miles, Garvey; Miletta, Michael S.; Milgrom, Albert; Milnazik, Robert S.; Miller, Alan; Miller, Douglass; Miller, Grant; Miller, Harold R.; Miller, Jack; Miller, Jacob; Miller, Lou; Miller, Max; Miller, Richard; Miller, Solomon; Milliken, Steve; Millinoff, Stanley; Mills, Ger-ald J.; Minor, Loye N.; Minter, George; Mitchell, Edward T.; Mitchell, Patrick C.; Mitgang, Herbert; Mooney, James L.; Moora, Robert L.; Moore, Dickie; Moore, Gayle L.; Moore, Henry L.; Moore, H. Wallace; Moore, Jack; Moore, Myles P.; Moran, William; Morgan, Robert L.; Morey, Donald I.; Morrison, Allan M.; Morrison, David C.; Morrison, Donald C.; Morrison, Ewell; Morris, George A.; Morriss, Ewell O.; Morriss, R. C.; Morrissey, Alfred L.; Morse, Ralph

H.; Morton, John W.; Mosleth, Ray B.; Motiska, John J.; Moyniham, John C.; Muehlbauer, Ernst; Muehlbauer, Johann; Mueller, Francis G.; Muglia, Arthur J.; Mulle, Joseph S.; Mullahay, T. Vincent; Muller, Richard; Mulligan, Leslie; Mulvehill, Thomas; Murar, Bela; Murphy, Mildred; Murphy, Neil P.; Murphy, William B.; Musleh, Ray J. and Myers, Robert L.

N

Nader, Charles A.; Nadle, Walter; Nail, Earl J.; Naughton, William E.; Nault, Alpheget; Neal, Harry C.; Nellums, James M.; Nellums, Margaret; Neth, Cecil B.; Neumyer, John; Neville, Robert; Newstead, Dennis; Newstead, John O.; Newman, Ralph A.; Nicholls, Ralph; Nickerson, Roy A.; Nieheiser, Walter A.; Nitz, Elizabeth; Nitzberg, Morton; Niven, Arthur; Nixon, John E.; Noble, Gerald S.; Noblit, Lawrence; Noel, Ralph; Norcross, Charles; Norfield, Barbara; Norton, James; Nottet, Rene; Novak, Eugene; Noviec, Peter J. and Noyes, Arthur A.

O

O'Brian, Patrick M.; O'Connor, John S.; Odom, Bruce S.; O'Farrell, Catherine; Offner, Simone; Ohlson, Gus W.; O'Kearney, John J.; Olenick, Lawrence; Olsen, Rolf; Olson, Harold C.; Olson, Lloyd A.; Olt, Robert J.; O'Neill, Patrick C.; Onuskas, Albert; Ooms, Adam; Opdyke, Hal F.; Oppenheim, W.; Orgel, Seymour; Orpen, Donald J.; Ornstein, Herman; O'Rourke, George; Ott, John C., Sr., and Oviatt, Warren E.

P

Padover, S. K.; Pagel, Everd H.; Pagen-Brown, William H.; Palermo, Louis S.; Palmer, Allan; Palmer, Clarence A.; Palmer, Douglas; Palmer, Herbert; Palmer, James O.; Palmer, Merle E.; Palmer, T. Norman; Parenti, Leo S.; Parker, Archie; Parker, James C., Sr.; Parker, Paul L.; Parks, James G.; Parkton, Raymond W.; Parman, Quentin; Parris, Paul; Parrish, James M.; Partain, John M.; Patterson, Lee M.; Patterson, Remington; Patterson, Richard E.; Patton, Hugh B.; Peace, John N.; Pecharo, Thomas; Peckham, Fred W., Jr.; Pedro, John M.; Peel, Harris; Pelkingston, William; Pelligrino, Frank; Penn, George A. M.; Peppard, Harley; Perez, Frank; Pernod, Maurie H.; Perisho, Robert; Perl, Norbert; Perretta, Harry F.; Perzely, Gabriel G.; Parry, Theodore A.; Petrakis, George R.; Petruzzelli, Saverio; Peyton, Wesley G.; Pfeifer, Delmer I.; Phares, Don; Phillips, Arnie M.; Phillips, J. A., Jr.; Phillips, Theodore M.; Pieratt, Afton; Pierce, Vincent W.; Pierson, Carl; Pingerelli, Paul W.; Pinkerton, William N.; Pinkett, Kate M.; Pilney, Bernard J.; Pizzolato, Salvador; Platanitis, Steve; Platt, Cray M.; Platts, Peter C.; Pletcher, Vernon; Podeswa, Harold; Poff, William; Pogwizd, Richard J.; Pohle, Harry; Pohlenz, Dean; Poirier, Ferdinand A.; Pollock, Reyburn; Pollock, Sol; Pomber, Ivor J.; Pons, Suzanne; Popham, George; Pormen, Paul, Sr.; Posegga, Willi; Posner, Seymour J.; Post, Charles H.; Potter, Catherine; Potulny, John; Poulson, Albert G.; Powers, John; Pratt, Frank R.; Praznovzky, G. L.; Pregaldin, Charles V.; Pretzer, Norman L.; Price, Benjamin F.; Price, James C.; Priest, Russell E.; Pringle, Murray T.; Priscu, Daniel; Pritchett, Farmer L.; Pritchett, Logan; Prochaska, Oswald; Proctor, William G.; Prokav, Ferenc; Prutsman, Alden; Pryne, Richard K.; Pryk, Joseph F.; Pryor, Tyler W.; Przybylo, Albin J.; Pulliam, Walter; Purvis, Virgin; Putnam, Delmar B.; Pye, Joseph and Pyle, Robert.

Q

Queenan, Charles F.; Quigley, James M.; Quinn, Joseph and Quint, James.

R

Rabinovich, Joseph; Radosta, John S.; Raffalele, Fred J.; Ragen, Dorothy May; Railsback, Leonard E.; Raita, John, Jr.; Raiuk, Walter; Rakiewicz, Joseph S.; Rakin, Louis; Rakitt, Martin S.; Randolph, Robert A.; Rasche, Margareta; Raskin, Herman; Rathburn, William D.; Raupfer, Robert J.; Ravich, Samuel S.; Raymond, Jack; Raymond, Jean R.; Raymond, Nicholas; Raymond, Walter H. T.; Read, Milton H.; Reddy, George O.; Redman, Joseph C.; Redman, Paul; Redman, Reginald; Reed, Ernest R.; Reed, Stanley; Rees, James A.; Regan, Daniel; Regan, Neil T.; Reger, Alice; Rehse, Margareti; Reid, Alyce; Reilly, Thomas F.; Reilly, Richard D.; Reinhardt, Siegfried; Reining, Wilhelm; Renner, Edouard; Renne, Peter; Resnik, Albert L.; Resnik, David; Resnik, Rudolph F.; Respess, George V., Jr.; Reque, David; Reynolds, Andrew J.; Reynolds, Ray P.; Reynolds, Samuel; Reznek, David; Rhodes, Ernest J.; Riccardi, August; Ricchiuti, Andrew J.; Riccio, Dominick; Richardson, Marvin D.; Richardson, Monroe; Richmond, Harvey H.; Riemer, Joseph L., Sr.; Rieser, Roderick N.; Rimes, Jackie A.; Ring, Willard; Riordan, Larry; Rios, Ernie; Ritz, Al; Roark, Loren F.; Roark, Rexford E.; Roberts, Eric; Roberts, Ira J.; Robertson, Nan; Robinette, Carlish; Robinson, Cyril D.; Robinson, Robbie; Rodesta, John; Rodgers, Robert P.; Rodgers, Robert R.; Roessner, Elmer; Rogers, Herbert D.; Rogers, John; Rogers, Peter; Rogers, Woodrow W.; Rohde, Theodore R.; Rohner, Dean E. A.; Rollins, Horace W.; Rollins, Lowell; Rollins, William; Romaine, Joseph D.; Romany, Walter A.; Romero, Emilio P.; Rooney, Andy; Rooney, Edmund J.; Rosa, Alfred; Rosbotham, John; Rose, Margaret; Rose, Ralph G.; Rosen, Abe S.; Rosenbaum, Irving H.; Rosenthal, Edwin; Rosenthal, Harry F.; Ross, Doug; Rosseter, John; Rossman, Ed; Rowan, John M.; Rowan, Timothy E.; Rubin, Bernard; Rubin, Sheldon S.; Ruder, Leonard T.; Ruddock, Theodore B.; Ruff, John A. L.; Ruhlin, Roger R.; Rukeyser, Louis; Runge, Hans; Ruppino, John D.; Rush, Audrey; Russ, John; Russell, Dorothy N. S.; Russell, James; Russell, John T.; Russick, Donald; Rutherford, Junior E.; Ryan, Charles W., Jr. and Ryan, John J.

S

Saal, Herbert; Sachs, Josef; Sack, Nyla; Safter, Solomon; Sahlman, Inge Maria; Salamie, Lew; Salistian, John W.; Salk, Ronald D.; Salkowski, John; Sanchez, Jesus; Sanchez, Manuel J.; Sand, Charles R.; Sanders, Archibald C.; Sanders, Rhea E.; Sanderson, Harvey D.; Sanderson, James D.; Sandrof, Ivan; Sandoval, Vincent; Sanford, Victor B.; Santora, Dominick L.; Santora, Edward F.; Santora, Paul; Santo, Ben J.; Sapir, Philip; Saterlee, Charles; Saunders, Howard F.; Saunders, Reg; Savary, Gerald L.; Sawatzke, Beryle D.; Saxon, Robert A.; Scanlon, Robert J.; Scarlett, Harold T.; Schaefer, Heinz; Schalata, Thomas E.; Schapiro, Sidney; Schear, Dwight B.; Scheffner, Warren H.; Scheuermann, Georg; Schiemer, Martin; Schifino, Jerry; Schleider, Leonard; Schmidt, Emil K.; Schmidt, Eugene C.; Schmidt, Grace; Schmidt, Harry; Schmidt, Wesley H.; Schnabel, Margot; Schneider, Herbert; Schneider, Hub; Schneider, Werner; Schoepflin, Ludwig; Scholl, John H.; Schouman, Frederick S.; Schowehel, William; Schroeder, Kenneth; Schroeter, Leonard W.; Schrum, William G.; Schuette, George W.; Schultz, Norman E.; Schultz, Whitt N.; Schuman, Francis E.; Schwarz, Helmut; Schwarwarzkopf, Maria; Schwartz, Nathan; Schwertner, Gerhard H.; Schwoebel, William, Jr.; Sconce, Robert E.; Scorgie, Fred; Scott, David J.; Scott, Edwin M.; Scott, Edward R.; Scott, Wallace H.; Scudder, Robert J. F.; Searfoss, Howard;

Seeger, Gunther; Seebol, Robert; Sellow, Donald R.; Seely, Charles; Seidl, George W.; Seifert, Norman; Seligsohn, Jerome; Selmanoff, E. S.; Sempill, John D.; Seney, Edgar F.; Senft, Louis; Senigo, Mark E.; Sergeson, William E.; Sevensky, Edward R.; Shaner, Ernest J.; Shaheen, Edmund F.; Shapiro, Raymond S.; Shapiro, Sidney; Sharnik, John Seymour; Shaw, Fred; Shaw, Robert M.; Shea, Richard E.; Shea, Robert J.; Sheil, Thomas L.; Sheldon, John; Sheldon, Robert; Sherlock, Dee; Shipley, William F.; Shipmann, James F.; Sheppard, Donald L.; Shershow, Harry; Shilling, Karl; Short, John D.; Shrum, William G.; Shuman, Ben; Sibert, Lother B.; Siegel, Jerome; Siegmund, John H.; Sikes, George R.; Silvano, Samuel; Silveria, Raymond M.; Silvestro, Nicholas P.; Simmons, James A.; Simmons, Theodore R.; Sinder, David A.; Singer, Albert; Singer, Hershel S.; Singer, Leonard; Singer, Philip; Sirani, Anthony; Sisk, Alvin B.; Skean, Gordon A.; Skelton, Paul R.; Skok, Roman R.; Skolnick, Edward; Slavikosky, Andrew P.; Slemmons, Guy A.; Sletson, Isaac M.; Sliman, Samuel; Sliman, Michael L.; Slimmer, Burton; Slinger, George F.; Sloniger, Jerrold E.; Small, Donald N.; Small, Jean A.; Smiley, Joseph; Smith, Al G.; Smith, Clarence; Smith, Fitzgerald; Smith, George L.; Smith, Harold; Smith, Henry M.; Smith, Leonard; Smith, Leroy; Smith, Martin; Smith, Oroville; Smith, Robert E.; Smith, Robert J.; Smith, Robert T.; Smith, Stanley; Smith, Steward W.; Smith, Stuart L.; Smith, Walter B.; Smith, Wilson T.; Smock, William G.; Sneed, Lester N.; Soblik, Benjamin; Soditis, Anthony W.; Solis, Gilberto; Sontag, Robert; Sorensen, Carl; Sorensen, Robert E.; Spait, Emma; Sparks, John; Sparrow, Ernest L.; Speake, Joseph; Spear, William R.; Speier, Robert W.; Spence, Donald; Spiegel, George; Spiess, Walter; Spink, Chester H.; Sprague, Carrol; Sprinkle, Karl; Sponner, Rosemary; Spry, Paul; Stadler, Maury T.; Stanley, Leonard W.; Stanley, Wilson P.; Stapleton, W.; Starkey, John R.; Starkey, Richard; Stauter, George A.; Steffen, Vernon; Stein, Yale; Steinberg, Ludwig C.; Steinberg, Sid; Steingasser, Karl; Steinwalt, J. Wells; Stenzel, Karl; Stephens, Duane P.; Stephenson, Stan; Stephensky, Bernard; Stern, Alfred; Stern, Lawrence; Stern, Phil; Stern, David III; Stettner, Max H.; Stevenson, Stanley; Stewart, John P.; Stinzing, Maja; Stirts, Guy E.; St Julian, Donald A.; St John, Mary; St John, Wattie T., Jr.; Stockton, Arthur M.; Stoil, Theodore; Stokes, La Verth; Stone, Lawrence L.; Stone, Marc; Storck, Gertrud; Stoti, Edward; Strazicich, Mirko G.; Strickland, J. R.; Strombeck, Wesley L.; Stuart, Margaret; Suddles, Fred J., Jr.; Suizo, Chester R.; Sullivan, Jack; Sullivan, John V. B.; Sullivan, John B.; Sullivan, Peter J.; Summers, William M.; Sumrall, Calvin; Suter, Myron E.; Sutherland, Floyd; Sutherland, Henry A.; Svinis, Albin; Swafford, James C.; Swan, Curtis D.; Sweeney, Bernard; Sweeney, Gilbert; Sweeney, Raymond G.; Swigart, Peter; Swihart, George H.; Swinton, Stanley; Sylvester, Edward J.; Symonds, Gene D. and Szekely, Istvan.

T

Taarup, Georg T.; Talmage, George S.; Tankerdley, Preston; Taormina, Salvatore C.; Tapisco, Harry; Tarbi, Frank J.; Tatai, Koh; Taubkin, Irvin S.; Taubman, Howard; Taylor, A. S., Jr.; Taylor, Donald J.; Taylor, Philip W.; Taylor, Ralph P.; Taylor, William F.; Teague, John G.; Tellis, Richard; Terry, Buddy; Tessier, Maurice E.; Teutscher, Alfred; Textor, Kurt; Tewksbury, Grayson D.; Thoman, James C.; Thomas, John F.; Thomas, "Tex"; Thompson, John J.; Thompson, Paul W.; Thornberry, Monica H.; Thornburn, John; Thrush, Roland J.; Thurber, George H.; Tiffany, Earl J.; Timmons, William G.; Tinker, William;

Todd, Norman V.; Toepfer, Robert; Tognini, Aldo C.; Tolluzzi, Henry E.; Tominey, Francis J.; Toney, Glen G.; Toparek, John; Torredelfino, Michael; Tosti, Adele; Tout, William; Towe, Lonnie E.; Towler, Lillian; Townsend, Campbell; Townsend, Richard; Tramasure, John H.; Trautfelter, Peter R.; Traux, Norman; Treleven, Charles; Trescott, Henry W.; Troop, Joseph H. P., Jr.; Truman, Edward C.; Tsouprake, Ted E.; Tuck, George W.; Tucker, George; Tuite, John F.; Turnblad, John; Twining, W. R. and Tyer, Arnold J.

U

Ullian, Lewis; Ulmer, Irene; Ulmer, John R.; Ullmann, Karl; Umans, George; Umeda, Takashi; Unwin, Fred E. and Upson, Robert R.

V

Vaccaro, Michael; Valenti, Michael J.; Van Abshoven, Reiner; Van Deerlin, Lionel; Van den Bosch, Riet; Van den Maas, Joost; Van der Akker, Arie; Van der Ploeg, Jan; Van Erp, Frits; Van Ginkle, Joseph; Van Heule, William; Van Pelt, Fred; Van Waas, Lucien; Van Wingerden, Stewart; Vaughn, William T.; Vebell, Edward T.; Vermanders, Maurice; Vennard, Polly; Venturelle, Nicholas; Verdon, Richard W.; Verfaillie, John D.; Verfaillie, Roy A.; Veronico, Nicholas A.; Verzqyvelt, Herbert J.; Vestal, Samuel; Vigil, Richard A.; Villano, Samuel C.; Villapiano, John; Villapiano, Samuel C.; Villency, Charles; Vintalora, Bernard J.; Visser, Kenneth E.; Vitterito, Michael; Voisin, Gerard; Von Behren, J.; Von Behren, Fred; Von Rospach, Cecil F.; Von Rospach, Marion; Voulas, Harry C.; Vourlas, Charajambe A. and Vrotsos, Johnny.

W

Wachter, Wally; Wacker, John; Waechter, Willy; Wagman, Jules; Walden, Russell O.; Walker, Alfred J.; Walker, James H.; Walker, Joan F.; Walker, Maurice J.; Walker, Nadeanne; Wall, Clarence W.; Wallace, Bertram E.; Waller, Gerald; Walter, Albert; Walter, Donald; Walters, Jack; Wander, Howard; Ward, Emory; Ward, James; Ward, Thomas; Warnk, Friedrich; Warren, Billie; Warren, George K.; Warren, James P.; Warren, Mark; Wartenbee, Kenneth D.; Waters, Frank; Waters, John W.; Waters, William; Waterman, Frank; Waterman, Samuel A.; Watkins, William T.; Watson, Harry S.; Watson, Lonnie; Watts, Steve L.; Waugh, Fred E.; Weaver, Glenn; Webb, Martin B., Jr.; Webbere, George; Webbere, Mary; Webster, Ellsworth J.; Webster, Larry; Wechsberg, Joseph; Wedel, Karl; Weiland, Ria; Weinberg, Curt; Weinrott, Hershal; Weinstein, William R.; Weintrobe, Louis; Weir, Max Hill; Weissberg, Samuel; Weissman, Harold; Weiss, David; Weiss, Jack; Weisz, Hedi; Weisz, Kurt; Wehrwein, Austin C.; Welsh, John III; Weniger, Virginia; Wentworth, John; Wentzel, Jacob; Wentz, John R.; Wentzig, Jenny; Werner, Martin H.; Wesolek, Paul R.; West, Floyd; Weston, Joseph; Wexton, Stan; Wheeler, James B.; Wheeler, Victor J.; White, Argil; White, Arthur W.; White, Bert; White, Charles W.; White, Dale; White, Egbert; White, Jeff W.; White, Stoddard; White, Walton S.; White, William; Whitfield, George; Whiteman, Philip; Whitman, Hamilton; Whittick, Anthony; Whittlesey, Merrell W.; Wible, Everett E.; Wickham, Paul H.; Wickliffe, Willard E.; Widem, Allen M.; Wieder, Myrlin H.; Wiemann, Gustav R.; Wiener, Leigh A.; Wiessman, Harold; Wilber, Dick; Wilcox, Edwin II; Wilensky, Louis; Wiley, James F.; Wilhelm, Gail C.; Wilkinson, John C.; Wilkey, Lewis H.; Williams, Arthur R.; Williams, Cecil; Williams, Donald; Williams, Eleanor A.; Williams, Frank M.; Williams, James;

Williams, John; Williams, Laura; Williams, Les; Williams, Oscar; Williams, Richard A.; Williams, Robert; Williams, Robert F.; Williams, William F.; Williams, William; Willig, John M.; Willner, Neil E.; Wilson, Theodore L.; Windfurh, Ernest; Wing, Jesse; Winger, Dick; Wingert, Rader W.; Wisniewski, Edward M.; Wolf, Earl H.; Wolfe, Burton; Wolfe, Chester; Wolfe, George, Jr.; Wolfe, George H.; Wolff, Lothar; Wondolowski, John; Wondoloski, Regina; Wong, Andrew Q.; Wood, Robert B.; Wood, Sidney R.; Wood, Wilford; Woods, Shirley; Worley, Virgil E.; Wray, Raymond A.; Wright, Donald O.; Wright, John M.; Wright, Mitchell; Wright, Raymond; Wronker, Robert; Wujek, Bole Slaw and Wysong, Robert.

Y

Yates, Thomas; Yfzem, Lawrence C.; Young, George; Young, James and Yudain, Bernard L.

Z

Zachow, Willy; Zaitz, Clarence; Zalenski, William E.; Zaluzki, Michael; Zanto, Robert; Zbytniewski, Ernest B.; Zellanack, John J.; Ziccarelli, James A.; Ziegfield, Arthur F.; Ziff, Richard I.; Zimmerman, Chester; Zimmerman, Constantine; Zimmerman, Paul B.; Zipt, Theodor; Zlonkiewicz, Michael; Zueckowski, Casimir and Zumwalt, Kenneth D.

★ ★

Bibliography

★ ★

[Sources consulted]

Adleman, Robert H., and Col. George Walton. *The Champagne Campaign.* Boston: Little, Brown & Co., 1969.

Butcher, Capt. Harry C., USNR. *My Three Years With Eisenhower.* New York: Simon and Shuster, 1946.

Clay, Lucius D. *Decision in Germany.* New York: Doubleday & Co., Inc., 1950.

Collier, Richard. *Bridge Across the Sky.* New York: McGraw-Hill, 1978.

Donovan, Frank. *Bridge in the Sky.* New York: David McKay Co., 1968.

Eisenhower, Dwight D. *Crusade in Europe.* New York: Doubleday & Co., Inc., 1948.

Hutton, Bud, and Andy Rooney. *The Story of The Stars and Stripes.* New York: Rinehart & Co., Ltd., 1946.

Meyer, Robert, Jr. *The Stars and Stripes.* New York: David McKay Co., 1960.

Sharnik, John, and Oliver Gregg Howard. *Stripes, The First Five Years.* Pfungstadt, Germany: The Stars and Stripes, 1947.

Weizmann, Chaim. *Trial and Error.* New York: Harper and Brothers, 1949.

Winterich, John T. *Squads Write!* New York: Harper and Brothers, 1949.

Woods, Oliver, and James Bishop. *The Story of The Times.* London: Michael Joseph Ltd., 1983.

Newspapers:

The Christian Science Monitor
The Stars and Stripes

Magazines:

Colliers
Life
Saturday Evening Post

NORTHERN IRELAND 1942: From left, Carl Larsen, Tony Cordaro, Bryce Burke, Maj. Harry Harcher (officer in charge), Bert Marsh, Fred Ferrara, and unidentified Belfast telegraph printer.

LONDON 1944: From left, Ben Price, Hamilton Whitman, Andy Rooney, Bud Hutton, Russ Jones, and Bob Moora in *London Times* newsroom.

LIEGE 1945: From left, Carl Larsen, Charles Kiley, "Blackie" Blackman, Dan Regan, Johnnie Brown, Capt. Max Gilstrap (officer in charge), 1st/Lt. Robert Brown. Seated: Arthur Force, Ken Zumwalt, Larry Griffing, Frank Waters, John Sharnik, Al Ritz, and Cray Platt. Standing: Capt. Victor Meluskey (censor), Bert Marsh, Dick Jones, Nick Cinquemani, and "Tex" Thomas.

ROME 1945: From left, Julius Grazer, unidentified, Tony Iannacio, Maj. Robert Neville (officer in charge), Vin Pierce, Irving Levinson, Ed Rossman, John Welch III, Harry Shershow, and Bill Mauldin.

PFUNGSTADT 1945: This is how the brewery town looked when *The Stars and Stripes* printed the first free newspaper in Hitler's Germany. The war ended a month later.

LONDON 1945: Eager staffers and British pressmen pull V-E Day edition off press at *London Times*.

GRIESHEIM 1952: From left, John Livingood, Russ Braley, Mort Nitzberg, and James Quint. Ken Zumwalt and Howard Katzander are standing in front of map. Second copy desk is in rear.

GRIESHEIM 1952: Visitors sign in at entrance to the European edition of *The Stars and Stripes*. Security at left, message center in building 24, distribution in building 20, and administration, production, and editorial in rear structure.

BING CROSBY came calling at Griesheim May 27, 1953. From left, Jack Ellis (sports editor), Ken Zumwalt, the crooner, John Livingood, and Ernie Reed.

IKE AND RED MEET: A year after *Stripes* photographer Francis "Red" Grandy took the photo of General Eisenhower's reaction to the news that Truman had fired MacArthur, they met at Rhine-Main Air Base March 12, 1952. They were introduced by managing editor Ken Zumwalt while Gen. Thomas T. Handy looked on.

"I'LL BE DARNED!" That's what Ike said when told April 11, 1951, that President Truman had fired General MacArthur. *Stripes* photographer Frances "Red" Grandy snapped this prize-winning picture.

"Don't look now but there's old 'Cooshay Awvec' back in town!"

One of many cartoons appearing in issues of The Stars and Stripes *drawn by GI staffers, this one by Dick Wingert.*

AUTHOR 1945: Ken Zumwalt as a corporal and managing editor of the Nice edition of *The Stars and Stripes*.

AUTHOR 1987: With Eric Paul Zumwalt, his eighteen-month-old grandson.

Index

A

A. W. Faber pencil factory, 106
"Abbie and Slats," 11
Aberdeen Proving Ground, Md., 152
Able Company, 185
Adams, Franklin P., x
Adleman, Robert H., 68
Adler, Larry, 70
  Milton, 126
Ahlberg, Bill, 74
Air Force Daily, 226
Air Gunner, 63
Air Lift Task Force, 176
Albert & Company, 196
Albin, Francoise, 61
  Paul, 61
  Paulette, 61, 71, 89, 100 (*see also*
    Zumwalt, Paulette)
Allied Control Council, 170
Allied War Shipping Pool, 69
Alter, John E., 147
Amaroc News, 119
American Daily, 225, 226–227, 228, 229
American Federation of Government
    Employees (AFGE), 254
American Red Cross, 15, 19, 37–38,
    61, 101, 136, 194, 221, 250
Ampurex, 135
Anderson, John W., 23
  Omer, 207
Anderson-Martini, 198
Andrea Doria, 252
Aquitania, 69, 77
Armattoe, Raphael E. G., 99
Armed Forces General Welfare Fund,
    127

Armed Forces Network (AFN), 121,
    127
Armed Forces Radio, 35
Army News Service (ANS), 140
Army Times Publishing Company,
    155, 225, 226
Arnold, Henry H. (Hap), 32, 45
Asbury, John, 171
"As Pegler Sees It," 205
"atomic cannon," 151–152
Attlee, Clement R., 64, 69, 79
Avedon, Charles, 60, 93
Axis Sally, 53

B

Back, Lor Lizabeth, 189–190
Bacon, Robert L., 29
Badiner, Jacob (Jack), 91
Bailey, Eunice, 167
Baird, Jean, 32, 63, 184
Baitz, Stan, 63, 67
Baker, Anna Elizabeth, 101
Baku, Lina, 83
Baldwin, Hanson W., 96
Balmain, Pierre, 244
Barclay, Anne Elizabeth (*see* God-
    dard, Anne E.)
Barnes, Alfred J., 77
Barr, John E., 180–181
Barriac, George, 183
Bartl, Elizabeth, 168
Bartoni, Donald A., 250, 251, 253
Bates, Raymond B., 170
Battle of the Bulge, 22–25, 35, 103,
    107
B-Bag, 5, 10, 13, 39, 44, 114, 128, 129,
    145, 222, 223, 239

Beachhead News, 153
Bean Blossom Bugle, 58
Beattie, Edward W., Jr., 242
Bednavska, Sophia, 83–84
Beecher, Richard, 183
Bell, Red, 18
Bennett, Ivan Loveridge, 139
Benny, Jack, 70
Benoit, William Robert (Willy), 54,
    184, 185–186
Bergman, Ingrid, 70
Berlin Airlift, 149
Berliner, The, 170
Berlin Press Club, 74
Berlin Radio, 33, 176
Bernstein, Lester, 86
    Victor, 98
Bevans, James M., 142, 194
Biancone, Anthony (Tony), viii, 227,
    228, 229, 249
    Elizabeth Medart, 229
Bikini, 124
Bishop, James, 141
Black, Creed, x, 101
Blackman, Morris (Blackie), 21–22
black market, 14, 74–75, 118, 119,
    161–165, 242
Blomkwist, Marie, 83
"Blondie," 11, 64, 114
Blue Coast Final, 63
Boes, Hal, 100
Bolling, Alexander W., 126
Bolmey, Roger H., 88
Boni, Bill, 116, 118
Bor, Otto, 88
Borcx, John, 83
"Boris Pasternak," x
Bormann, Martin, 86
Bourgin, Simon, 20
Boyd, Roy W., Jr., 219
Bradshaw, William, 114
Brady, James, 211
Brasier, Renee, 182, 183
Braun, Eva, 133
    Gretl, 133
Breen, Bobby, 70
Breger, Dave, 11
Brett, Lloyd C., 199

Brewer, Angus, 170
Brignola, Joe, 71, 72–74, 75, 221
"Bringing Up Father," 230
Brinkley, Bill, 52
Briscoe, Claude, 10
British King's Medal, 192
Brody, Mariam Jean, 15
Bromwell, James E., 125–128, 135
Brooks, Morton P., 253
Brown, Bob, 32, 34
    Johnny, 34, 62
    Louis H., 137, 197, 198
    Vanessa, 140, 141
Browne, Beatrice A. Dahl, 103, 109
    Jack, 89, 103, 109, 112, 122, 150,
        191, 193
    Roberta, 122, 214
Brownjoy, N. C. D., 171
Buchwald, Art, 225
Bucknell, Philip, 118, 123, 203
Buckwach, Aaron, 93
Bull, H. R., 98
Bunnelle, Robert, 60
Burchard, Albert, 234
    James, 28
Burke, Bryce, 10
Burnett, Arnold, 254–255
    Viola, 254–255
Burress, Cynthia, 245–246
    William A., 245–246
Burzinski, Joseph S., 103–104
    Noma Sakowiez, 103–104
Buschner, Johanna, 192–193
Butcher, Harry C., 59, 239–240
Butler, Chris, 221, 234

C
Cable, Homer, 76, 89
Caldwell, Jack, 20
Campbell, James W., 254–255, 256
Camp Des Loges, 156
Caniff, Milton, 227
Cannon, Jimmy, 7, 23, 26, 32, 223
Carlton, Roy C., 160
Carmichael, Thomas H., 164
Carroll, Earl J., 135
    Madeline, 70
Casky, Laurence L., 179
Casner, Maurice "Mike," Jr., 234

Cassini, Igor, 20
Castle Tours, 223
Cauvin, Jacqueline, 183
C-Day, 118–121
censorship, 24, 60, 92–93, 95–96, 97,
    115, 241–242, 254, 257–259
Chamberlain, Edward Pye, 107, 113
Chambliss, W. M., 157
Champagne Campaign, The, 68
Chaplin, George, 60
Charisse, Cyd, 138
Cherokees of the Old South, 136
Childs, George T., xi
Christenson, Bob, 52
Christie, John, 20
Christmas bonus, 197–200
Churchill, Winston, 64, 69
Ciano, Count Galeazzo, 30
Cinquemani, Nick, 34
Cisielska, Maria, 83
Clark, A. D., 97
    Edgar, 16, 18–19, 28, 36, 43–44,
        56–57
    Mark, 110
Clay, Lucius D., 130–131, 165, 166,
    167, 170, 171, 172–173, 174, 181,
    202, 204, 211, 240
    Marjorie, 164–165, 173
Clift, John, 70
Close, George, 228, 248
Cluff, Hector, 180
Cohen, Abe, 47
    Richard L., 132–133
Coleman, William W., 254
Collingwood, Charles, 3
Collins, Mary, 140
    Robert, 10
Colonna, Jerry, 70
Combined Air Lift Task Force, 176
Combs, Thomas S., 157
Comite National de Defense Contrelat
    Tuberculosis, 199
Conner, John H., 222
Connors, Paul, 233
Continental Assurance Company, 253
Conway, Hugh, 28, 51
Conybear, Ken, 3
Cook, Jeffrey M., 257

Cornell, George W., 115
Cotton, Joe, 46
Coupe, Jay, 258
Crawford, Broderick, 35
Cullen, Ann Kathleen, 10
Cunningham, Thomas J., Jr., 253
Curtis Publishing Co., 127
Cushing, Charles P., xi

D
Dahlquist, John E., 242–243
Daily Pacifican, 115
Dallaire, Victor J., 16, 18–19, 28, 52,
    84, 152–153
Dankeschon, Veronica, 142–143
Danziger, David, 223
Darlan, Jean, 29–30
David, Lester, 7, 47
Davidson, Arthur R., 94
Davis, Morrow, 7
Dean, Ben, 28
de Gaulle, Charles, 156
De Mazo, William, 28
Dempsey, Casey, 35
Deojay, George, 254
Department of Defense, 256
de Ridder, Yvonne, 191–192
Der Stuermer, 108
Der Verfasser, 201
Desmond, Johnnie, 70
de Thier, Maurice, 183
Detiere, Lucien, 18
DeVone, James C., 110–111
Dewey, Thomas, 12–13
"Dick Tracy," 11, 114
Diehl, Joe, 62
Dietrich, Josef (Sepp), 107
    Marlene, 140
Dilley, John R., 243–245
Dilliard, Irving, 106, 113
Doan, Leander L., 43
Doenitz, Karl, 54
Dog Company, 40–41
Dolan, Tom, 21–22
Dondero, George A., 201–204, 209
Donnelley, Dick, 225–226
Donovan, Robert J., x, 66, 77
Dorsey, George, 28, 52
Dowell, Edwin E., 76–77, 85–86,

102, 112–113, 115, 119, 121, 123, 128, 129
  Suzanne Berthe Pons, 121
Drenick, Ernest, 142
Dreyfuss, Allan, 106
Dubois, Josiah E., 204
Dumper, Robert, 67
Duncan, Greg, 28, 233
Durant, Jack W., 160
Dwan, E. J., 94

E

Early, Steve, x, 4
Easter Parade, 179
Eathorne, Jim, 46
Eberling, Edwin, 8
Eddy, Manton E., 205, 246
  Mrs. Manton E., 246
Editor and Publisher, 217, 224, 258
Edwards, Julia, 120, 174
Ehrenfreund, Norbert, 234
Eis, Lillian, 66
Eisenhower, Dwight D., 3, 32, 39, 44, 63, 69, 82, 87, 93, 96, 97, 192, 194, 205, 210, 217–219, 220, 221, 239, 240
Eldridge, Fred, 60, 109, 134
Elliott, Margie, 186–187
  Paul, 44, 64, 67, 72, 238
Emery, Daphne, 188
  Stan, viii, 187–188
Encyclopedia Britannica, 216, 217
English, Marla, 141
Enola Gay, 65
Epstein, Henry, 118, 155
Ericson, Earl, 28, 115, 126
Ernest, Anna-Maria, 193–194
Esperanto, 128
Estoff, William D. (Bill), 46–47, 52
Europa, 69
Europakable, 193
Everett, Robert P., 257
Eyster, George S., 121, 142, 206, 243

F

Faber, Baron Lothar, 106
Faldini, Franca, 140
Faller, Kenneth E., 110
Fanning, Win, 120, 174

Farben, I. G., 204
Feature Section, 134, 155, 225
Federal Bureau of Investigation, 216
Feiberger, Rolf, 197
Feldmuehle paper mill, 155
Files, Roger, 192
Fisher, Ella M., 184
"Flash Gordon," 230
Fleming, Joseph B., 7, 74, 75, 78, 116, 118, 120, 169, 173–174, 175, 180, 185
Foisie, Jack, x, 28
Force, Arthur, 31, 38, 45, 46, 78, 109, 238
Forrestal, James V., 173
Frank, Elmer D., 123, 145, 147, 152, 155, 187, 196, 197, 198
Frankfurter Rundschau, 133, 145, 196, 232
Frankfurter Zeitung, 44, 72
Frankfurt Military Post, 119
Frankfurt Press Club, 129, 241
Frederick, Robert T., 62, 68
Freedom of Information subcommittee, 256
Freidin, Seymour, 61
French Liaison Mission, 199
French Ministry of Health, 19
French Red Cross, 19
Friedrich, Otto, x, 246
Fritzsche, Hans, 106
Frost, Jim, 79, 182
  William, 180
Frye, William R. (Bill), 34, 38, 74
Funk, Walter, 105
Furst, Peter, 51
Furstenfeldbruck Air Base, 246
Furuholmen, Bjorne, 243

G

Gaither, Ralph, 250
Gallagher, Philip E., 146, 156
Ganeval, Jean, 176
Gans, Sidney, 7, 47, 79, 116–117, 121, 123, 126, 198, 199, 205
Gardner, Ava, 138
Garrell, Norman, 37
"Gasoline Alley," 114
Gass, Kathleen, 111

Gay, Hobart R., 87
Gen. R. E. Callan, 233
General Motors, 199
German Association of Paper Manu-
    facturers, 155
German Radio, 54
Giblin, Leonard P., 50, 52, 58, 70–71
Gilstrap, Max, 2, 5, 20, 21, 31, 34–35,
    64, 81–82
Goddard, Anne E., 188–189
Godfrey, Arthur, 63
Goebbels, Joseph Paul, 36, 122
Goering, Hermann, 56, 78, 86, 105,
    106, 124
Goodfriend, Arthur, 5, 60, 70, 240
Grad, Jules B., 7, 22
Graff, Gene, 11
Graf Zeppelin, 146
Graham, Billy, 139
Grandy, Francis "Red," vii, 216–220
Great Falls Air Lift Training School,
    178
Green, Paul, 28, 30, 51
Greenough, Marie Anne, 185
Green Project, 69
Gridley, 66
Griffing, Larry, 65, 78
Groth, John, 61
Gudebrod, Morton, 60, 116, 117
"Gumps, The," 64
Gustowska, Helena Anna, 84
Guy M., 19
H
Haeger, Robert, 171–172
Hagar, Jon, 208, 210, 211
Haindl, Bavaria, 130, 131
Hakin, George, 52
Halloran, Vincent, 185
Halvorsen, Gale S., 178
Handy, Mrs. Thomas T., 246–247
    Thomas T., 211, 220, 242
Hansen, Peter, 20
Harcher, Harry, 28
Harding, Richard, 3
Harmon, Ernest, 242
Harrigan, James J., 52, 66
Harriott, Joyce, 185, 188
Harris, Martin, 44

Truitt W., 210
Hart, H. Peter, 113
Harty, Hugh F., 222
Harvey, Joe, 90
"Hashmarks," 11–12, 37
Hawkins, Eric, 22, 225
Hawley, Hudson, xi
Hayes, Andrew, 250
Hayworth, Rita, 140
Heidelberg University Clinic, 208
Hemingway, Ernest, 3
Hemsing, Albert, 255
Henkin, Daniel Z., 152
Herron, Frances, 20
Hertzog, Laurence, 234
Hess, Rudolf, 78, 86, 105, 106
Hessler, Charles W., 84
Heyligens, Jacques, 183
Hickey, Doyle O., 43
Higgins, Marguerite, 172
High Commission of Germany
    (HICOG), 205, 208
Higuchi, George, 109–110
Hilda, 142
Hill, Ed, 51
Himmler, Heinrich, 62
Hiroshima, 65
Hitler, Adolf, 33, 44, 54, 132, 133, 160
Hitpass, Kathe, 235
Hocking, Dean, 28
Hodenfield, G. K., 7, 21, 28, 69
Hofricter, Georg, 152, 196
Hogan, Charles, 52
    Edmund, 70
Hoge, Thomas, 56
    William, 38, 229
Holdway, Elmer, 111
Holzhausen, Germany, 41
Hope, Bob, 70
Horowitz, Paul, 31
Horvath, Richard L., 257
Hottelet, Richard C., 40
House Committee on Un-American
    Activities, 202, 203
Howard, Oliver Gregg, 134
Howland, Kenneth, 145
Howley, Frank L., 242
"Hubert," 11, 59

Huberts, Harm, 83, 104
    Maria Drewniak, 104
    Rinus, 83
Hubmann, Hans, 192
    Lisa, 192
Huebner, Clarence Ralph, 126, 131,
    241
Hughes, Kathleen, 138, 140
Husted, Frances Mae, 61
Hutton, Betty, 70
    Bud, 2, 4–5, 20, 23, 35–36, 45, 50,
    52, 54, 58, 59, 63

I

Iannacio, Anthony (Tony), 29–30,
    31, 52–53
Ile de France, 69
Il Messaggero, 30
Imhof, Roland, 221–222
Immell, Perry, 181
Imprimerie Centrale du Croissant So-
    ciete Nationale, 155–156
Imprimerie Chateaudun, 156
Imprimerie Parisienne Reunies, 155
Imprimerie Richelieu, 155
Information Journal, The, 117
"Inquiring Photographer," 88
International Military Tribunal, 78
Irwin, Joel, 93
    Margaret, 61
Iteen, David, 222

J

Jandoli, Russell J., 94
"Jane," 11
Janetchko, Stefanie, 83
Jardin Albert, 50
Jelke, Minot (Mickey) III, 231
Jennings, Douglas K., 222
"Joe Palooka," 114
Johnson, Lyndon B., 256
Jolley, Bill, 182
Jones, Alton, 55, 63
    Dick, 26, 34, 46, 132, 133, 134
    Russell F., x, 7, 21, 26, 28, 34, 40,
    118, 172
    Wade, 28, 52
Jorgensen, Christine, 231
Jorgenson, Arthur L., 139, 151–152,

    227, 248
    Inez, 152
Judge, John P., 52

K

Kaltenbrunner, Ernst, 86
Kane, Bud, 46, 221
    Matthew W., 37
Katz, Julius Peter, 183
Katzander, Howard, 134, 186, 216
    Shirley, x, 216
Kaufman, Larry, 223
Kay, E. D., 66
Kaye, Betty, 217
Keck, Myrna, 140
Kefauver, Estes, 220
Keitel, Wilheim, 105
Kennedy, Edward, 54, 60, 117
Kent, C. S., 141
Kestler, Hal C., 97, 115
Kieffer, Jeanette Augusta (Gussie),
    84, 85
Kiessling, Guenter, 257–258
Kiley, Charles F., 10, 20, 55
Kilian, James A., 107
Killpack, Ed, 221
King, Byron R., 250
    Ernest J., 32
King Features Syndicate, 242
Kinman, Duane N., 8–9
Kirchhoff, Bernard (Barney), vii, 254,
    255, 258
Kirkpatrick, Helen, 16
Kirkwood, Anne, 135
    Maurice R., 134–135, 145, 151,
    188, 211
Kline, Phil, 52
Knorr, Betty Luros, viii, 121, 131,
    135, 165
    Richard E., 102, 111, 115, 116–117,
    118, 121, 123, 126, 129, 130–131,
    134, 135
Knowland, William R., 231
Koenig, Dick, 221
Kohl, Helmut, 258
Kohlross, Guenter, 222
Kohn, Al, 28, 233
Konzelman, Carl, 43, 79–80, 108
Koop, Guenter, 221–222

Korb, Rose I., 111
Kraatz, Hans, 85
Kraft, Sigrid, 195
Krakowianka, Bronya, 83
Kuchel, Thomas, 231
Kugelmas, Elizabeth, 215
  Joseph Alvin, 215–216
L
Label, Sydney, 228, 249
La Colline, 67
Lamb and Lark pub, 182, 187
La Meuse, 20–21, 31
Lampron, Emil, 214
  Jacqueline, 214
  Nancy Elaine, 214
Lance, Bert, 136
Landau, Joe, 72–73, 76, 89
Landsberg Air Base, 246
Lanham, Charles T., 95
Laque, George, 29
Larsen, Carl, 22, 38, 43
LaSalle, Angelo A., 234
Laurence, Geoffrey, 86
Lawson, Richard, 257–258
Leahy, William D., 32
Lear, Ben, 239
Learned, George, 134
LeClef, Rene, 192
Le Doux, Ferdinand, 37
Lee, James, 18
  John C. H., 95–96, 97–98, 114–
    115, 119
  Ray, 36
Lehman, Milton, 28, 51
Leiser, Carolyn Camp, 118
  Ernest, x, 14, 34, 35, 36, 56, 62, 64,
    116, 118
LeMay, Curtis S., 177
le Moel, Monique, 186
Lende, Charles, 88
Lerner, Max, 38
Levin, Gene, 120
Levinson, Irv, 51
Lewicki, Alexander, 83
Lewis, Kate B., 237
  Katharine T., 237
  Katherine Baldwin, 122
  Mrs. Crosby, 122

Richard, 7, 32
Ley, Robert, 78, 86
Liddle, Joan, 184, 188
Liebes, Bernard H., 210, 211
Liepa, Dzidra (Ina), 189
Life, 127, 217
"Li'l Abner," 11, 64, 114
Lilley, Charley, 2
Lisagore, Peter, 62, 66, 79
Litchfield, England, 90, 107
Livingood, Ina, 249
  John W., vii, 107–108, 112, 113,
    119, 120, 123, 129, 150, 169, 189,
    210, 218, 249–250
Llewellyn, Ensley Maxwell, 9–10, 242
Lock, Edwin P., 103
Logan, Joshua, 247
Lomeshie Research Center, 99
London Daily Express, 244
London Daily Mail, 155
London Daily Mirror, 120
London Times, 141
Long, Wellington, 171–172, 258
Lord, Sterling, x, 134
Louis, Prince, 68
Luce, Claire Booth, 204
Luckman, Sid, 11
lucky bucks campaign, 224–225
Ludwig II, 174
Lukianchenko, G. S., 169–170
Lyon, Leonard, 219, 230
M
Maastricht, Holland, 19, 34
MacArthur, Douglas, 32, 66, 94, 209,
  217, 218
McAuliffe, Anthony C., 25, 242, 252
McBride, Joseph, 20, 118, 141, 243
McCloy, John J., 154, 205
McConnell, Harold, viii, 114, 210
McCormick, Otis, 138–139, 183, 241,
  248
McDonald, Marie, 140
  Warren F., 9–10
McDowell, John, 202
McGee, George, 255
  Michael, 255
McGowan, James, 44, 108
McGrath, Edward G., 257

McGraw, E. J., 115
McGuigan, Bernard J., 125–128, 131, 135, 136–137
  Dorothy Gies, 131, 136
  Michael John, 136
McInteer, Hugh, 52
McLean, James V., 108, 113, 132
McNamara, Robert S., 254, 255
  W. C., 10
McNarney, Joseph T., 87, 90, 119, 120, 121, 194–195, 240
Madsen, Andrew E., 167
  Dana, 167
  Nancy, 167
  Yvette, 166, 167
Mahoney, Arthur, 164
Maid of Konnersreuth, 190
Mail Call, 97
Malone, Henry Thompson (Hank), 126, 135–136
  Perrillah, 135–136
Manning, Larry, 157
Maquis, 51
Mara, Adele, 140
Maranda, George E., 255–256
Margareta, Princess (see von Hesse, Countess)
Margolin, Nathan J., 73, 76, 89, 119, 120, 187, 253–254
Marie, Anna, 18
Marsh, Bert E., 12, 34, 36–37, 58, 66
  Sam, 37
Marshall, George Catlett, 6, 32, 87, 238–239
Marshall Plan Conference, 202
Martin, Ralph G., 7, 28, 36, 51
Martinez, Fernand, 183
Martino, Nino, 70
Mason, John S., 114–115
Mastin, Robert C., 23
Matteo, Dorothy, 117
  Henry, 116–117
  Marcia, 117
Mauldin, Bill, x, 11, 28, 30, 51, 53, 56–58, 202, 203, 239
Maxey, Bill, 40
Mayo, Virginia, 140
Mazo, Earl, 7–8, 10

Mazur, Robert F., 84–85
Meckes, Carl, 199
Mecklin, John M., 19
Melcher, Jack, 10, 64–65
Meluski, Victor (Molly), 31
Memphis, 66
Merchant, Larry (see Kaufman, Larry)
Mercier, Chez, 31
Merritt, Bob, 88, 221
Mertinke, Fred, 7, 20
Michael, F. S., Jr., 256
  William K., xi
Mid-Pacifican, 59
Midweek, 132
military payment certificates (scrip), 118, 119–121
Miller, C. L., 37
  Glenn, 23, 70
  Jacob, 10
Misevich, Charles P., 64
Miss Cheesecake, 140–141
Mitchell, Pat, 23
Mitgang, Herbert, x, 28, 47
Mitts, David L., 64
Mogan, James W., 23
Monaco, 68
Monroe, Marilyn, 140
Monte Carlo, 68
Montfort, Joseph, 183
Montgomery, Bernard L., 63
"Moon Mullins," 64, 114
Moora, Robert L. (Bob), 4, 6, 10, 13, 15–16, 36, 43, 238
Moore, Grace, 70
  Terry, 140
Moran, Gussie, 140
  William R., 210
Morgenthau, Henry A., 204
Morrison, Allan M., 7
Morrow, Ed, 172
Moss, John E., 256
Moyers, Sam, 184
"Mr. Roberts," 246–248
Muench, Aloisius J., 139
Mulligan, Moe, 108
Munster, B. F., 156
Murphy, Mildred, 172

Robert D., 172
Musmanno, Michael A., 133–134
Mussolini, Benito, 52–53
My Three Years With Eisenhower, 239

N

Nagasaki, 65
Nash, Kathleen B., 159–161
National Catholic Community Service, 138, 140
Neth, Cecil, 222
Neue Zeitung, 206, 207
Neumann, Theresa, 190, 191
Neville, Robert, 28, 30, 39, 52–53
Newfield, Wally, 10
Newman, Ralph, 12
Newstead, Dennis, 191
Doreen, 191
Newsweek, 127
New York Times, 127, 156
Nimitz, Chester W., 32
Noce, Daniel, 210
Noel, Ralph, 10, 15
Norden bombsight, 24
Nottingham, John D., 253–254
Now, 134
Noyes, Arthur, Jr., 86, 115, 150–151, 171, 185, 218, 235–237
Dennis, 236
Geraldine (daughter), 236
Geraldine (wife), 236
Nuremberg trials, 78, 86–87, 103, 105–106, 143

O

Occupation Chronicle, 118–119
O'Farrell, Kathleen, 111
Offner, Simone, 84, 85
O'Hara, David B., 257
O'Kearney, John, 153
Olagnier, Rosette, 100
Oldfield, Barney, 34, 243
O'Leary, Colonel, 211
O'Malley, Richard, 218
"Once Over Lightly," 11
Operation Little Vittles, 178–179
Operation Meat Grinder, 209
Operation Santa Claus, 179
Operation Sleigh Bells, 179

Operation Vittles, 169, 176
Orphan Fund, 19
Osborn, Frederick H., 85
Ott, Edward R., vii, 227, 253
Overseas Family, 232
Overseas Press Club, 256
Overseas Traveler, 232
Overseas Weekly, 230, 244, 251

P

Pachier, Francis, 255
Packard, Reynolds, 8
Palais de la Mediterranee, 50
Palmer, Herb, 221
Paris Herald-Tribune, 116
Parks, Floyd L., 202
Parris, Paul, 76
Patch, Alexander M., Jr., 40, 51
Patch Kaserne, 246
Patterson, Dale K., 257
Lee, 222
Robert P., 79, 91–92, 96, 97, 203
Patton, George S., 7, 25, 57–58, 87–88, 223
Pegler, Westbrook, 201, 204–206, 209
Peiper, Joaquin, 107
Pelletier, William H., 126, 136
Penn, George, 221
Pepper, Claude, 115–116
Peron, Eva, 202
Pershing, John J., xi, 6, 239
Petacci, Clara, 53
Pett, Norman, 11
Pettus, Kenneth, 94–95
Philipp, Prince, 160, 161
Phillips, Warren, x
Picnic Tours, 174
Platt, Cray, 34
Poldre, Eliu, 84
Pons, Suzanne, 84, 85 (*see also* Dowell, Suzanne Berthe Pons)
"Popeye," 11
Popov, Major, 170
Potsdam Conference, 204
Power, Tyrone, 246
Price, Ben, 13, 43, 140, 141
"Prince Valiant," 230
Proctor, Eulalie, 127
Mert, Jr., 255, 256, 258

William G., vii, 90, 109, 111–113, 116, 117, 121, 123, 125, 126, 127, 128–129, 131, 134, 136, 144, 187
Proxmire, William, 258–259
Pyle, Ernie, 3, 57

Q

Queen Elizabeth, 69, 77
Queen Mary, 69, 77
Quigley, James M., vii, 207
Quint, Anne, 253
    James, 250, 251, 253

R

Rabinovich, Joseph, 114, 191
Rache, Greta, 193
Radosta, John, 52, 108–109
Raita, John, 222
Rakin, Lou, 10
Raymond, Jack, x, 43, 52
    Nicholas, 222
Reader's Digest, 127
Reber, Miles M., 116
Reed, Ernie, vii, 115, 121, 218, 219
    Janet, 163
    Katherine G., 162–163
Regan, Dan, 7, 22, 32, 35, 62
    Neil T., 78, 98–99, 100, 101
Reinhardt, Django, 191
Renaud, Monsieur, 65
Republican Party, 124
retirement plan, 250–251, 253
Reuter, Ernst, 180
Rhodes, Charles, 35
Rice, Grantland, x, 4, 230
Rich, C. K., 210
Richardson, Robert C., Jr., 92–93
    Walter B., 42–43
Richter, Henry J., 149, 150–151, 211, 248
    Janet, 149, 151
Ridgway, Matthew B., 209, 218
Riordan, Larry, 34–35, 37, 38, 221
Ritz, Al, 20, 31
Robertson, Nan, 190
Robinson, Robbie, 28
Rodgers, Robert R., 120
Roessner, Elmer, 12–14
Rogers, Bernard, 257

Rohde, Ted, 221
Romany, Walter, 66
Rome Daily American, 115, 227, 228, 229, 249
Rooney, Andy, x, 7, 10, 36, 37, 52, 58, 62, 63
    Mickey, 70
Roosevelt, Elliott, 33
    Faye Emerson, 33
    Franklin D., 12–13, 32–33, 45, 98
Rose, Billy, 230
    Maurice, 42
Rosen, Milton, 156
Ross, Harold, x, 4
Royall, Kenneth C., 173
Rubin, Barnard, 94–95
Rue, Larry, 236
Rukeyser, Louis, 223
Rumsfeld, Donald, 256
Ryder, Melvin, 225–226, 229

S

Sad Sack, 132
St. John, Mary, 149
    Wattie T., 123, 149
Sanders, Rhea, 191
Sanderson, Harvey, 174
Sanford, Vic, 52
Schacht, Hjalmar, 106
Scheffner, Warren H., 151, 227, 248
Schiffer, Hans, 164
Schloss Friedrichof, 161
Schneider, Herb, 10
Schouman, Frederic S., 108
Schreiner, Marie-Odile, 84
Schreuder, O. B., 142
Schwammenauel dam, 35
Scites, Horace, 180
Seaton, Fred A., 229
Seidentopf, Robert, 195, 196
Seney, Ed, 87, 113
Serramoglia, George, 183
Seven, Toni, 140
716th Railway Operating Battalion, 14
Shafer, Paul, 204
Shapiro, Sidney, 118
Sharnik, Seymour (John), x, 34, 35, 38, 46, 74, 89, 116, 118, 129, 191

Shaunce, Glen, 42
Shaw, Fred, 226, 229
Sheil, Tommy, 89
Sheldon, Robert, 113
Sheppard, Don, 141–143
Shershow, Harry, 28
Shinn, Robert, 243
Short's Bar, 187
Shrum, Bill, 222
Sibert, Lother B., 228, 229, 248–249,
    250
Sikora, Berwin R., 89
Simpson, Arthur, 18
Sinatra, Frank, 70
Sixth Fleet edition, 156–157
Skean, Gordon, 119, 193–194
Skelton, Paul R., 110–111
Slanger, Frances, 10
"Slants on Sports," 118
Smiley, Joseph, 214
Smith, Joseph E., 176
    Kingsbury, 242
    Ridgway, Jr., 254
    Walter Bedell, 7, 34, 54–55, 65, 77
soap box derby, 214
Solbert, O. N., 12, 60
Solomon, J. C., 236
Sontag, Bob, 66, 87
    Robert, 76
Sophia, Princess, 161
Sorbonne, 67
Spaatz, Carl, 3
Spangler, Billy E., 257
Spann, Charles, 225
Spear, Bill, 20, 31, 38
Spellman, Francis Cardinal, 139
Sprague, Carrol, 233–234
Sprague Barracks, 234
Stalin, Joseph, 64
Stars and Stripes in Rebeldom, xi
State Department, 208
Staub, Wilbur, 198
Stauber, Ruby Rose, 257
Stedman, Don, 127
"Steve Canyon," 227
Stevenson, Adlai, 128, 240
Stilwell, Joseph W., 60
Stimpson, Harry L., 14

Stone, Lawrence (Larry), 76
Storey, Alf, 182
    Gertie, 182
Story of the Stars and Stripes, 63
Story of the Times, The, 141
Streicher, Julius, 62, 108
Stubbs, Maurice G., 227
Stucnskaite, Alfreda, 83
Summers, Sadie, 216
    William M., 133, 134, 135, 144–
        146, 149, 185, 187, 215–216, 226,
        234, 248
Super Albert 60, 152, 196
Swan, Curtis, 12
Swideruwna, Leonarea, 83
Swinton, Stan, 53
T
Taegliche Rundschau, 244
Taft, Robert A., 210, 220
Taft-Hartley Labor Act, 202
"tausch ring," 165
Taylor, James H., 257
Tedder, Arthur W., 3
"Terry and the Pirates," 11, 114
Textor, G. E., 206
"This Is Your Life," 192
Thomas, Jim, 64
    "Tex," 34
Thompson, Paul W., 60, 78, 90–91,
        98–99, 103, 127, 238
    Stan, 10
Thornberry, Monica, 185, 188
Thrush, Roland, vii
Tiffney, Earl H., 187
Tilley, Reade, 243
Time, 127
Timmons, William R., 110–111
Todd, Norman, 66
Toluzzi, Anne Helene, 222
    Henry, vii, 221–222
    Peter Michael, 222
Tomorrow, 20
Towe, Lonnie, 222
Trescott, Henry Wilbur, 235
    Paul, 235
Trial and Error, 76
Trizonal Towns, 223
Truman, Harry S., 13, 45, 64, 71, 79,

87, 97, 139, 217, 218, 220
  Martha E., 71
TRUST forces, 199
Tully, Andrew, 61
Tunner, William H., 176–177

U

U.S. Air Force, 209–212
U.S. Riviera Recreational Area, 50
Ulmer, John, 78
United Nations Relief and Rehabilitation Administration (UNRRA), 128
United States Forces European Theater (USFET), 76
United States Riviera Recreational Area, 47
University of Maryland, 214, 237
Unwin, Fred, 52
"Up Front," 11
"Up Front With Mauldin," 57
USS *Missouri*, 66
USS *Wakefield*, 2

V

Vaccaro, Michael A., 132–133
  Tony, 221
van Abshoven, Reiner, 83
Van Pelt, Fred, 49, 50, 63, 186
VDK, 199
Vebell, Ed, 52, 62
"Veronica Town," 143
Vestal, Sam, 221
VI Corps News, 153
Victoria, Queen, 158, 159
Vinson, Fred, 204
Virden, John M., 229
Vir Den, Ray, 227, 228–229, 249
Viskniskki, Guy T., xi
V-J Day, 66
Vogeler, Lucille, 217, 219–220
  Robert A., 217, 219–220
von Bismarck, Otto, 36
von Bohlen und Halbach, Gustav Krupp, 86
von Braun, Wernher, 241
von Faber-Castell, Alexander, 106
von Hesse, Countess, 158, 160, 161
von Knoblock, Doris, 195–196

von Papen, Franz, 106
von Ribbentrop, Joachim, 62, 105, 106
von Rospach, Cecil, 230–231
  Marion, 229, 230–231, 232
von Rundstadt, Gerd, 33
Voolar, Kamilla, 84
Vorwaerts, 170

W

Wacker, John, 109
Wage, Dan P., 168
  Martha Joan, 166, 168
Wallenberg, Hans, 206–207, 209
Waller, Jerry, 189, 190, 217, 221
  Lor Lizabeth, 221
"Wall Street Week," 223
Walton, George, 68
Ward, Pat, 231
Warsaw, Poland, 130–131
Warweek, 20
Washington, 205
Waters, Frank, 31, 46, 109
Watson, Charles, 66
  David F., 160
  Harry, 52, 108
  Mark, x
  Melville E., 13
Weaver, Glenn, 214
Webster, Flossie, 234
Wechsberg, Joseph, 20
Weekend, 108, 118, 123, 131–134, 136, 143, 184
Weinberg, Curt, 76, 89
Weinstein, William, 101, 107, 109, 111–113
Weir, Max Hill, 223
Weiss, Ludwig, 160
Weizmann, Chaim, 75–76
Weston, Joe, 20
Wheeler, George S., 204
  Victor, 223
White, Arthur, 7, 10, 101, 120
  Charles W., 7, 20
  Charley (Trooper), 58–59
  Dale, 226, 229
  DeWitte, 163
  Egbert, 28, 59, 85–86, 96, 152
  Stoddard, 76, 86, 100, 102

White-Addison, Hattilu, 243
Whitman, Hamilton, 20
Wilcox, Ed, 20
Wilhelm, Kaiser, 35, 158
Wilkinson, John Cornish, 12
Williams, Don, 51
  Eugene T., 179
"Willie and Joe," x, 56, 57–58
Willig, John, 51
Willoughby, Charles A., 94–95
Wilson, Charles E., 231
  Earl, 230
Winant, John G., 79
Winchell, Walter, 243, 247
Wingert, Dick, 11, 12, 59
Winget, Rader, 15, 16, 80–81
Woerner, Manfred, 257
Wolfgang, Prince, 160, 161
Women's Army Corps, 158

Woods, Oliver, 141
Woollcott, Alexander, x, 4
World Series, 121–122
Wright, John, 157
Y
Yank, 132
Ybarbo, Jimmie, 166
  John, 166
  Wilma E. (Billie), 166–167
Z
Zhukov, Marshal Gregory, 33
Ziccarelli, James A., 230, 251
Zimmerman, Herbert, 41
  Paul, 60
Zucca, Rita, 53
Zumwalt, Paulette, 100–101, 102,
    103, 109, 148–149, 216, 251, 252
  Richard Albin, 251, 252
  Roger Clay, 240, 251, 252